CW00552448

797,885 Books

are available to read at

www.ForgottenBooks.com

Forgotten Books' App
Available for mobile, tablet & eReader

ISBN 978-1-331-30449-4
PIBN 10171712

This book is a reproduction of an important historical work. Forgotten Books uses
state-of-the-art technology to digitally reconstruct the work, preserving the original format
whilst repairing imperfections present in the aged copy. In rare cases, an imperfection in
the original, such as a blemish or missing page, may be replicated in our edition. We do,
however, repair the vast majority of imperfections successfully; any imperfections that
remain are intentionally left to preserve the state of such historical works.

Forgotten Books is a registered trademark of FB &c Ltd.
Copyright © 2015 FB &c Ltd.
FB &c Ltd, Dalton House, 60 Windsor Avenue, London, SW19 2RR.
Company number 08720141. Registered in England and Wales.

For support please visit www.forgottenbooks.com

1 MONTH OF
FREE
READING

at

www.ForgottenBooks.com

By purchasing this book you are
eligible for one month membership to
ForgottenBooks.com, giving you
unlimited access to our entire
collection of over 700,000 titles via
our web site and mobile apps.

To claim your free month visit:

www.forgottenbooks.com/free171712

* Offer is valid for 45 days from date of purchase. Terms and conditions apply.

English
Français
Deutsche
Italiano
Español
Português

www.forgottenbooks.com

Mythology Photography **Fiction**
Fishing Christianity **Art** Cooking
Essays Buddhism Freemasonry
Medicine **Biology** Music **Ancient
Egypt** Evolution Carpentry Physics
Dance Geology **Mathematics** Fitness
Shakespeare **Folklore** Yoga Marketing
Confidence Immortality Biographies
Poetry **Psychology** Witchcraft
Electronics Chemistry History **Law**
Accounting **Philosophy** Anthropology
Alchemy Drama Quantum Mechanics
Atheism Sexual Health **Ancient History**
Entrepreneurship Languages Sport
Paleontology Needlework Islam
Metaphysics Investment Archaeology
Parenting Statistics Criminology
Motivational

Gloomy Memories

IN THE

HIGHLANDS OF SCOTLAND:

VERSUS

𝔐rs. ℌarriet 𝔅eecher 𝔖towe's

SUNNY MEMORIES

In (England) a Foreign Land:

OR A FAITHFUL PICTURE OF THE

EXTIRPATION of the CELTIC RACE

FROM THE HIGHLANDS OF SCOTLAND.

GLASGOW :—ARCHIBALD SINCLAIR, 10 BOTHWELL STREET.
EDINBURGH :—JOHN GRANT, GEORGE IV. BRIDGE.
INVERNESS :—JOHN NOBLE, CASTLE STREET.
OBAN :—HUGH MacDONALD, ESPLANADE.

1892.

LIBRARY
FEB
8
1988
UNIVERSITY
OF TORONTO

PUBLISHER'S PREFACE.

In publishing a new edition of Donald Macleod's "Gloomy Memories" it may be interesting to submit a few facts regarding previous editions. The first edition, printed for the author at the *Chronicle* Office, Edinburgh, in 1841, consisted of a reprint of a number of letters addressed to the *Edinburgh Weekly Chronicle.* A second edition was published in Greenock in 1856, while a third edition, enlarged and improved, was published in Toronto, Canada, in 1857.

Despite the fact that three editions were published, the work was within recent years all but impossible to procure. The idea of publishing the present edition, which is a reprint of that published in Canada, is due to Mr. John Campbell, a patriotic Mull man resident in Greenock, who, impressed with the educative value of the "Gloomy Memories," set about collecting subscriptions with the view of having an edition published at a price that would place the work within the reach of all. To his efforts therefore, conjoined with the patriotism of a number of Celts and others interested in the Highlands, the public are indebted for the present re-issue of the "Gloomy Memories."

PREFACE TO THE PRESENT EDITION.

MANY things have happened in the County of Sutherland, as well as in the Highlands generally, since 1840-41, when Donald MacLeod wrote to the *Edinburgh Weekly Chronicle* about "the Sutherland Clearances," and even since the later portions of this work were called forth by Mrs. Beecher Stowe's attempt in her "Sunny Memories" to whitewash the house of Sutherland after its defilement from contact with the fire and crow-bar brigade of that county. To many interested in the Highlands of Scotland, the title of this book has been long familiar, and the name of Donald MacLeod has long been esteemed and honoured. Few, however, of the present generation have read the "Gloomy Memories" as the earlier editions are long out of print, and but comparatively few of the Canadian edition, published in 1857, reached this country. In these circumstances it may be interesting to give a few facts regarding the author of this patriotic work, and the causes which led him to publish his "Gloomy Memories."

Donald MacLeod was born at Rossal, Strathnaver, where his father, William MacLeod, was at the time a farmer. When Donald was about twenty years of age, his father was obliged to leave his little farm in order that it might form part of a gigantic sheep run, and was obliged to accept a croft among others at the foot of the Strath, in *Aird-an-iasgaich*. Afterwards, the family were removed to Strathy Point, whence Donald had to make another move at the instance of Patrick Sellar's successor. He removed southward, keeping as long as he could within the bounds of the county. The last employment he had in his native shire was as a mason building the breast on the north side of the Kyle, and to the east of the bridge of Bonar.

From this he went to Edinburgh, where he found access to the press, but such an " agitator " was not likely to receive much encouragement in that city of " law and order," and accordingly Donald MacLeod went to Canada, where he ended his days. In Woodstock, Ontario, he prepared for the press, the edition which was published for him in 1857, by Thomson & Coy., *Colonist* Office, Toronto.

No one who reads the "Gloomy Memories" and considers the author's environments and opportunities, can fail to observe the marked ability with which he states his facts, and the firmness displayed at a time when his sentiments could find but little support and scanty approval. Despite the attempts of Mrs Harriet Beecher Stowe, and Commissioner James Loch, M.P., to whitewash the Sutherland escutcheon, and the various efforts of the Sellar family to vindicate the memory of their father, yet the statements made by Donald MacLeod have never been overturned or refuted —indeed they have in these latter days been fully substantiated. The Royal Commission appointed in 1883 to enquire into the condition of the Highland Crofters had ample evidence submitted to it in the county regarding the Sutherlandshire clearances, their extent and attendant cruelties. At its sittings in Edinburgh, the Commission heard the evidence of two witnesses of these cruel evictions, as well as received fifteen duly attested affidavits of old men then living who had been eye-witnesses of the clearances, and of the accompanying atrocities.

The conduct of the clergy during the period of these evictions must call forth the censure of all right thinking persons. Instead of pleading the cause of the poor and defending the widow and orphan, they, with one or two exceptions, aided and abetted the evictors and sought to justify their conduct. Nor is the attitude of the clergy towards the Crofter Agitation in our own day much better. As a rule—with just sufficient exceptions to prove the rule—they have either sided with the oppressors of the people and condemned the agitators, or displayed a callous indifference when the most vital interests of their people were at stake. Even many of the successors of those who protested so vehemently against "site refusers" in 1843, are frequently found attempting to justify the oppression and extortion of modern landlordism. It is therefore a matter of profound thankfulness that the people have asserted their rights and demanded a restitution of privileges long denied them. Till within recent years the Highland people were denied iii

a voice in the making of those laws under which they lived. An extended franchise has recently endowed them with a new existence and their sufferances are now sought for with a persistency indicative of their importance in the domain of politics. *

The Crofters' Act of 1886, despite its imperfections and aggrivating limitations, is based on the historic rights of the Celts, and is therefore but an earnest of what must yet be conceded, if the Highlanders are united in their desires and persistent in their demands. How it would have cheered the heart of Donald MacLeod had he lived to see the passing of the Crofters' Act, and he would have been gratified beyond measure to find that the electors of his native county had, at the last general election, declined the blandishments of those in authority and sent a crofter's son, Mr Angus Sutherland to Parliament to represent them—and so furnished all other constituencies with an example well worthy of imitation.

GLASGOW, 1892.   FIONN.

* In 1884 the Sutherland constituency was 325, in 1885 the extended franchise raised it to 3180.

John MacKay
Newland
Bettyhill
Thurso
Sutherlands

INTRODUCTION

TO CANADIAN EDITION.

To DONALD MATHESON, Esq., M.P.P., for North Oxford, Canada West, and WILLIAM MANSON, Esq., Captain of the Highland Guards, New York, Scottish Highlanders, and their descendants in the Canadas, and in the United States of America.

GENTLEMEN,—In dedicating the following narrative to you, the author has not the vanity to suppose that you will be honoured thereby, containing as it does a narration of painful facts, connected with the suffering and depreciation of a *once* mighty race of people, who had largely contributed to the renown of Britain as a nation, and instrumental in raising her to her present proud position among the nations of the earth.   It is not the object of the author to dilate here upon the antiquity and character of the Celtic race, but expose the cruelty and injustice to which they have been subjected by the aristocracy of Great Britain, and tolerated by the Government, seemingly with the avowed intention to extirpate them root and branch from the land of their birth and home of their forefathers, and to convert the fertile valleys of Caledonia, " the land of the brave," into hunting and sheep walks.   Doubtless the cruel dealings of Highland aristocracy to the down-trodden sons and daughters of Caledonia, will find apologists, and even at the present time they have procured an American literary luminary, who promises well to whitewash their foul deeds, particularly the Sutherlandshire depopulators (*of the long purse*); and endeavouring to make it appear that all the author and others have written about the Sutherlandshire clearances, were malicious accusations and groundless grievances; *but she will not get Scot free away with it.* I know, experimentally, that the advocates of the poor man's rights do labor under many disadvantages ; still the author of this work rejoices that he has it in his power to appeal to hundreds of his countrymen to attest the veracity of all the statements he advances, and has confidence in his own abilities to bring home every charge of cruelty and oppression practised upon the Sutherlandshire Highlanders by their ruthless and tyrannical lords of the soil and their underlings.   This unvarnished narrative, imperfect as it may be, in regard to its literary character, is however, inscribed not from any mercenary motives, but as a humble tribute of regard for your well known sympathies for the wrongs of your oppressed countrymen : trusting, that a liberal allowance will be made for the limited literary attainments of

Yours respectfully,
DONALD M'LEOD.

Woodstock, 20th Feb., 1857.

GENTLEMEN AND FELLOW COUNTRYMEN :—

It is true, as many of you said, that we have had at one time a nativity, and a native country, to which we and our forefathers were married and loved—where we have kindred feelings and associations, as sacred to our memory as almost our very existence. It is true that we are the genuine descendants of a race of whom we have much cause to be proud, and boast of—for we may turn up the pages of antiquity and ransack modern and ancient history in vain, to find out a race of people, among whom bravery and patriotism existed equal to the Celtic race, or among whom Civilization, Science, Literature, Morality, Benevolence, and Humanity, made such progress as among the Celtic, who occupied the Highlands of Scotland. But alas, alas ! It is true, that all that they were—all that they have done for ungrateful Britain, went for nothing when their enemies got the upper hand of them. It is now a lamentable truth, that the Highlands of Scotland (Tìr mo ghràidh. Tìr nam beann, nangleann's nan gaisgeach) which the Roman army in their victorious days failed to conquer —which the brutal Edwards, and Cromwell, and many other formidable invaders failed to subdue—are now converted to a howling solitary wilderness, from which joy and rejoicing are fled for ever. Where the martial notes of the bag-pipes, echoed by mountains and glens, ceased to be heard—and where no sweeter strains to cheer the stranger who may happen to travel there, are heard, than the yell of shepherds and foxhunters the bleating of sheep, the barking of collie dogs, and the screeches of the owl and eagle.

It is true my friends, that I have devoted all my spare time and means, for the last thirty-four years, expostulating, remonstrating with, and exposing the desolators of my country, and extirpators of my race, from the land of their birth, and advocating the cause of the suffering people, during these trying, murdering, and desolating times—considering that I could not serve God in a more acceptable way, than to help those who could not help themselves. Thousands of my countrymen in this country, and elsewhere, will bear me witness in what I have suffered at the hands of the scions of Highland aristocracy, for performing what I considered my incumbent duty.

Not knowing my position in life, especially my pecuniary circumstances, many of my countrymen in the Canadas, say—Why not come out DONALD M'LEOD with your long promised *Highland Cabin*, that the cruel conduct, and ungodly oppression of Highland oppressors, may be immortalized in the Canadas.

Your importunities are most agreeable to me, for I bear in my mind an undying desire to gratify you, and I hope in the course of some time, that I will accomplish it.

The only excuse I can plead for the delay, is my circumscribed circumstances. I have been peeled and plucked so often, that there was scarcely a feather in my wings when I left Scotland, and they are but slowly progressing as yet—but there is hope of their restoration. To solicit aid was hitherto foreign to my mind, but now I am old and have learnt, (nach sluagh duine na ònar) that one man is not a people.

The time is now come when I consider I have to perform my part to gratify you. The conflicting opinions and ideas regarding the *rights* of property, more especially property in land, and what constitutes property in land, is a great barrier in my way : all who read and believe sacred history, I think will agree with me, that the whole creation of *God* was at one time public property. How is the most part of God's creation now taken out of His hands, and converted to individual private property ? Since history took notice of the movement of nations, I can trace only three fundamental, feasible laws, which constitute right of property in land, viz :—the laws of discovery, of conquest, and of purchase. For instance. when a seafaring captain discovers a continent, or an island, he takes possession of it in the name of his Sovereign and Government. On his return he is rewarded. Government transports, with soldiers, surveyors, pioneers, &c., are dispatched to ascertain the mineral wealth and various resources of the land, and all expenses for discovery, and of the expedition are paid out of the public treasury, hence the discovered land becomes national property. Emigration will follow, commissioners are appointed by government, (and paid out of the public purse) to sell the land. The land is sold, but under certain stipulations, and these conditions must be observed, or the purchase right is forfeited. Though you purchased the land legally, and pay for it punctually, still government has a perfect right, (at least should have) to compel the obstinate and vicious to cultivate, or use the land for the greatest good or benefit of the lieges ; wise governments do in all cases retain for themselves the power that no right of property in land shall be a barrier to public good and prosperity ; railways and canals can be driven through your land, quarries and gravel pits can be opened in your corn-fields, whether you will or not, so that in my opinion land cannot be, nor should be, private property that a man can do what he pleases with it.

There are many vicious, inhumane, and unconstitutional men in this world, and to be found among land owners in greater ratio than any other classes I know or read about. Now supposing that one or any number of them took it into their heads to convert their estates into hunting parks, lays, and preserves of wild and destructive animals, which could neither be enclosed nor prevented from depradatory inroads upon other people's property—purposely to afford themselves, their rich friends, and favourite companions amusement, or to let their domains upon rent to sportsmen, should not government interfere. But to find these men boldly entering both Houses of Parliament with a bill demanding an Act of Parliament to protect them in their wicked and unconstitutional scheme, and to punish by banishment or long imprisonment, any one who would even trespass upon the preserves or lays of these animals to annoy them. But this is not all, but an act whereby they could seize upon the property of their poorer co-proprietors and neighbours, burn down their habitations, banish themselves from the land, and add their property to their own extensive game preserves. You surely would consider this effrontery without a parallel in the annals of plunderers ; and I am sure you will agree with me that the imbecillity, yea, insanity of the Legislature or Government who would enact such laws and grant such liberties, are beyond the comprehension of rational beings; likewise that the shortsightedness, culpable carelessness, and cowardice of a nation boasting of their civilization, intelligence, and christianity, who would tolerate such unwise and ungodly proceedings are beyond description. But you say *Donald* are you *raving*, where did such enormities take place? I tell you in Scotland; yes in beloved and never to be forgotten Scotland, in Caledonia *Tir nam beann, nan gleann's nan Gaisgeach*,—"the land of the mountains, the cataracts, and heroes" still worse than this took place, and I will make it as clear as noonday to you in my narrative,—yes, after the union of England and Scotland, far more insane and unconstitutional laws were enacted, and to the everlasting disgrace of the British Parliament and nation are still allowed a stain upon the statute book, and in full operation, to rob the poor to make the rich richer—to gratify a few avaricious minions who, constitutionally speaking, forfeited their rights of property, (with very few exceptions) their rights and privileges of communion with christians, and who should long ere now be arraigned before the highest *tribunal* of the nation, and dealt with as conspirators and traitors. Men who have neither bravery, ancestry, virtue, or honour to boast of; men who cannot claim the rights of *discovery*, of *conquest*, of defending, nor of purchase to the land they now hold as their private property, and considering their rights to these lands *sacred*.

Very few Historians, however unprincipled and partial, ever attempted to deprive the Celtic race of their right of discovery to Scotland, and we have ample proof in history of how the Celts defended Scotland from every invader from the first invasion of the Romans down to the ignoble union or alliance with England; so that Scotland stands alone among the nations of the known world *unconquered*. No doubt the Lowlands of Scotland have been invaded and conquered more than once; but when these powerful invaders came to exchange blows with the (unmixed in blood) Celtic Caledonians, they met with more than their match, were repelled, had to retrace their steps, and often not many of them left to retrace their steps. If this is admitted, (and who can deny it) I maintain that the lineal descendents of the discoverers and defenders of Scotland, are the real proprietors of the land, and that every one of that lineage from John O'Groat to Maiden Kirk, has as good a right to a portion of the land as the Dukes of Roxburgh, Buccleuch, Hamilton, Athol, Argyle, Gordon, or Sutherland, who (along with other nine or ten Earls, Marquises and Lords) hold more than the two-thirds of Scotland, as their private property, exclusively for themselves and their families' agrandizement, luxury and amusement, and three-fourths of their domains devoted to rear brute animals. How the legitimate heirs of children of the soil were dispossessed and expelled, and how aliens and cruel bastards got possession of the Scottish soil, is to be explained. To trace the history of the Celtic race down from the Garden of Eden to Cape-wrath, in Sutherlandshire would be the work of supererogation, hence I must confine myself to the time since history took hold of their movements and system of Government; and however complicated, conflicting, and partial

historians are upon the genealogy, customs and government of this race, it is evident that braver men never existed, and no other race on record who excelled them in literature, science, and civilization.

I would in particular solicit the attention of my readers to what they should all know—the chain of Scottish historians, whose works are still extant, though suppressed and locked up from those who should be edified by them—works sufficient to convince the most obdurate, that learning and civilization always followed our race from the earliest ages, not only in Scotland but in other nations where they made a distinguished figure. "I am tired," says Julius Leichton, "of hearing the Roman authors quoted, when the commencement of our civilization is spoken of, while nothing is said of the Celts, or of our obligation to them. It was not the *Latins*, it was the *Gauls* who were our first instructors. Aristotle declared that philosophy was derived by the Greeks from the Gauls, and not imparted to them. The Gauls were truly of sharp wit and apt to learn. So much did the Briton Celts excel in profound learning, that the youths of the continent came hitherto to study by a course of no less than twenty year's probation." (See *Tacitus's* life of *Agricola*.) Read the same Roman historian's admiration and description of the Caledonian Celts under the command of Corbred the Second, surnamed Galgacus and twenty-second King of Scotland, when they confronted the Romam army under the command of Agricola, at the foot of the Grampian hills, where a most sanguinary battle was fought; and though the Romans by stratagem gained a partial victory, and when Agricola proposed to pursue them, "No," said Tacitus (his son-in-law) "be content that you have so many of the Roman soldiers to lead off the field that if you pursue the defeated Caledonians one league further, you shall not have one Roman soldier to guard your person going home. These are the most formidable, and bravest enemy that ever Rome had to confront, every one of them will die before they yield, they are true patriots, Agricola, make all haste to your strongholds or you are done." So the Romans had to retrace their steps, and the Calenonians pursued them until the Romans were ultimately driven into the sea. Columba burned many of these Celtic records, yet many survived his ravages. St. Patrick burned one hundred and eighty-nine of those works at Tara, Ireland, all written in the Gaelic language, with a little mixture of Latin. Edward the First, of England, destroyed many of them, and after the ignoble union with England, what portion of them were preserved extant from these ravages, are now suppressed so as to deprive Scotland of their Celtic record and of the history of their grandfathers. I find thirty-seven of these records suppressed, and locked up in libraries where only a few favorites are admitted, and those say very little about them, except what they say to mutilate and violate them. To enumerate all the works in the Gaelic, Latin, and English language, now suppressed, would require more room or space than I can spare in this small narrative. Among these works, we find the ancient annals of Scotland; the Pictish Chronicle of high antiquity; the register of St. Andrew, beginning with 827, when that university was founded by the primitive Celtic christians of Scotland; the works of Ncuius in the

seventh century; the annals of Dunbarton, beginning with the Colum-
bian period; the Chronicle of Melrose, partly written in Gaelic, and
partly in Latin; the Obituary and Chartularly of Glasgow; the History
of Scotland by Vermandus, Arch-Deacon of St. Andrew, in 1079,
Hector Boethius, first principal of Aberdeen College, his history cut deep
and is on that account abhorred by the English, (on the savage charge
given by Edward the First to his no less savage son, to boil him after he
was dead, and to carry his bones with him to frighten the Scots)—Boethius
remarks that after he was boiled, " few would sup the broth." The black
book of Paisley, the last part of which is a continuation of Scots' Chroni-
con. Also Lord Elibank's Treatise on the Scottish League with France
in the reign of Charlemange; and the vast collection of Scottish Annals
collected by Sir James Balfour, still preserved, particularly his registers
of Scone and Cambuskeneth, now locked up in the Advocates' Library,
Edinburgh, besides his history of Fergus the First to Charles the First;
together with the Monastic Chronicles, under the appropriate title of
Scottish Annals.

But all these and as many more are suppressed, and locked up, but still
extant; besides this we have about one hundred manuscript volumes in the
Gaelic language, collected and in the possession of the Highland Society,
Edinburgh, some of which were transcribed in the fifth century, and is
allowed by competent judges, to be the oldest document written in any
living language; the document itself is sufficient to prove its author. He
was named *Fithil*, rector of the High School of *Iona*. The volume consists of two poems, inculcating the only true guide to well-doing here, and
eternal happiness hereafter, viz. : that spotless morality which is alone
founded on the word of God; there is also a critical dissertation on a
singular poem, *Tain Bo*, or the cattle spoil, an event which happened only
five years after the Ascension. All of these Gaelic volumes consists of
treatises on Botany, Anatomy, Astronomy, Astrology, Theology, Economy,
Science, Literature, and Politics; all in the Gaelic language, but all (as I
said before) suppressed or lying useless, locked up in universities' and
societies' libraries. It is a very natural enquiry :—Why are these works
suppressed or locked up? or by whom, and what is the cause for it?—
They are suppressed by the British Government, and the cause is obvious
but ignoble in the extreme.

Previous to the miscalled union of Scotland and England it is evident
that England could never conquer Scotland until the Caledonians were
subdued; they often made bloody attempts, but were as often defeated; but
England had recourse to intrigues, her favourite weapons, and after securing her alliance with Scotland, she found it a very easy task to conquer.
What her arms, and her bloody and murderous kings and generals could
never achieve, her treacherous intrigues and money did for her. She got
Scot to fight against Scot, Caledonian against Caledonian. She then
laughed in her sleeve, and exulted like the lion in the fable when he
saw the two bulls in the same park with him quarrelling and fighting;
knowing they would soon become his pray, for she (*stretched upon a
couch of down*) had her soul satisfaction to see the two d—— stupid

Scottish bulls fighting between death and life until they ultimately conquered and subdued one another in 1746, upon the murderous and unfortunate field of Culloden, when the English insatiable Lion seized upon
them both, and Scotland, who, before this, was the *pride* and protectoress
and faithful ally of all the reformed christian nations of the world, and
the terror of England; and all other cruel ambitious nations, her name
became now *Ichabod*, her glory departed, she forfeited her proud position
among nations, aud ceased forever to be numbered among them or recog-
nized as a nation.   England seized her Government, her laws, and in
short her all.   The duped, affected, and the disaffected, shared alike.
No doubt the Duke of Cumberland, the most obnoxious, cowardly monster,
that ever disgraced humanity, commissioned his followers to acts of murder, plunder, and violence.   Thank God, unprecedented in the histories of
nations (excepting England) plunder which some of them do enjoy to this
day, Argyle among the noblest of them.   In that unfortunate year the
Black Act was enacted, which deprived the Caledonians of their national
garb, of their arms, and forbade them to wear either under the
pains and penalties of heavy fines, long imprisonment, and banishment.
This nefarious act was in force, and strictly watched for thirty-two
years, which is equal to a generation.   Our poets, the reprovers of evil
cowardly deeds, and the recorders of the deeds of valiant men, were
silenced, and many of them made a narrow escape from the gallows, for
their *pensive* memoirs of the fallen at Culloden, on the day when Scotland was prostrated, at the foot of her avowed enemy, a day pregnant with
degradation, slavery, and the desolation and misery I have to record ; all
the Gaelic manuscript and history that could be discovered, by hook or
by crook, was seized, destroyed, or locked up, among which was the
national records, from Fergus the First, to William the First, and none
who understood the language were admitted to see them ; and after the
elapse of thirty-two years of this *Reign of Terror* very few were found
to peruse or understand the language.
   There were various motives for these outrageous proceedings, against the
Caledonians in particular, and they answered their various designs to the
aristocrats heart's desire.   England knew that the most effectual way to
subdue the Celts, was to crush their loyalty to their legitimate sovereign,
to crush their kindred feeling, habits and customs, and extirpate the
patriarchial system of government from among them ; but there was
another primary cause, viz. : the Celtic history of Scotland recorded the
feudal brutality of English invaders in Scotland, which is indeed too
horrifying to speak of, hence would need to be suppressed, that England's
barbarity might be obliterated, and that Scotland and Ireland might be
saddled with all her sins.   Moreover that Scotland might be left defenceless from the attacks of England's hired historians, to defame her in her
government and her chivalry, in her patriotism, her customs, her science,
and literature, and to make everything that was great and good, English.
It is a notorious fact that so far as the ingenuity of these *hired* emmisaries
could go, they were faithful to their employers ; and that these noted
calumniators of Scotland were chosen from among her own treacherous

sons, beginning with Robertson, under the dictation and command of Horace Walpole, the notorious *Dupe* of Chaterton, down to infamous Babington Macaulay. Limits will not permit me to detail the injustice done to Cedonians by these *hired* literary scourges, yet with all that they have done, there is still extant of the history of our noble race, enough to make these mutilators blush, and more than enough to make their spurious sarcasm and unfounded calumny stink in Scottish and in the world's nostrils. Five hundred years before the Christian Era, the Celts took possession of Scotland, and down from that period they governed themselves under the Patriarchial system, until the last remnant of it was destroyed upon the unfortunate muir ef Culloden ; they had their kings and chieftains, who were entrusted with their government, not by hereditary rights, but as they were found competent to discharge their duties. They obeyed and ardently loved and respected their kings and chieftains while they behaved themselves, but no further ; never allowed them to interfere with the rights of the land any further than to parcel it out to their followers impartially, and the people parcelled out to them what they considered sufficient to keep them comfortable and respectable. The chieftains or captains were amenable to the king in all their proceedings ; when a dispute arose between the people and their chief, that could not be settled otherwise, it was submitted to the king as their umpire ; his decision was final.

When the king required men to defend the nation, each chief had to appear with so many trained men, in proportion to the number entrusted to them ; and in proportion as they distinguished themselves on the battle field, they were honoured and rewarded by the king. According to our Celtic Annals, the founder of the noble family of Sutherland (after which now an Englishman takes his name, and who will make a conspicuous figure in my narrative) flourished in the year seventy-six, and fought under Galgacus, the hero of the Grampians, (see Nicholl's Scottish Peerage) and we find another of that noble family of Thanes, Barons, and Earls, who kept their history unsullied from any acts of cruelty or injustice for more than nineteen hundred years, and their memory dear to those under them for ages. I say we find him joining Bobert Bruce upon the memorable field of Bannockburn, leading a powerful and resolute body of his retainers to the field of slaughter ; upon this great occasion they distinguished themselves so well that the king complimented their noble leader upon the field of battle, and shortly afterwards presented him with a *charter* of lands in Morayshire, Caithness and Sutherland Shires ; but upon the express conditions that he would attend to the military discipline of those brave man, and that he and his offspring, and they and their offspring, would possess those lands while he and them continued loyal subjects, and attached to the crown of Scotland ; many similar distinctions were made and charters granted by Robert Bruce after the battle of Bannockburn, but all on the same conditions. Many of the Scotch Kings and Queens who succeeded Bruce were still more strict upon the chief or captains ; they were restricted to only a few acres of pleasure ground, and no piece of land susceptible of cultivation was to remain uncultivated, or unoccupied, and the mountains and forests were free to all. Kings, queens, and captains, knew that men, faithful adherents, who had an interest in the soil, were their safeguard and protectors in the hour of need and of danger, and they valued their services. This is the fundamental Patriarchial laws of property in land in Scotland. How were these laws reversed, and that now, a very few men claim every inch of land in Scotland, as their private property, and their rights to these sacred? Have they purchased their lands from the rightful owners? No. Have they got it from *Heaven*? No; but by taking the advantage of the revolts, and revolutions which followed the dethroning of the legitimate Sovereigns, and the treacherous union with England, they managed to plunder the people of it. After the union a new sacred perishable parchment right of property was cousecrated, and not a vestige of right or of protection was left for the people only that the land was bound to maintain the disabled poor in so much of the necessaries of life as was considered sufficient to sustain life, and so far was this same vestige neglected, that it was for one hundred and twenty years lying under dust, unmolested, in the Advocates' Library, Edinburgh, and the poor throughout Scotland perishing and dying in want, and might sleep there yet, was it not for that *God fearing* man, Mr Charles Spence, Solicitor, Supreme Court, at the entreaties of many, made a search, and found it and took an active part in putting it in force. I myself went to Sutherlandshire and supplied Mr. Spence with seventy-two cases of the Ducal Estate, besides what I supplied from the neighbouring Counties and Estates; we took action in some of them and were successful, the Court of Session was crowded with poor cases, there the *hue* and *cry* got up, Highland landlords will be ruined and lowland landlords will not escape. Sir Duncan MacNeil was then Lord Advocate for Scotland. He was solicited to prepare a poor law bill to parliament to save Highland landlords from ruin and bankruptcy. Sir Duncan went to work, prepared an *admirable* bill, or rather a compilation of complications, of crook and straights, hollows and bolds, short and long, mockery and realities, sense and nonsense, heaped up in a voluminous volume, he hurried the bill through both Houses of Parliament, and behold the result; the poor were deprived of the only vestige of right they had, and poverty made a crime, no man however charitably disposed can interfere in their behalf now; but Sir Duncan like a wise philosopher secured a luxurious situation for his brother Sir John, who sits at the head of the Board of Supervision in Edinburgh, gauging the stomachs of the Scottish poor to know to a nicety how much food they require to sustain life. The operation of this bill is a disgrace to christianity, as you will see when I come to shew it up in its proper place. But sinful and unjust as this bungling bill is, yet Highland landlords found a loop-hole to get rid of it untouched. They had a long established law by which they could expel the poor of the soil, to foreign lands or to large towns where they had to be sustained by people who had no right to do it, and who had no hand in impoverishing them and besides they have an arbitrary power, (which none durst contend) to tax the rest of their retainers, who in most cases are not much better off than the paupers, they are taxed for their maintainance; but they dare not whisper a complaint or off they go; in this way the Highland minions got of *Scot free.* But their unhallowed schemes are constituted in their edicts forbidding marriages on their estates. I have before me a letter from a friend stating that there are in the parish of Clyne, Sutherlandshire, a parish of small size, seventy-five bachelors, the oldest of them seventy-five years; and the youngest of them thirty-five years of age, only two marriages, and three baptisms registered; in another parish one baptism no marriage, and so on. It is not very likely that they would tell Mrs. B. Stowe, or that she enquired about this edict, in order to give it a place in her sunny memories, but she must have it. More of this afterwards. In 1846, the result of expelling the people from their fertile valleys and straths, and huddling them (those who could not make their escape to foreign lands or elsewhere) together in motley groups upon patches of barren moors, precipices, and by corners upon the sea shore, exposed to all the casualities of the seasons; places with few exceptions never designed by God for cultivation, nor for the abode of man, without the least encouragement for improvement, all tenants at will ready to be turned away for the least offence, or when a grazier or huntsman envied their places.

This is a cursed scheme which was adopted by every Highland lahdlord, from Cape-wrath to the Mull of Kintyre, with one or two honourable exceptions, (it would be more applicable if I called these Highland scourges). I say in the year 1846-'47, when the miserable unnourishing potatoe crop which was reared upon these patches failed, then the cry of famine in the Highlands got up like the voice of thunder, sounded and resounded, to the outmost skirts of Europe, India, and America; public meetings were called to see what could be devised and done to save the people. The first meeting was held in the Music Hall, Edinburgh, the Lord Provost Black, presided; the Rev. Norman M'Leod, junior, moved the first resolution, which ran nearly thus :— "As it pleased God in his mysterious providence to visit the Highlands and Islands of Scotland with Famine on account of their sin, that it behoved Christians of all denominations who were blessed with the means to come forward liberally that the Highlanders might be saved." The resolution was seconded and supported when his Lordship rose to put it to the meeting, I got up and announced that I had a few words to say before it was put to the meeting, being in my moleskin working dress every eye was fixed upon me, the same as if I was a wolf that had sprang up; however I got a hearing and said that I was a Highlander, and knew the cause of distress and famine in the Highlands, and that I had devoted all my spare time for many years back proclaiming it publicly in their ears, and the ears of the nation, predicting that ultimately it would arrive at this fearful crisis, and now I cannot sit quiet in this great assembly of learned men, and hear the sins and heavy guilt of Highland proprietors saddled upon my GOD, and that by his well paid servant. Will the Rev. mover of this resolution tell me what cause he supposes the Lord has against the poor Highlanders for so long a time (for they were not in a much better state for the last twenty-six years than they are now), that he should send a famine among them to destroy them ; or do the leaders of this movement consider themselves more humane and merciful than God, or that puny man or men can contend with him in doing what He in His mysterious providence, purposed to do ; methinks, that if God was to visit sinners with famine or any other calamity for their sins, that He would begin in London and with Highland proprietors, and not with the poor people who were more sinned against than sinners. Highland landlords are the legitimate parents, and the guilty authors of this and of former distress and famine in the Highlands of Scotland, and should be made responsible for it and for future calamities which they are storing up for the unfortunate victims of their boundless avarice. I did not come to this meeting, my Lord Provost, with a view to obstruct the proceedings, for I rejoice to see such steps taken to save the the people, not from the famine God sent among them to destroy them, but from the famine entailed upon them by their wicked unworthy landlords. But if God is not exonerated from the charge brought against Him, publicly here this day, and entirely separated from an ungodly association of Highland aristocrats, who were bent for years upon the destruction of Highlanders, and upon the extermination of the race from the soil, I will be under the necessity of proposing a counter resolution." His Lordship pledged himself that the committee would take it into consideration. I did not press my motion and the meeting proceeded. The appeal went forth, and was responded to in a manner creditable to the nation, the ·colonies and the United States of America. In less time than could be expected, the unprecedented sum of £300,000 was subscribed, and the legitimate parents of this distress were not behind with their subscriptions. Lord Macdonald subscribed, among the first, one thousand pounds sterling, Duke of Sutherland, two thousand pounds, other Dukes, Lords, Earls, and notorious Colonel Gordon, followed the example so far. The sole management of this enormous sum of money was placed in the hands of Government for distribution ; Lord Trevelyan, the Hero of the Test Starving Commission in Ireland, was appointed as commissioner for the distribution of this munificent gift of nations for the relief of Highlanders. He got a brig of war rigged out for his service, commanded by one Captain Elliot, an Englishman, an accomplished *tool* in the hands of tyrants and calumniators. The Highlanders were represented as dirty, lazy, untameable beings, who would do nothing to help themselves while they would be kept alive upon charity. Hence was decreed that every male and female considered by the local Boards of Relief able to work, were not to be relieved without working for it ; and to test their real need of relief, and their willingness to work, they were allowed *one pound of meal* as meat and wages for *ten hours' labour*, with the addition of one-half a pound of meal to each of their families, or children who could not work, and often the meal was so much adulterated that it was dangerous for even swine to eat it. Yes, reader, pregnant women whose husbands were not at home, and aged widows, were seen at this work, and treated in like manner.

I was then suggested by some known knave, that Highland proprietors would get so much of the money for improving their estates, as they knew best who was worthy of relief, and willing to work ; and these sums to be in proportion to their subscriptions ; then you may easily guess who got the lion's share of it. From their own reports we find, that Lord Macdonald got £3,000 in return for his £1,000 subscription, what he has done with it is not known, and never will, (and I durst not say that he pouched it). His Grace of Sutherland got £6,000 in return for his £2,000 subscription, (good return) but his Grace built a splendid hunting booth, in a secluded Glen, in the north-west portion of his domains, and he made a road to this booth from Lairg, through a solitary wilderness, a distance of at least thirty miles, entirely for the accommodation of his gamekeepers, huntsmen, and sportsmen ; any other travellers were seen only as rare as a pelican in the deserts of Arabia. But very few of the Sutherlanders reaped any benefit from these works, as on former occassions strangers were preferred. We could not expect to see this in Mrs. H. B. Stowe's Sunny Memories. Neither need we expect to see in her future Memories of the House of Sutherland, that during these distressing times a large quantity of meal was deposited in some of his Grace's stores and entrusted to some of his factors for distribution, and that that meal was concealed or unrighteously kept from the people for a whole twelvemonth, and used for feeding dogs, swine, poultry, and cattle, until it became so rotten that it was found dangerous to the health of these animals, then men were employed to hurl it out to *middens* and to the sea in rotten blue lumps ; great quantities of it were disposed of in this way, while the poor were chiefly feeding upon shell fish and sea weeds. This is a grave charge against his Grace and his wicked servants, who were, at all hazards, determined to destroy the people ; I have seen them living in Canada, and not far from me, who were employed for days at this work. Whether his Grace or his head commissioner, James Loch, dictated, or at least supplied Mrs. H. B. Stowe with all the information she required to make up chapter seventeenth of her Sunny Memories, (a lady whom I will use the liberty to address afterwards, but to whom I am not, at present afraid to tell her if she founded the information in Uncle Tom's Cabin upon no better evidence than she had on this occasion, that very little credence can be placed in it). I say whether these personages, along with Lord Trevelyan and his Quarter Deck Inspector were collectively or seperately connected with this diabolical outrage upon justice and humanity, is better known to themselves ; but one thing is evident, the crime was committed by their underlings, and let the reproach remain, among them as an immortal stain upon their character. Black and deformed as their deeds were, they were not without their precedents in the history of distributions in Sutherlandshire, which you will see as we proceed. To be brief, I believe that if a correct history of the distribution of this munificent gift of nations, the squandering away of the money and its misapplications could be obtained, it would be the most disgraceful which ever has been recorded, and that it would be the astonishment of mankind, how could men professing christianity and of good standing in society, be hardened so much as to commit such villany, or how could they ever afterwards have the effrontery to shew their face in society. At the closing up of the affair the public requested the trustees and officials to render an account of their stewardship. Accountants were employed for months examining their books. It was found out that six or seven thousand pounds sterling were wanted that could not be accounted for at all, and their accounts and disbursements so much confounded and confused that scrutiny was given up, and the infamous affair hushed up, and the wholesale plunderers allowed to escape with the booty, unblushingly to mix with society. This is all the satisfaction the liberal contributors got, or ever will, excepting Highland Dukes, Lords, &c., no doubt satisfactory to them, for they got for certainty the benefit of one hundred and thirty thousand pounds of it; take along with this, Captain Elliot with his crew of marines and sailors, him receiving his £1 10s. per day, and his subordidates receiving equal sums, according to their rank, and a host of agents and officials on full pay, you may easily believe that a very small portion of this extraordinary public bounty ever reached the stomachs of the poor for whom it was intended. Indeed it is a question with me if the poor realised any benefit at all from it, except those who had been transported to Canada and other colonies with it. I know for a certainty that after the funds were exhausted, that the people were in a worse state than they were before, and that the misapplication of these funds sealed the public bowels of compassion against them in future. For many years I was expostulating with the late and present Dukes of Sutherland in my own humble way, for their policy towards their people. In 1841 I published so many of my letters in the form of a pamphlet, which is here reprinted—some may think that I have some particular private spleen against the House of Sutherland, when I lay so heavy at them. To disabuse the mind of such, permit me to say (honestly) that I have no such private spleen to gratify, and that I have no more animosity towards the House of Sutherland than I have towards all other Highland depopulators. That I was persecuted and suffered much at the hands of the underlings of the House of Sutherland I do not deny nor conceal. But it is the ten-times *cursed* system which desolated Caledonia, beggared and pauperised the people, which broke down and scattered to the four winds of heaven the best portion of the materials of our national bulwarks, which robbed the people of their righteous rights, and left them the victims of their avaricious spoilers and defamers. This is the system to which I will be an avowed enemy and antagonist while I breathe the breath of life. You have now my former productions before you.

INTRODUCTION TO MY FIRST PAMPHLET.

FAMINE and destitution in the Highlands of Scotland have become proverbial, and if not altogether continuous, are at least the rule, while any little gleams of improvement or partial alleviation form the exception. There are, however, there as elsewhere, a considerable number who suffer few of the evils that flesh is heir to, but who thrive and fatten on the miseries of their victims—the poor natives, whom they insult, oppress, and expatriate, without apparently the least compunction for the extreme distress they occasion.

Every effect must have a cause, and that cause I shall only glance at here, as it will be sufficiently apparent in the course of my narration.

During the Peninsular war an uncommon demand for provisions of all description arose, and when, on the return of peace, this temporary demand was subsiding, the landlords, being the legislators, contrived to keep up the extravagant war prices, by a system of prohibitions against all foreign produce, so as to make a permanent artificial scarcity, and consequent dearth throughout the country, that they might continue to pocket the increased rents the war prices had enabled them to realise in a depreciated currency. This, then, was the moving spring which led to the general conspiracy of landlords against the before undisputed rights of the inhabitants, to a residence on their paternal soil which they had so often defended with their blood, and to a subsistence from its produce in return for their industry. Hence the severities exercised in the most reckless manner, against the aborigines of the Highlands in general, and those of Sutherlandshire in particular; severities which have almost annihilated that habitual fidelity to, and respect for his superiors, for which the Gael was always so remarkable, and which formed the leading moral trait in his character, and was identified with his very existence. These bonds have been rudely severed; the immediate descendants of those serfs and retainers whose attachment to their chiefs was a passion, and for whom they were at any time, ready to lay down their lives, have been robbed, oppressed, and driven away, to make room for flocks and herds to supply the intense demand of the English market, excited by the legal prohibition of continental produce, and the wants of a rapidly increasing population.

The motive of the landlords was self-interest; and in the Highlands it has been pursued with a recklessness and remorselessness to which the proverbial tyranny and selfishness of that class elsewhere furnishes no parallel. Law and justice, religion and humanity, have been either totally disregarded, or what was still worse, converted into instruments of oppression.

The expulsion of the natives and the substitution of strange adventurers—sheep farmers, generally from England and from the English border—being, as it were, simultaneously agreed upon by the Highland proprietors, instruments were readily found to carry their plans into effect, who soon became so zealous in the service—not, however, forgetting to profit by the plunder in the meantime—that they carried their atrocities to a height which would have appalled their employers themselves, had they been witnesses of them. Every imaginable means, short of the sword or the musket, was put into requisition to drive the natives away, or to force them to exchange their farms and comfortable habitations, erected by themselves or their forefathers, for inhospitable rocks on the sea shore, and to depend for subsistence on the produce of the watery element in its wildest mood, and with whose perils they, in their hitherto pastoral life, were totally unacquainted and unfitted to contend.

This state of things, which I have reason to know, has prevailed more or less in all the Highland districts for more than 20 years, has carried to the greatest height in Sutherland. That unfortunate country was made another Moscow. The inhabitants were literally burnt out, and every contrivance of ingenious and unrelenting cruelty was eagerly adopted for extirpating the race. Many lives were sacrificed by famine and other hardships and privations ; hundreds stripped of their all, emigrated to the Canadas and other parts of America ; great numbers especially of the young and athletic, sought employment in the Lowlands and in England, where, few of them being skilled workmen, they were obliged— even farmers who had lived in comparative affluence in their own country— to compete with common labourers as hewers of wood and drawers of water, in communities where their language and simple manners rendered them objects of derision and ridicule. The aged and infirm, the widows and orphans, with those who could not think of leaving them alone in their helplessness ; and a number whose attachment to the soil which contained the ashes of their ancestors, and the temples where they had worshipped, in hopes of some change for the better, were induced to accept of the wretched allotments offered them on wild moors and barren rocks. These and their offspring remain in the country and form the *poor*, whose constant destitution and periodical famine is beginning to exercise more attention, than is agreeable to those who have been the cause of their miseries, lest many dark and infamous deeds should, by an authorised enquiry be revealed in open day. Hence the violent opposition to a Government enquiry conducted by impartial persons. The lairds have no objection to an enquiry to be conducted by themselves and the resident clergy, knowing that in that case, they would be quite safe, and the report would of course lay all the blame on the inveterate sloth, and vicious habits they have unceasingly laboured to assign as the causes of Highland destitution. Such a course of dark and inhumam policy as that so long going on in the Highlands, could not have existed if the public had been properly aware of it, but among a simple illiterate people, speaking a provincial dialect, it was easy for landlords, clergy, factors, and new tenants combined, who constituted the local administrators of both the law and gospel—men possessed of wealth, influence, talents and education—it was easy for them to effect their purposes, and stiffle all enquiry, while the mild nature, and religious training of the poor Highlanders, prevented their resorting to that determined resistance and wild revenge which sometimes sets bounds to the rapacity of landlords and clergy in the sister island. The Highlanders had not language to make his wrongs known through the press, nor did he resort to the ruthless deed ; hence he has been oppressed with impunity, while his persecutors hold up their heads as honourable gentlemen, and goodly ministers ! I am truly sorry that truth has obliged me to represent the character of these latter gentlemen in such an unfavourable light, but I am convinced that had they done their duty, in denouncing the wrongs perpetrated before their eyes, instead of becoming auxiliaries, the other parties would in most cases, have been unable to proceed. The oppressors always appealed to them for sanction and justification and were not disappointed. The foulest deeds were glossed over, and all the evil which could not be attributed to the natives themselves, such as severe seasons, famine, and consequent disease, was by these pious gentlemen ascribed to Providence, as a punishment for sin—the other parties who were enriching themselves, of course never sinned, for they were rolling in wealth and luxury at the expense of the poor sinners! Such was the holy teaching of these learned clerks. They had always the ear and confidence of the proprietors, and I put it to their consciences to say how often, if ever, they exerted that influence in favor of the oppressed, To the tribunal of that Master whose servants they pretend to be I cite them, where hypocrisy and glaring perversions will not avail! At this same tribunal also I might arraign those unjust men who perverted the judgment seat, and made what should have been a protection, an instrument of oppression. But at present I must beg the reader's attention to the following narrative, in which I have endeavored, by a recital of uncomtradicted and undeniable facts, to bring these parties to the bar of public opinion. Hitherto, during all the time that has passed in the publication of these letters, no attempt has been made to deny the facts I have alleged, though I have repeatedly challenged such contradiction.

Instead of my narrative exceeding truth, it has in reality fallen far short of it ; for no language that I am able to use, can convey an adequate idea of the wrongs and sufferings of my unfortunate countrymen. While I feel myself called on by a sense of duty to bring these wrongs and sufferings before the public, I regret that the subject has not fallen into abler hands; but, silence in the face of such a mass of cruelty and iniquity would be enough to make the very stones cry out! Having by the kindness of the Editor of the *Edinburgh Weekly Chronicle* been furnished with a vehicle, and assisted by other kind friends and correspondents, these letters have already met the public eye in the columns of that excellent paper, to the Editors and Proprietors of which I and my countrymen are so much indebted. I am now induced to comply with the urgent request of great numbers of my countrymen and others, to re-puplish the letters in the form of a pamphlet. I have engaged in this undertaking in the full confidence of the kind support of my countrymen and fellow-sufferers and their descendants, in whatever place or country, here or across the Atlantic, divine Providence may have fixed their destiny, in the fervent hope that He—

> " Who sees with equal eyes, as Lord of all,
> The hero perish and the sparrow fall,"

will so overrule events as to bring ultimate good out of the severe trials which He hath permitted to overtake my dear country, and that—

> " Though harsh and bitter is the root,
> Yet sweet will be the flower ! '

DESTITUTION IN SUTHERLANDSHIRE.

-------------------÷-------------------

LETTER I.

(To the Editor of the Edinburgh Weekly Chronicle.)

SIR :—I am a native of Sutherlandshire, and remember when the inhabitants of that country lived comfortably and happily, when the mansions of proprietors and the abodes of factors, magistrates, and ministers, were the seats of honor, truth, and good example—when people of quality were indeed what they were styled, the friends and benefactors of all who lived upon their domains. But all this is changed. Alas, alas! I have lived to see calamity upon calamity overtake the Sutherlanders. For five successive years on or about the term day, has scarcely anything been seen but removing the inhabitants in the most cruel and unfeeling manner, and burning the houses which they and their forefathers had occupied from time immemorial. The country was darkened by the smoke of the burnings, and the descendants of those who drew their swords at Bannockburn, Sheriffmuir, and Killicrankie—the children and nearest relations of those who sustained the honor of the British name in many a bloody field—the heroes of Egypt, Corunna, Toulouse, Salamanca, and Waterloo—were ruined, trampled upon, dispersed, and compelled to seek an asylum across the Atlantic; while those who remained from inability to emigrate, deprived of all the comforts of life, became paupers—beggars—a disgrace to the nation whose freedom and honour many of them had maintained by their valour and cemented with their blood.

To those causes the destitution and misery that exists in Sutherlandshire are to be ascribed; misery as great, if not the greatest to be found in any part of the Highlands, and that not the fruit of indolence or improvidence, as some would allege, but the inevitable result of the avarice and tyranny of the landlords and factors for the last thirty or forty years; of treatment, I presume to say, without a parallel in the history of this nation. I know that a great deal has been done to mitigate the sufferings of the Highlanders some years back, both by Government aid and public subscriptions, but the unhappy country of Sutherland was excluded from the benefits derived from these sources, by means of false statements and public speeches, made by hired agents, or by those whose interest it was to conceal the misery and destitution in the country of which themselves were the authors. Thus the Sutherlandshire sufferers have been shut out from receiving the assistance afforded by Government or by private individuals ; and owing to the thraldom and subjugation in which this once brave and happy people are to factors, magistrates, and ministers, they durst scarce whimper a complaint, much less say plainly, "Thus and thus have you done."

On the 20th of last April, a meeting of noblemen and gentlemen, connected with different districts of Scotland, was held in the British Hotel, Edinburgh, for the purpose of making inquiry into the misery and destitution prevailing in Scotland, and particularly in the Highlands, with a view to discover the causes and discuss means for meeting the prevailing evil. Gentlemen were appointed to make the necessary inquiry, and a committee named, with which these gentlemen were to communicate. At this meeting a Sutherlandshire proprietor made such representations regarding the inhabitants of that county, that, relying, I suppose, on his mere assertions, the proposed enquiry has never been carried into that district. Under these circumstances, I, who have been largely a sufferer, and a spectator of the sufferings of multitudes of my countrymen, would have felt myself deeply culpable if I kept silence, and did not take means to lay before the committee and the public the information of which I am possessed, to put the benevolent on their guard respecting the men who undertake to pervert, if they cannot stifle, the inquiry as to the causes and extent of distress in the shire of Sutherland. With a view to discharging this encumbent duty, I published a few remarks, signed 'A Highlander,' in the *Edinburgh Weekly Journal* of 29th May last, on the aforesaid proprietor's speech; to which he made a reply, accusing me of singular ignorance and misrepresentation, and endeavouring to exonerate himself. Another letter has since appeared in the same paper, signed, "A Sutherlandshire Tenant," denying my assertions and challenging me to prove them by stating facts. To meet this challenge, and to let these parties know that I am not so ignorant as they represent; and also to afford information to the before-mentioned committee, it being impossible for those gentlemen to apply an adequate remedy till they know the real cause and nature of the disease, I addressed a second letter to the editor of the *Weekly Journal*; but, to my astonishment, it was refused insertion; through what influence I am not prepared to say. I have, in consequence, been subjected to much reflection and obloquy for deserting a cause which would be so much benefitted by public discussion; and for failing to substantiate charges so publicly made. I have, therefore, now to request, that, through the medium of your valuable and impartial paper, the public may be made acquainted with the real state of the case; and I pledge myself not only to meet the two opponents mentioned, but to produce and substantiate such a series of appalling facts, as will sufficiently account for the distress prevailing in Sutherlandshire; and, I trust have a tendancy towards its mitigation.

LETTER II.

SIR,—Previous to redeeming my pledge to bring before the Public a series of facts relating to the more recent oppressions and expatriation of the unfortunate inhabitants of Sutherlandshire, it is necessary to take a brief retrospective glance at the original causes.

Down from the feudal times, the inhabitants of the hills and straths of Sutherlandshire, in a state of transition from vassalage to tenancy, looked upon the farms they occupied from their ancestors as their own, though subject to the arrangements as to rent, duties and services imposed by the chief in possession, to whom, though his own title might be equivocal, they habitually looked up with a degree of clannish veneration. Every thing was done "to please the Laird." In this kind of patriarchal dominion on the one side, and obedience and confidence on the other, did the late tenantry and their progenitors experience much happiness, and a degree of congenial comfort and simple pastoral enjoyment. But the late war and its consequences interfered with this happy state of things, and hence a foundation was laid for all the suffering and depopulation which has followed. This has not been peculiar to Sutherlandshire; the general plan of almost all the Highland proprietors of that period being to get rid of the original inhabitants, and turn the land into sheep farms, though from peculiar circumstances this plan was there carried into effect with more revolting and wholesale severity than in any of the surrounding counties.

The first attempt at this general *clearing* was partially made in Ross-shire, about the beginning of the present century; but from the resistance of the tenantry and other causes, has never been carried into general operation. The same was more or less the case in other counties. Effects do not occur without cause, nor do men become tyrants and monsters of cruelty all at once. Self-interest, real or imaginary, first prompts; the moral boundary is overstepped, the oppressed offer either passive or active resistance, and, in the arrogance of power, the strong resort to such means as will effect their purpose, reckless of conse-quences, and enforcing what they call the rights of property, utterly neglect its duties. I do not pretend to represent the late Duchess or Duke of Sutherlandshire in particular, as destitute of the common attri-butes of humanity, however atrocious may have been the acts perpetrated in their name, or by their authority. They were generally absentees, and while they gave-in to the general clearing scheme, I have no doubt they wished it to be carried into effect with as little hardship as possible. But their prompters and underlings pursued a more reckless course, and, intent only on their own selfish ends, deceived these high personages, representing the people as slothful and rebellious, while, as they pre-tended, every.thing necessary was done for their accomodation.

I have mentioned above, that the late war and its consequences laid the foundation of the evils complained of. Great Britian with her immense naval and military establishments, being in a great measure shut out from foreign supplies, and in a state of hostility or non-intercourse with all Europe and North America, almost all the necessaries of life had to be drawn from our own soil. Hence, its whole powers of production were required to supply the immense and daily increasing demand; and while the agricultural portions of the country were strained to yield an increase of grain, the more northern and mountainous districts were looked to for additional supplies of animal food. Hence, also, all the speculations to get rid of the human inhabitants of the Highlands, and replace them with cattle and sheep for the English market. At the conclusion of the war, these effects were about to cease with their cause, but the corn laws, and other food taxes, then interfered, and by excluding foreign animal food altogether, and grain till it was at a famine price, caused the increasing population to press against home produce, so as still to make it the interest of the Highland lairds to prefer cattle to human beings, and to encourage speculators with capital, from England and the south of Scotland, to take the lands over the heads of the original tenantry. Thus Highland wrongs were continued, and annually augmented, till the mass of guilt on the one hand, and of suffering on the other, became so great as almost to exceed description of belief. Hence the difficulty of bringing it fully before the public, especially as those interested in suppressing inquiry are numerous, powerful, and unsparing in the use of every influence to stop the mouths of the sufferers. Almost all the new tenants in Sutherlandshire have been made justices of the peace, or otherwise armed with authority, and can thus, under colour of law, commit violence and oppression whenever they find it convenient—the poor people having no redress, and scarce daring even to complain. The clergy, also, whose duty it is to denounce the oppressor, and aid the oppressed, have all, the whole seventeen parish ministers in Sutherlandshire, with one exception, found their account in abetting the wrongdoers, exhorting the people to quiet submission, helping to stifle their cries, telling them that all their sufferings came from the hand of God, and was a just punishment for their sins! In what manner those reverend gentlemen were benefitted by the change, and bribed thus to desert the cause of the people, I shall explain as I proceed.

The whole country, with the exception of a comparatively small part of one parish, held by Mr Dempster of Skibo, and similar portions on the outskirts of the county held by two or three other proprietors, is now in the hands of the Sutherland family, who, very rarely, perhaps only once in four or five years, visit their Highland estates. Hence the impunity afforded to the actors in the scenes of devastation and cruelty—the wholesale expulsion of the people, and pulling down and burning their habitations, which latter proceeding was peculiar to Sutherlandshire. In my subsequent communications I shall produce a selection of such facts and incidents as can be supported by sufficient testimony, to many of which I was an eye-witness, or was otherwise cognizant of them. I have been, with my family, for many years, removed, and at a distance from those scenes, and have no personal malice to gratify, my only motive being a desire to vindicate my ill-used countrymen from the aspersions cast upon them, to draw public attention to their wrongs, and if possible to bring about a fair inquiry, to be conducted by disinterested gentlemen, as to the real cause of their long-protracted misery and destitution, in order, that the public sympathies may be awakened in their behalf, and something effected for their relief. With these observations I now conclude, and in my next letter I will enter upon my narration of a few of such facts as can be fully authenticated by living testimony.

LETTER III.

Sir,—In my last letter, I endeavoured to trace the causes that led to the general clearing and consequent distress in Sutherlandshire, which dates its commencement from the year 1807. Previous to that period, partial removals had taken place, on the estates of Lord Reay, Mr. Honeyman of Armidale, and others: but these removals were under ordinary and comparitively favourable circumstances. Those who were ejected from their farms, were accommodated with smaller portions of land, and those who chose to emigrate had means in their power to do so, by the sale of their cattle, which then fetched an extraordinary high price. But in the year above mentioned, the system commenced on the Duchess of Sutherland's property; about 90 families were removed from the parishes of Farr and Larg. These people were, however, in some degree provided for, by giving them smaller lots of land, but many of these lots were at a distance of from 10 to 17 miles, so that the people had to remove their cattle and furniture thither, leaving their crops on the ground behind. Watching this crop from trespass of the cattle of the incoming tenants, and removing it in the autumn, was attended with great difficulty and loss. 'Besides, there was also much personal suffering, from their having to pull down their houses and carry away the timber of them, to erect houses on their new possessions, which houses they had to inhabit immediately on being covered in, and in the meantime, to live and sleep in the open air, except a few, who might be fortunate enough to get an unoccupied barn, or shed, from some of their charitable new come neighbours.

The effects of these circumstances on the health of the aged and infirm, and on the women and children, may be readily conceived—some lost their lives, and others contracted diseases that stuck to them for life.

During the year 1809, in the parishes of Dornoch, Rogart, Loth, Clyne, and Golspie, an extensive removal took place; several hundred families were turned out, but under circumstances of greater severity than the preceding. Every means were resorted to, to discourage the people, and to persuade them to give up their holdings quietly, and quit the country; and to those who could not be induced to do so, scraps of moor, and bog lands were offered in Dornoch moor, and Brora links, on which it was next to impossible to exist, in order that they may be scared into going entirely away. At this time, the estate was under the management of Mr. Young, a corn-dealer, as chief, and Mr. Patrick Sellar, a writer, as under-factor, the later of whom will make a conspicuous figure in my future communications. These gentlemen were both from Morayshire; and, in order to favour their own country people, and get rid of the natives, the former were constantly employed in all the improvements and public works under their direction, while the latter were taken at inferior wages, and only when strangers could not be had.

Thus, a large portion of the people of these five parishes were, in the course of two or three years, almost entirely rooted out, and those few who took the miserable allotments above mentioned, and some of their descendants, continue to exist on them in great poverty. Among these were the widows and orphans of those heads of families who had been drowned in the same year, in going to attend a fair, when upwards of one hundred individuals lost their lives, while crossing the ferry between Sutherland and Tain. These destitute creatures were obliged to accept of any spot which afforded them a residence, from inability to go elsewhere.

From this time till 1812 the process of ejection was carried on annually, in a greater or less degree, and during this period the estates of Gordon-bush and Uppet were added, by purchase, to the ducal property, and in the subsequent years, till 1829, the whole of the country, with the small exceptions before mentioned, had passed into the hands of the great family.

In the year 1811 a new era of depopulation commenced ; summonses of removal were served on large portions of the inhabitants. The lands were divided into extensive lots, and advertised to be let as sheep farms.

Strangers were seen daily traversing the country, viewing these lots, previous to bidding for them. They appeared to be in great fear of rough treatment from the inhabitants they were about to supersede; but the event proved they had no cause ; they were uniformly treated with civility, and even hospitality, thus affording no excuse for the measures of severity to which the factors and their adherents afterwards had recourse. However, the pretext desired was soon found in an apparently concerted plan. A person from the south, of the name of Reid, a manager on one of the sheep farms, raised an alarm that he had been pursued by some of the natives of Kildonan, and put in bodily fear. The factors eagerly jumped at this trumped-up story; they immediately swore in from sixty to one hundred retainers, and the new inhabitants, as special constables, trimmed and charged the cannon at Dunrobin Castle, which had reposed in silence since the last defeat of the unfortunate Stuarts. Messengers were then dispatched warning the people to attend at the castle at a certain hour, under the pretence of making amicable arrangements. Accordingly, large numbers prepared to obey the summons, ignorant of their enemies' intentions, till, when about six miles from the castle, a large body of them got a hint of their danger from some one in the secret, on which they called a halt and held a consultation, when it was resolved to pass on to the Inn at Golspie, and there await the rencontre with the factors. The latter were much disappointed at this derangement of their plans; but on their arrival with the sheriff, constables, &c., they told the people, to their astonishment, that a number of them were to be apprehended, and sent to Dornoch Jail, *on suspicion* of an attempt to take Mr. Reid's life ! The people, with one voice, declared their innocence, and that they would not suffer any of their number to be imprisoned on such a pretence. Without further provocation, the sheriff proceeded to read the riot act, a thing quite new and unintelligible to the poor Sutherlanders so long accustomed to bear their wrongs patiently ; however, they immediately dispersed and returned to their homes in peace. The factors, having now found the pretext desired, mounted their horses and galloped to the castle in pretended alarm, sought protection under the guns of their fortress, and sent an express to Fort George for a military force to suppress the rebellion in Sutherlandshire ! The 21st Regiment of foot (Irish) was accordingly ordered to proceed by forced marches, night and day, a distance of fifty miles, with artillery, and cart-loads of ammunition. On their arrival, some of them were heard to declare they would now have revenge on the Sutherlanders for the carnage of their countrymen at Tara-hill and Ballynamuck; but they were disappointed, for they found no rebels to cope with; so that, after having made a few prisoners, who were all liberated on a precognition being taken, they were ordered away to their barracks. The people meantime, dismayed and spirit-broken at the array of power brought against them, and seeing nothing but enemies on every side, even in those from whom they should have had comfort and succour, quietly submitted to their fate. The clergy, too, were continually preaching submission declaring these proceedings were fore-ordained of God, and denouncing the vengeance of Heaven and eternal damnation on those who should presume to make the least resistance. No wonder the poor Highlanders quailed under such influences; and the result was, that large districts of the parishes before mentioned were dispossessed at the May term, 1812.

The Earl of Selkirk hearing of these proceedings, came personally into Sutherlandshire, and by fair promises of encouragement, and other allurements, induced a number of the distressed outcast to enter into an arrangement with him, to emigrate to his estates on the Red River, North America. Accordingly, a whole shipful of them went thither; but on their arrival, after a tedious and disastrous passage, they found themselves deceived and deserted by his lordship, and left to their fate in an inclement wilderness, without protection against the savages, who plundered them on their arrival, and, finally massacred them all, with the exception of a few who escaped with their lives, and travelled across trackless wilds till they at last arrived in Canada.

This is a brief recital of the proceedings up to 1813; and these were the only acts of riot and resistance that ever took place in Sutherlandshire.

LETTER IV.

In the month of March, 1814, a great number of the inhabitants of the parishes of Farr and Kildonan were summoned to give up their farms at the May term following, and, in order to ensure and hasten their removal with their cattle, in a few days after, the greatest part of the heath pasture was set fire to and burnt, by order of Mr. Sellar, the factor, who had taken these lands for himself. It is necessary to explain the effects of this proceeding. In the spring, especially when fodder is scarce, as was the case in the above year, the Highland cattle depend almost solely on the heather. As soon, too, as the grass begins to sprout about the roots of the bushes, the animals get a good bite, and are thus kept in tolerable condition. Deprived of this resource by the burning, the cattle were generally left without food, and this being the period of temporary peace, during Buonaparte's residence in Elba, there was little demand for good cattle, much less for these poor starving animals, who roamed about over their burnt pasture till a great many of them were lost, or sold for a mere trifle. The arable parts of the land were cropped by the outgoing tenants, as is customary, but the fences being mostly destroyed by the burning, the cattle of the incoming tenant was continually trespassing throughout the summer and harvest, and those who remained to look after the crop had no shelter; even watching being disallowed, and the people were haunted by the new herdsmen and and their dogs from watching their own corn! As the spring had been severe, so the harvest was wet, cold, and disastrous for the poor people, who under every difficulty, were endeavouring to secure the residue of their crops. The barns, kilns, and mills, except a few necessary to the new tenant, had, as well as the houses, been burnt or otherwise destroyed and no shelter left, except on the other side of the river, now overflowing its banks from the continual rains; so that, after all their labour and privations, the people lost nearly the whole of their crop, as they had already lost their cattle, and were thus entirely ruined.

But I must go back now to the May term and attempt to give some account of the ejection of the inhabitants; for to give anything like an adequate description I am not capable. If I were, the horrors of it would exceed belief.

The houses had been all built, not by the landlord as in the low country, but by the tenants or by their ancestors, and, consequently, were their property by right, if not by law. They were timbered chiefly with bog fir, which makes excellent roofing but is very inflammable: by immemorial usage this species of timber was considered the property of the tenant on whose lands it was found. To the upland timber, for which the laird or the factor had to be asked, the laird might lay some claim, but not so to the other sort, and in every house there was generally a part of both.

In former removals the tenants had been allowed to carry away this timber to erect houses in their new allotments, but now a more summary mode was adopted, by setting fire to the houses! The able-bodied men were by this time away after their cattle or otherwise engaged at a distance, so that the immediate sufferers by the general house-burning that now commenced were the aged and infirm, and the women and children. As the lands were now in the hands of the factor himself, and were to be occupied as sheep-farms, and as the people made no resistance, they expected at least some indulgence, in the way of permission to occupy their houses and other buildings till they could gradually remove and meanwhile look after their growing crops. Their consternation, was, therefore, the greater when, immediately after the May term day, and about two months after they had received summonses of removal, a commencement was made to pull down and set fire to the houses over their heads! The old people women, and others, then began to try to preserve the timber which they were entitled to consider as their own. But the devastators proceeded with the greatest celerity, demolishing all before them, and when they had overthrown the houses in a large tract of country, they ultimately set fire to the wreck. So that timber, furniture, and every other article that could not be instantly removed, was consumed by fire, or otherwise utterly destroyed.

These proceedings were carried on with the greatest rapidity as well as with most reckless cruelty. The cries of the victims, the confusion, the despair and horror painted on the countenances of the one party, and the exulting ferocity of the other, beggar all description. In these scenes Mr. Sellar was present, and apparently, (as was sworn by several witnesses at his subsequent trial,) ordering and directing the whole. Many deaths ensued from alarm, from fatigue, and cold; the people being instantly deprived of shelter, and left to the mercy of the elements. Some old men took to the woods and precipices, wandering about in a state approaching to, or of absolute insanity, and several of them, in this situation, lived only a few days. Pregnant women were taken with premature labour, and several children did not long survive their sufferings. To these scenes I was an eye-witness, and am ready to substantiate the truth of my statements, not only by my own testimony, but by that of many others who were present at the time.

In such a scene of general devastation it is almost useless to particularize the cases of individuals—the suffering was great and universal. I shall, however, just notice a very few of the extreme cases which occur to my recollection, to most of which I was an eye witness. John M·Kay's wife, Ravigill, in attempting to pull down her house, in the absence of her husband, to preserve the timber, fell through the roof. She was in consequence, taken with premature labour, and in that state, was exposed to the open air and the view of the by-standers. Donald Munro, Garvott, lying in a fever, was turned out of his house and exposed to the elements. Donald Macheath, an infirm and bed-ridden old man, had the house unroofed over him, and was, in that state, exposed to wind and rain till death put a period to his sufferings. I was present at the pulling down and burning of the house of William Chisholm, Badinloskin, in which was lying his wife's mother, an old bed-ridden woman of near 100 years of age, none of the family being present. I informed the persons about to set fire to the house of this circumstance, and prevailed on them to wait till Mr. Sellar came. On his arrival I told him of the poor old woman being in a condition unfit for removal. He replied, " Damn her, the old witch, she has lived too long; let her burn." Fire was immediately set to the house, and the blankets in which she was carried were in flames before she could be got out. She was placed in a little shed, and it was with great difficulty they were prevented from firing it also. The old woman's daughter arrived while the house was on fire, and assisted the neighbours in removing her mother out of the flames and smoke, presenting a picture of horror which I shall never forget, but cannot attempt to describe. She died within five days.

I could multiply instances to a great extent, but must leave to the reader to conceive the state of the inhabitants during this scene of general devastation, to which few parallels occur in the history of this or any other civilized country. Many a life was lost or shortened, and many a strong constitution ruined;—the comfort and social happiness of all destroyed;

and their prospects in life, then of the most dismal kind, have, generally speaking, been unhappily realized.

Mr. Sellar was, in the year 1816, tried on on indictment for a part of these proceedings, before the circuit court of Justiciary at Inverness.

LETTER V.

At the spring assizes of Inverness, in 1816, Mr. Seller was brought to trial, before Lord Pitmilly, for his proceedings, as partly detailed in my last letter. The indictment, charging him with culpable homicide, fire-raising, &c., was prosecuted by his Majesty's advocate. In the report of the trial, published by Mr. Sellar's counsel, it is said "To this measure his lordship seems to have been induced, chiefly for the purpose of satisfying the public mind *and putting an end* to the clamours of the country." If this, and not the ends of justice, was the intention, it was completely successful, for the gentleman was acquitted, to the astonishment of the natives and of all who understood anything of the true state of the case, and the oppressors were thereby emboldened to proceed in their subsequent operations with a higher hand, and with perfect impunity, as will be seen in the sequel.

It is a difficult and hazardous attempt to inpugn proceedings carried on by his Majesty's advocate, presided over by an honourable judge, and decided by a jury of respectable men; but I may mention a few circumstances which might have a tendency to disappoint the people. Out of forty witnesses examined at a precognition before the sheriff, there were only eleven, and those not the most competent, brought forward for the crown; and the rest, some of whom might have supported material parts of the indictment—as, for instance, in the case of Donald Monro—were never called at all. Besides, the witnesses for the prosecution, being simple, illiterate persons, gave their testimony in Gaelic, which was interpreted to the court; and, it is well-known, much depends upon the translator, whether evidence so taken, retains its weight and strength or not. The jury, with very few exceptions, was composed of persons just similarly circumstanced with the *new* tenants in Sutherlandshire, and consequently, might very naturally have a leaning to that side, and all the exculpatory witnesses were those who had been art and part, or otherwise interested, in the outrageous proceedings. Mr. Sellar was a man of talent, an expert lawyer, and a justice of the peace, invested with full powers, as factor and law agent to a great absentee proprietor, and strongly supported by the clergy and gentry in the neighbourhood: he was also the incoming tenant to the lands which were the scene of his proceedings—too great odds against a few poor simple Highlanders, who had only their wrongs to plead, whose minds were comparatively uncultivated, and whose pecuniary means were small.

The immediate cause which led to these legal proceedings was, that several petitions from the expelled tenants had been sent to the noble proprietors, representing the illegal and cruel treatment they had received ; and, in consequence of the answers received expressing a wish that justice might be done, the case was laid before the sheriff-depute, Mr. Cranstoun, who sent an express injunction to Mr. Robert M'Kid, sheriff-substitute for the county, to take a precognition of the case, and if there appeared suffcient cause, to take Mr. Seller into custody. The sheriff-substitute was a man of acknowledged probity, but from the representations he had previously received, was considered unfavourable to the cause of the people. On examining the witnesses, however, a case of such enormity was made out as induced him to use some strong expressions contained in a letter to Lord Stafford, which I here subjoin, and which, with some false allegations, were urged against him on the trial, so that, under the direction of the court, the advocate-depute passed from his evidence on the grounds of malice and unduly expressed opinion, and thus Mr. M'Kid's important testimony was lost. On the whole, this case furnishes an instance of successful chicanery, undue influence, and the "glorious uncertainty of LAW."

TO LORD STAFFORD.

My LORD,—I conceive it a duty I owe to your Lordship, to address you upon the present occasion, and a more distressing task I have seldom had to perform.

Your Lordship knows, that in summer last, an humble petition, subscribed by a number of tenants on Mr. Sellar's sheep farm in Farr and Kildonan, was presented to Lady Stafford, complaining of various acts of injury, cruelty and oppression, alledged to have been committed upon their persons and property, by Mr. Sellar, in the spring and summer of that year.

To this complaint, her Ladyship, upon the 22nd of July last, was graciously pleased to return an answer in writing. In it, her Ladyship, with her usual candour and justice, with much propriety observes, "That if any person on the estate shall receive any illegal treatment, she will never consider it as hostile to her if they have recourse to legal redress, as a most secure way to receive the justice which she always desires they should have on every occasion." Her Ladyship also intimates, "That she had communicated the complaint to Mr. Sellar, that he may make proper inquiry and answer to her."

It would appear, however, that Mr. Sellar still refused, or delayed, to afford that redress to the removed tenants to which they conceived themselves entitled, which emboldened them to approach Earl Gower with a complaint, similar to the one they had presented to Lady Stafford.

To this complaint his Lordship graciously condescended, under date 8th February last, to return such an answer as might have been expected from his Lordship. His Lordship says that he has communicated the contents to your Lordship and Lady Stafford, who as his Lordship nobly expresses himself, "Are desirous, that the tenants should know, that it is always their wish that justice should be impartially administered." His Lordship then adds, that he has sent the petition, with directions to Mr. Young, that proper steps should be taken for laying the business before the sheriff-depute ; and that the petitioners would therefore be assisted by Mr. Young, if they desired it, in having the precognition taken before the sheriff-depute, according to their petition.

Soon after receipt of Earl Gower's letter, it would appear that a copy of the petition, with his Lordship's answer, had been transmitted to the sheriff-depute by the tenants. Mr. Cranstoun, in answer, upon 30th March last, says, "that if the tenants mean to take a precognition immediately, it will proceed before the sheriff-substitute, as my engagement will not permit me to be in Sutherland until the month of July."

In consequence of these proceedings, on an express injunction from his Majesty's advocate-depute, and a similar one from the sheriff-depute, I was compelled to enter upon an investigation of the complaints.

With this view I was induced to go into Strathnaver, where, at considerable personal inconvenience and expense, and with much patient perseverance, I examined about forty evidences upon the allegations stated in the tenants' petition; and it is with the deepest regret I have to inform your Lordship, that a more numerous catalogue of crimes, perpetrated by an individual, has seldom disgraced any country, or sullied the pages of a precognition in Scotland.

This being the case, the laws of the country imperiously call upon me to order Mr. Sellar to be arrested and incarcerated, in order for trial, and before this reaches your Lordship this preparatory legal step must be put in execution.

No person can more sincerely regret the cause, nor more feelingly lament the effect, than I do; but your Lordship knows well, and as Earl Gower very properly observed, " Justice should be impartially administered."

I have, in confidence, stated verbally to Mr. Young my fears upon this distressing subject, and I now take the liberty of stating my sentiments also to your Lordship, in confidence.

The crimes of which Mr. Sellar stands accused are,—

1. Wilful fire-raising; by having set on fire, and reduced to ashes, a poor man's whole premises, including dwelling-house, barn, kiln, and sheep-cot, attended with most aggravated circumstances of cruelty, if not murder.

2. Throwing down and demolishing a mill, also a capital crime.

3. Setting fire to and burning the tenants' heath pasture, before the legal term of removal.

4. Throwing down and demolishing houses, whereby the lives of sundry aged and bed-ridden persons were endangered, if not actually lost.

5. Throwing down and demolishing barns, kilns, sheep-cots, &c., to the great hurt and prejudice of the owners.

6. Innumerable other charges of lesser importance swell the list.

I subjoin a copy of Mr. Cranstoun's letter to me upon this subject, for your Lordship's information, and have the honour to be, &c.

(Signed)   ROBT. M'KID.

Here, then, I must part with Messrs. Young and Sellar as agents for the noble family of Sutherland, for about this time they ceased to act as such. I shall in my next, proceed to describe the davasting removals of 1819 and '20—those which happened in the intermediate years between these and the year 1815, being similar in character to the removals I have already described. Mr. Sellar shall hereafter only figure in my narrative as a leviathan tenant, who individually supplanted scores of the worthy small farmers of the parish of Farr.

LETTER VI.

SIR,—The integrity manifested by the sheriffs, Cranstoun and M'Kid, led to their dismissal from office, immediately after the trial. This dismissal operated as a sentance of banishment and ruin to Mr. M'Kid—his business in Sutherlandshire was at an end; he retired to Caithness with a large family, and commenced business as a writer, where every malignant influence followed him from the ruling powers in the former county. It is to be hoped that this upright gentleman has since surmounted his difficulties ; he must at all events have enjoyed a high reward in the testimony of a good conscience.

I have hitherto given the noble proprietors the title they bore at the time of the occurrences mentioned, but in order to avoid ambiguity, it may be necessary to give a brief historical sketch of the family. The late Duchess of Sutherland, premier peeress of Scotland, in her own right, succeeded to the estates of her father, William, 21st Earl of Sutherland, with the title of Countess, in the year 1766, being then only one year old. In 1785 she married the Marquis of Stafford and took his title in addition.

In the year 1833, the Marquis was created a Duke, and his lady was subsequently styled Duchess-Countess of Sutherland. She was a lady of superior mind and attainments, but her great and good qualities were lost to her Highland tenantry, from her being non-resident, and having adopted the plan of removing the natives, and letting the land to strangers. Their eldest surviving son, Lord Leveson Gower, also a prominent person, succeeded to the titles and estates of both parents on their decease, and is now the Duke of Sutherland.

The family mansion, Dunrobin Castle, is situated on the southern border of the county, and in the rare case of any of the noble family coming to the Highlands during the period of the removals, they only came to the castle and stopt there, where the old tenants were strictly denied access, while the new occupiers had free personal communication with the proprietors. When any memorial or petition from the former could be got introduced, there was no attention paid to them if not signed by a minister; and this was next to impossible, as the clergy, with one honourable exception, had taken the other side. In every case it appeared that the factors and ministers were consulted, and the decision given according to their suggestions and advice.

On the resignation or dismissal of Messrs. Young and Sellar, Mr. Loch, now M. P. for the Northern Burghs, came into full power as chief, and a Mr. Suther as under factor. Mr. Loch is a Scotsman, but not a Highlander. He had previously been chief agent on the English estates, and general adviser to the proceedings relative to the Sutherland tenantry, and cognizant of all the severities towards them. This gentleman has written a work entitled, " An account of the Improvements on the estates of the Marquis of Stafford, in the counties of Stafford and Salop, and on the estate of Sutherland," in which he has attempted to justify or palliate the proceedings in which he bore a prominent part. His book is, therefore, scarce ever to be relied on for a single fact, when the main object interfered ; he vilifies the Highlanders, and misrepresents every thing to answer his purpose. He has been fully answered, his arguments refuted, and his sophistries exposed by Major-General Stewart, in his "Sketches of the Character and Manners of the Highlanders of Scotland," to which excellent work I beg to call the attention of every friend to truth and justice, and especially those who take an interest in the fate of the expatriated tenantry. The General has completely vindicated the character of the Highland tenantry, and shown the impolicy, as well as cruelty, of the means used for their ejection. The removal of Messrs. Young and Sellar, particularly the latter, from the power they had exercised so despotically, was hailed with the greatest joy by the people, to whom their very names were a terror. Their appearance in any neighbourhood had been such a cause of alarm, as to make women fall into fits, and in one instance caused a woman to lose her reason, which, as far as I know, she has not yet recovered; whenever she saw a stranger she cried out, with a terrific tone and manner, *Oh! sin Sellar!*—" Oh! there's Sellar!"

Bitter, however, was the people's disappointment when they found the way in which the new factors began to exercise their powers. The measures of their predecessors were continued and aggravated, though, on account of unexpired leases, the removals were but partial till the years 1819 and 1820. However, I must not pass over the expulsion and sufferings of forty families who were removed by Mr. Sellar, almost immediately after his trial. This person, not finding it convenient to occupy the whole of the 6,000 or 7,000 acres, which he had obtained possession of, and partially cleared in 1814, had agreed to let these forty families remain as tenants-at-will; but he now proceeded to remove them in the same unfeeling manner as he had ejected the others, only he contented himself with utterly demolishing their houses, barns, &c., but did not, as before, set fire to them till the inmates removed; they leaving their crops in the ground as before described. This year (1816) will be remembered for its severity by many in Scotland. The winter commenced by the snow falling in large quantities in the month of October, and continued with increased rigour, so that the difficulty—almost impossibility—of the people, without barns or shelter of any kind, securing their crops, may be easily conceived. I have seen scores of the poor outcasts employed for weeks together, with the snow from two to four feet deep, watching the corn from being devoured by the now hungry sheep of the incoming tenants; carrying *on their backs*—horses being unavailable in such a case, across the country, without roads, on an average of twenty miles, to their new allotments on the sea coast, any portion of their grain and potatoes they could secure under such dreadful circumstances. During labour and sufferings, which none but Highlanders could sustain, they had to subsist entirely on potatoes dug out of the snow; cooking them as they could, in the open air, among the ruins of their once comfortable dwellings! While alternate frosts and thaws, snow-storms and rain were succeeding each other in all the severity of mid-winter, the people might be seen carrying on their labours, and bearing their burdens of damp produce, under which many, especially the females, were occasionally sinking in a fainting state, till assisted by others, little better off than themselves. In some very rare instances only, a little humane assistance was afforded by the shepherds: in general their tender mercies, like those of their unfeeling masters, were only cruelty.

The filling up of this feeble outline must be left to the imagination of the reader, but I may mention that attendant on all previous and subsequent removals, and especially this one, many severe diseases made their appearance; such as had been hitherto almost unknown among the Highland population; viz: typus fever, consumption, and pulmonary complaints in all their varieties, bloody flux, bowel complaints, eruptions, rheumatisms, piles, and maladies peculiar to females. So that the new and uncomfortable dwellings of this lately robust and healthy peasantry, "their country's pride," were now become family hospitals and lazar-houses of the sick and the dying! Famine and utter destitution inevitably followed, till the misery of my once happy countrymen reached an alarming height, and began to attract attention as an almost national calamity.

Even Mr. Loch in his before-mentioned work, has been constrained to admit the extreme distress of the people. He says, (page 76,) "Their wretchedness was so great, that after pawning everything they possessed, to the fishermen on the coast, such as had no cattle were reduced to come down from the hills in hundreds, for the purpose of gathering cockles on the shore. Those who lived in the more remote situations of the country were obliged to subsist upon broth made of nettles, thickened with a little oatmeal. Those who had cattle had recourse to the still more wretched expedient of bleeding them, and mixing the blood with oatmeal, which they afterwards cut into slices and fried. Those who had a little money, came down and slept all night upon the beach, in order to watch the boats returning from the fishing, that they might be in time to obtain a part of what had been caught." This gentleman, however, omits to mention, the share he had in bringing things to such a pass, and also that, at the same time, he had armed constables stationed at Littleferry, the only place where shell-fish were to be found, to prevent the people from gathering them. In his next page he gives an exaggerated account of the relief afforded by the proprietors. I shall not copy his mis-statments, but proceed to say what that relief, so ostentatiously put forth, really consisted of. As to his assertion that "£3,000 had been given by way of loan to those who had cattle," I look upon it to be a fabrication, or, if the money really was sent by the noble proprietors, it must have been retained by those intrusted with its distribution; for, to my knowledge, it never came to the hands of any of the small tenants. There was, indeed, a considerable quantity of meal sent, though far from enough to afford effectual relief, but this meal represented to be given in charity, was charged at the following Martinmas term, at the rate of 50s. per boll. Payment was rigorously exacted, and those who had cattle were obliged to give them up for that purpose, but this *latter part* of the story was never sent to the newspapers, and Mr. Loch has also *forgotten* to mention it! There was a considerable quantity of medicine given to the ministers for distribution for which no charge was made, and this was the whole amount of relief afforded.

LETTER VII.

The *honourable* acquittal of Mr. Sellar, and the compliments he received in consequence from the presiding judge, with the dismissal of the sheriffs had the desired effect upon the minds of the poor Sutherlanders, and those who took an interest in their case. Every voice in their behalf was silenced and every pen laid down—in short, every channel for redress or protection from future violence was closed; the people were prostrated under the feet of their oppressors, who well knew how to take advantage of their position. It appeared that, for a considerable interval, there were no regular sheriffs in the county, and that the authority usually exercised by them was vested in Captain Kenneth M'Kay, a native of the county, and now one of the extensive sheep farmers. It was by virtue of warrants granted by this gentleman that the proceedings I am about to describe took place, and, if the sheriff-officers constables, and assistants, exceeded their authority, they did so under his immediate eye and cognizance, as he was all the time residing in his house, situated so that he must have witnessed a great part of the scene from his own front window. Therefore, if he did not immediately authorize the atrocities to the extent committed (which I will not assert), he at least used no means to restrain them.

At this period a great majority of the inhabitants were tenants-at-will and therefore liable to ejectment on getting regular notice; there were, however, a few who had still existing tacks (although some had been wheedled or frightened into surrendering them), and these were, of course, unmolested till the expiration of their tacks; they were then turned out like the rest; but the great body of the tenantry were in the former condition. Meantime, the factors, taken advantage of the broken spirit and prostrate state of the people—trembling at their words or even looks—betook themselves to a new scheme to facilitate their intended proceedings, and this was to induce every householder to sign a bond or paper containing a promise of removal: and alternate threats and promises were used to induce them to do so. The promises were never realised, but, notwithstanding the people's compliance, the threats were put in execution. In about a month after the factors had obtained this promise of removal, and thirteen days before the May term, the work of devastation was begun: they commenced by setting fire to the houses of the small tenants in extensive districts—part of the parishes of Farr, Rogart, Golspie, and the whole parish of Kildonan. I was an eye-witness of the scene. This calamity came on the people quite unexpectedly. Strong parties, for each district, furnished with faggots and other combustibles, rushed on the dwellings of this devoted people, and immediately commenced setting fire to them, proceeding in their work with the greatest rapidity till about three hundred houses were in flames! The consternation and confusion were extreme; little or no time was given for removal of persons or property—the people striving to remove the sick and the helpless before the fire should reach them—next, struggling to save the most valuable of their effects. The cries of the women and children—the roaring of the affrighted cattle hunted at the same time by the yelling dogs of the shepherds amid the smoke and fire—altogether presented a scene that completely baffles description: it required to be seen to be believed. A dense cloud of smoke enveloped the whole country by day, and even extended far on the sea; at night an awfully grand, but terrific scene presented itself—all the houses in an extensive district in flames at once! I myself ascended a height about eleven o'clock in the evening, and counted two hundred and fifty blazing houses, many of the owners of which were my relations, and all of whom I personally knew; but whose present condition, whether in or out of the flames, I could not tell. The conflagration lasted six days, till the whole of the dwellings were reduced to ashes or smoking ruins. During one of these days a boat lost her way in the dense smoke as she approached the shore; but at night she was enabled to reach a landing place by the light of the flames!

It would be an endless task to give a detail of the sufferings of families and individuals during this calamitous period; or to describe its dreadful consequences on the health and lives of the victims. I will, however, attempt a very few cases. While the burning was going on, a small sloop arrived, laden with quick lime, and when discharging her cargo, the skipper agreed to take as many of the people to Caithness as he could carry, on his return. Accordingly, about twenty families went on board, filling deck, hold, and every part of the vessel. There were childhood and age, male and female, sick and well, with a small portion of their effects, saved from the flames, all huddled together in heaps. Many of these persons had never been on sea before, and when they began to sicken a scene indescribable ensued. To add to their miseries, a storm and contrary winds prevailed, so that instead of a day or two, the usual time of passage, it was *nine days* before they reached Caithness. All this time, the poor creatures, almost without necessaries, most of them dying with sickness, were either wallowing among the lime, and various excrements in the hold, or lying on the deck, exposed to the raging elements! This voyage soon proved fatal to many, and some of the survivors feel its effects to this day. During this time, also, typus fever was raging in the country, and many in a critical state had to fly, or were carried by their friends out of the burning houses. Among the rest, a young man, Donald M'Kay of Grumbmorr, was ordered out of his parents' house; he obeyed, in a state of delirium, and (nearly naked) ran into some bushes adjoining, where he lay for a considerable time deprived of reason; the house was immediately in flames, and his effects burned. Robert M'Kay, whose whole family were in the fever, or otherwise ailing, had to carry his two daughters on his back, a distance of about twenty-five miles. He accomplished this by first carrying one, and laying her down in the open air, and returning, did the same with the other, till he reached the sea-shore, and then went with them on board the lime vessel before mentioned. An old man of the same name, betook himself to a deserted mill, and lay there unable to move; and to the best of my recollection, he died there. He had no sustenance but what he obtained by licking the dust and refuse of the meal strewed about, and was defended from the rats and other vermin, by his faithful *colly*, his companion and protector. A number of the sick, who could not be carried away instantly, on account of their dangerous situation, were collected by their friends and placed in an obscure, uncomfortable hut, and there, for a time, left to their fate. The cries of these victims were heart-rending—exclaiming in their anguish, "Are you going to leave us to perish in the flames?" However, the destroyers

B

passed near the hut, apparently without noticing it, and consequently they remained unmolested till they could be conveyed to the shore, and put on board the before-mentioned sloop. George Munro, miller at Farr, residing within 400 yards of the minister's house, had his whole family, consisting of six or seven persons, lying in a fever; and being ordered instantly to remove, was enabled, with the assistance of his neighbours to carry them to a damp kiln, where they remained till the fire abated, so that they could be removed. Meantime the house was burnt. It may not be out of place here to mention generally, that the clergy, factors, and magistrates, were cool and apparently unconcerned spectators of the scenes I have been describing, which were indeed prepetrated under their immediate authority. The splendid and comfortable mansions of these gentlemen, were reddened with the glare of their neighbours flaming houses, without exciting any compassion for the sufferers; no spiritual, temporal, or medical aid was afforded them; and this time they were all driven away *without being allowed the benefit of their outgoing crop?* Nothing but the sword was wanting to make the scene one of as great barbarity as the earth ever witnessed; and in my opinion, this would, in a majority of cases, have been mercy, by saving them from what they were afterwards doomed to endure. The clergy, indeed, in their sermons, maintained that the whole was a merciful interposition of providence to bring them to repentance, rather than to send them all to hell, as they so richly deserved! And here I beg leave to ask those Rev. gentlemen, or the survivors of them, and especially my late minister, Mr. M'Kenzie of Farr, if it be true, as was generally reported, that during these horrors I have been feebly endeavouring to describe—there was a letter sent from the proprietors, addressed to him, or to the general body, requesting to know if the removed tenants were well provided for, and comfortable, or words to that effect, and that the answer returned was, that the people were quite comfortable in their new allotments, and that the change was greatly for their benefit. This is the report that was circulated and believed; and the subsequent conduct of the clergy affords too much reason for giving it credence as I shall soon have occasion to show.

LETTER VIII.

The depopulation I have been treating of, with its attendant horrors and miseries, as well as its impolicy, is so justly reasoned upon by General Stewart, in the work formerly alluded to, that I beg to transcribe a paragraph or two. At page 168 he says:—"The system of overlooking the original occupiers, and of giving every support to strangers, has been much practiced in the highland counties; and on one great estate (the Sutherland) the support which was given to farmers of capital, as well in the amount of sums expended on improvements, *as in the liberal abatement of rents*, is, I believe, unparalleled in the United Kingdom, and affords additional matter of regret, that the delusions practised on a generous and public-spirited landholder, have been so perseveringly and successfully applied, that it would appear as if all feeling of former kindness towards the native tenantry had ceased to exist. To them any uncultivated spot of moorland, however small, was considered sufficient for the support of a family; while the most lavish encouragement has been given to the new tenants, on whom, and with the erection of buildings, the improvement of lands, roads, bridges, &c. upwards of £210,000 has been expended since the year 1808. With this proof of unprecedented liberality, it cannot be sufficiently lamented, that an estimate of the character of these poor people was taken from the misrepresentations of interested persons, instead of judging from the conduct of the same men when brought into the world, where they obtained a name and character which have secured the esteem and approbation of men high in honour and rank, and, from their talents and experience, perfectly capable of judging with correctness. With such proofs of capability, and with such materials for carrying on the improvements, and maintaining the permanent prosperity of the county, when occupied by a hardy, abstemious race, easily led on to a full exertion of their faculties by a proper management, there cannot be a question but that if, instead of placing them, as has been done, in situations bearing too near a resemblance to the potato-gardens of Ireland, they had been permitted to remain as cultivators of the soil, receiving a moderate share of the vast sums lavished on their richer successors, such a humane and considerate regard to the prosperity of a whole people, would undoubtedly have answered every good purpose." In reference to the new allotments, he says; "when the valleys and higher grounds were let to the shepherds, the whole population was driven to the sea shore, where they were crowded on small lots of land, to earn their subsistence by labour and by sea fishing, the latter so little congenial to their former habits." He goes on to remark, in a note, that these *one or two acre lots*, are represented as an *improved* system. "In a country without regular employment and without manufactures, a family is to be supported on one or two acres!!" The consequence was, and continues to be, that, "over the whole of this district, where the sea shore is accessible, the coast is thickly studded with wretched cottages, crowded with starving inhabitants." Strangers "with capital" usurp the land and dispossess the swain. "Ancient respectable tenants, who passed the greater part of life in the enjoyment of abundance, and in the exercises of hospitality and charity, possessing stocks of ten, twenty, and thirty breeding cows, with the usual proportion of other stock, are now pining on one or two acres of bad land, with one or two starved cows; and for this accommodation, a calculation is made, that they must support their families and pay the rent of their lots, not from the produce but from the sea. When the herring fishery succeeds they generally satisfy the landlords, whatever privations they may suffer; but when the fishing fails, they fall in arrears and are sequestrated, and their stock sold to pay the rents, their lots given to others, and they and their families turned adrift on the world. There are still a few small tenants on the old system; but they are fast falling into decay, and sinking into the class just described." Again, "we cannot

sufficiently admire their meek and patient spirit, supported by the powerful influence of moral and religious principle." I need not go further, but again beg the reader's attention to this most valuable work, especially the article "Change of Tenancy," as illustrative of the condition and exponent of the character and feelings of my poor countrymen, as well as corroborative of the facts to which I am endeavouring to call public attention, as causes of the distress and destitution still prevailing in Sutherlandshire.

By the means described, large tracts of country were depopulated, and converted into solitary wastes. The whole inhabitants of Kildonan parish (with the exception of three families), amounting to near 2,000 souls, were utterly rooted and burned out. Many, especially the young and robust, left the country; but the aged, the females and children, were obliged to stay and except the wretched allotments allowed them on the sea shore, and endeavour to learn fishing, for which all their former habits rendered them unfit; hence their time was spent in unproductive toil and misery, and many lives were lost. Mr. Sage, of evergreen memory, was the parish minister—

"Among the faithless, faithful only he !"

This gentleman had dissented from his brethren, and, to the best of his power, opposed their proceedings; hence he was persecuted and despised by them and the factors, and treated with marked disrespect. After the burning out, having lost his pious elders and attached congregation, he went about mourning till his demise, which happened not long after. His son had been appointed by the people minister of a chapel of ease, parish of Farr, and paid by them ; but, when the expulsion took place, he removed to Aberdeen, and afterwards to a parish in Ross-shire. On account of his father's integrity he could not expect a kirk in Sutherlandshire.

After a considerable interval of absence, I revisited my native place in the year 1828, and attended divine worship in the parish church, now reduced to the size and appearance of a dove-cot. The whole congregation consisted of eight shepherds, with their *dogs*, to the amount of between 20 and 30, the minister, three of his family, and myself ! I came in after the first singing, but, at the conclusion, the 120th psalm was given out, and struck up to the famous tune, "Bangor;" when the four-footed hearers became excited, got up on the seats, and raised a most infernal chorus of howling. Their masters then attacked them with their crooks, which only made matters worse; the yelping and howling continued till the end of the service. I retired, to contemplate the shameful scene, and compare it with what I had previously witnessed in the large and devout congregations formerly attending in that kirk. What must the worthy Mr. Campbell have felt while endeavouring to edify such a congregation ! The Barony of Strathnaver, parish of Farr, 25 miles in length, containing a population as numerous as Kildonan, who had been all rooted out at the general conflagration, presented a similar aspect. Here, the church no longer found necessary, was razed to the ground, and the timber of it conveyed to Altnaharrow, to be used in erecting an Inn (one of the new *improvements*) there, and the minister's house converted into the dwelling of a fox-hunter. A woman, well known in that parish, happening to traverse the Strath the year after the burning, was asked on her return, what news? "Oh," said she, "Sgeul bronach, sgeul bronach! sad news, sad news! I have seen the timber of our well-attended kirk, covering the Inn at Altnaharrow; I have seen the kirk-yard, where our friends are mouldering filled with tarry sheep, and Mr. Sage's study room, a kennel for Robert Gunn's dogs; and I have seen a crow's nest in James Gordon's chimney head!" On this she fell into a paroxysm of grief, and it was several days before she could utter a word to be understood. During the late devastations, a Captain John M'Kay was appointed sub-factor, under Mr. Loch, for the district of Strathnaver. This gentleman, had he been allowed his own way, would have exercised his power beneficially; but he was subject to persons cast in another mould, and had to sanction what he could not approve. He did all he could to mitigate the condition of the natives, by giving them employment, in preference to strangers, at the public works and improvements, as they were called; but finding their enemies too powerful and malignant, and the misery and destitution too great to be even partially removed, he shrunk from his ungracious task and went to America, where he breathed his last, much regretted by all who knew him on both sides of the Atlantic.

LETTER IX.

I have already mentioned that the clergy of the Established Church (none other were tolerated in Sutherland), all but Mr. Sage, were consenting parties to the expulsion of the inhabitants, and had susbtantial reasons for their readiness to accept wooly and bairy animals—sheep and dogs—in place of their human flocks. The kirks and manses were mostly situated in the low grounds, and the clergy hitherto held their pasturage in common with the tenantry; and this state of things, established by law and usage, no factor or proprietor had power to alter without mutual consent. Had the ministers maintained those rights, they would have placed in many cases, an effectual bar to the oppressive proceedings of the factors; for the strange sheep-farmers would not bid for, or take the lands where the minister's sheep and cattle would be allowed to co-mingle with theirs. But no! Anxious to please the "powers that be," and no less anxious to drive advantageous bargains with them, these reverend gentlemen found means to get their lines laid "in pleasant places," and to secure good and convenient portions of the pasture lands enclosed for themselves: many of the small tenants were removed purely to statisfy them in these arrangements. Their subserviency to the factors, in all things, was not for nought. Besides getting their hill pasturage enclosed, their tillage lands were extended, new manses and offices were built for them, and roads made specially for their accommodation, and every arrangement made for their advantage. They basked in the sunshine of favour; they were the bosom friends of the factors and new tenants (many of whom were soon made magistrates), and had the honour of occasional visits, at their manses, from the proprietors themselves. They were always employed to explain and interpret to the assembled people the orders and designs of the factors; and they did not spare their college paint on these occasions. Black was made white, or white black, as it answered their purpose, in discharging what they called their duty! They did not scruple to introduce the name of the Diety; representing Him as the author and abettor of all the foul and cruel proceedings carried on; and they had at hand another useful being ready to seize every soul who might feel any inclination to revolt. Indeed, the manifest works of the later in their own hands, were sufficient to prove his existence; while the whole appearance of the country, and the state of its inhabitants at this period, afforded ample proof that the principle of evil was in the ascendant. The tyranny of one class, and the wrongs and sufferings of the other, had demoralising effects on both; the national character and manners were changed and deteriorated, and a comparativly degenerate race is the consequence. This was already manifest in the year 1822, when George IV. made his famous visit to Edinburgh. The brave, athletic and gallant men, who in 1745, and again more recently, in 1800, rose in thousands at the call of their chief, were no longer to be traced in their descendants. When the clans gathered to honour His Majesty on the latter occasion, the Sutherland turn-out was contemptible. Some two or three dozen of squalid-looking, ill-dressed, and ill-appointed men, were all that Sutherland produced. So inferior, indeed, was their appearance to the other Highlanders, that those who had the management refused to allow them to walk in the procession, and employed them in some duty out of public view. If their appearance was so bad, so also were their accommodations. They were huddled together in an old empty house, sleeping on straw, and fed with the coarsest fare, while the other clans were living in comparative luxury. Lord Francis Leveson Gower, and Mr. Loch, who were present, reaped little honour by the exhibition of their Sutherland retainers on that great occasion. Moral degradation also, to some extent, followed that of physical. Many vices, hitherto almost unknown, began to make their appearance; and though the people never resorted to "wild savage justice," like those of Ireland in similar circumstances, the minor trangressions of squabbling, drunkeness, and incontinency became less rare—the natural consequence of their altered condition. Religion also, from the conduct of the clergy, began to lose its hold on their minds—and who can wonder at it?—when they saw these holy men closely leagued with their oppressors. "Ichabod," the glory of Sutherland had departed—perhaps never to return!

LETTER X.

I now proceed to describe the "allotments" on which the expelled and burnt-out inhabitants were allowed to locate during the pleasure of the factors. These allotments were generally situated on the sea-coast, the intention being to force those who could not or would not leave the country, to draw their subsistence from the sea by fishing; and in order to deprive them of any other means, the lots were not only made small, (varying from one to three acres), but their nature and situation rendered them unfit for any useful purpose. If the reader will take the trouble to examine the map of Sutherlandshire by Mr. Loch, he will perceive that the county is bounded on the north by the Northern Ocean, on the south by the county of Ross, on the west by the Mynch, on the north-east by Caithness, and on the south-east by the Moray Frith. To the sea-coasts, then, which surround the greatest part of the country were the whole mass of the inhabitants, to the amount of several thousand families, driven by their unrelenting tyrants, in the manner I have described, to subsist as they could, on the sea or the air; for the spots allowed them could not be called land, being composed of narrow stripes, promontories, cliffs and precipices, rocks, and deep crevices, interspersed with bogs and morasses. The whole quite useless to the superiors, and evidently never designed by nature for the habitation of man or beast. This was, with a few exceptions, the character of these allotments. The patches of soil where anything could be grown, were so few and scanty that when any dispute arose about the property of them, the owner could easily carry them away in a creel on his back and deposit them in another place. In many places, the spots the poor people endeavoured to cultivate were so steep that while one was delving, another had to hold up the soil with his hands, lest it should roll into the sea, and from its constant tendancy to slide downwards. they had frequently to carry it up again every spring and spread it upon the higher parts. These patches were so small that few of them would afford room for more than a few handfuls of seeds, and in harvest, if there happened to be any crop, it was in continual danger of being blown into the sea, in that bleak inclement region, where neither tree nor shrub could exist to arrest its progress. In most years, indeed, when any mentionable crop was realised, it was generally destroyed before it could come to maturity. by sea blasts and mildew. In some places, on the north coast, the sea is forced up through crevices, rising in columns to a prodigious height and scattering its spray upon the adjoining spots of land, to the utter destruction of any thing that may be growing on them. These were the circumstances to which this devoted people were reduced, and to which none but a hardy, patient and moral race, with an ardent attachment to their country, would have quietly submitted; here they, with their cattle, had to remain for the present, expecting the southern dealers to come at the usual time (the months of June and July) to purchase their stocks; but the time came and passed, and no dealers made their appearance; none would venture into the country! The poor animals in a starving state, were continually running to and fro, and frequently could not be prevented from straying towards their former pasture grounds, especially in the night, notwithstanding all the care taken to prevent it. When this occurred, they were immediately seized by the shepherds and impounded without food or water, till trespass was paid! this was repeated till a great many of the cattle were rendered useless. It was nothing strange to see the pinfolds, of twenty to thirty yards square, filled to the entrance with horses, cows, sheep and goats, promiscuously for nights and days together, in that starving state, trampling on and goring each other. The lamentable neighing, lowing, and bleating of these creatures, and the pitiful looks they cast on their owners when they could recognize them, were distressing to witness; and formed an addition to the mass of suffering then prevailing. But this was not all that beset the poor beasts. In some instances when they had been trespassing, they were hurried back by the pursuing shepherds or by their owners, and in running near the precipices may of them had their bones broken or dislocated, and a great number fell over the rocks into the sea, and were never seen more. Vast numbers of sheep and many horses and other cattle which escaped their keepers and strayed to a distance to their former pastures, were baited by men and dogs till they were either partially or totally destroyed, or became meat for their hunters. I have myself seen many instances of the kind, where the animals were lying partly consumed by the dogs, though still alive, and their eyes picked out by birds of prey. When the cattle were detained by the shepherds in the folds before mentioned, for trespass, to any amount the latter thought proper to exact, those of their owners who had not money—and they were the majority—were obliged to relieve them by depositing their bed and body clothes, watches, rings, pins, brooches, &c., many of these latter were the relics of dear and valued relatives, now no more, not a few of whom had shed their blood in defence of that country from which their friends were now ignominiously driven, or treated as useless lumber, to be got rid of at any price. The situation of the people with their families and cattle, driven to these inhospitable coasts, and harassed and oppressed in every possible way, presented a lamentable contrast to their former way of life. While they were grudged those barren and useless spots—and at high rents too—the new tenants were accommodated with leases of as much land as they chose to occupy, and *at reduced rents*; many of them holding farms containing many thousand acres. One farm held by Messrs. Atkinson and Marshall, two gentlemen from Northumberland, contained an hundred thousand acres of good pasture-land! Mr. Sellar had three large farms, one of which was twenty-five miles long; and, in some places, nine or ten miles broad, situated in the barony of Strathnaver. This gentleman was said to have lost annually, large quantities of sheep; and others of the new tenants were frequently making complaints of the same kind; all these depredations, as well as every other, were laid to the charge of the *small tenants*. An association was formed for the suppression of sheep-stealing in Sutherlandshire, and large rewards were held out—Lord Stafford himself offering £30 for the conviction of any of the offenders. But though every effort was used to bring the crime home to the natives (one gentleman, whom, for obvious reasons I will not name, said in my hearing, he would rather than £1000 get one conviction from among them): yet, I am proud to say, all these endeavours were ineffectual. Not one public conviction could they obtain! In time, however, the saddle came to be laid on the right horse; the shepherds could rob their masters' flocks in safety, while the natives got the blame of all, and they were evidently no way sparing; but at last they were found out, and I have reason to know that several of them were dismissed, and some had their own private stocks confiscated to their masters to make good the damage of their depredations. This was, however, all done privately, so that the odium might still attach to the natives. In concluding this part of the subject, I may observe that such of the cattle as strayed on the ministers' grounds, fared no better than others; only that, as far as I know, these gentlemen did not follow the practice of the shepherds in working the horses all day and returning them to the pinfold at night: and I am very happy in being able to give this testimony in favour of these reverend gentlemen.

I must not omit to mention here an anecdote illustrative of the state of things prevailing at that time One of the shepherds on returning home one Sabbath evening, after partaking of the Lord's Supper, in the church of Farr, observed a number of the poor people's sheep and goats trespassing at the outskirts of his master's hill-pasturage, and with the assistance of his dogs, which had also been at the kirk, drove them home and impounded them. On Monday morning he took as many of the lambs and kids as he thought proper, and had them killed for the use of his own family! The owners complained to his master, who was a magistrate; but the answer was, that they should keep them off his property, or eat them themselves, and then his servants could not do it for them, or words to that effect. One way or other, by starvation, accidents, and the depredations of the shepherds and their dogs, the people's cattle to the amount of many hundred head, were utterly lost and destroyed.

LETTER XI.

I have now endeavoured to shadow forth the cruel expulsion of my " co-mates and brothers in exile," from their native hearths, and to give a faint sketch of their extreme sufferings and privations in consequence. Few instances are to be found in modern European history, and scarce any in Britian, of such a wholesale extirpation, and with such revolting circumstances. It is impossible for me to give more than an outline ; the filling up would take a large volume, and the sufferings, insult, and misery, to which this simple, pastoral race were exposed, would exceed belief. But if I can draw public attention to their case, so as to promote that authorised inquiry, so much deprecated by Highland proprietors, my end will be attained. If the original inhabitants could have been got rid of totally, and their language and memory eradicated, the oppressors were not disposed to be scrupulous about the means. Justice, humanity, and even the laws of the land, were violated with impunity, when they stood in the way of the new plans on " Change of Tenancy;" and these plans, with more or less severity, still continue to be acted upon in several of the Highland counties, but more especially in Sutherland, to this day. But there is still a number left, abject, "scattered and peeled" as they are, in whose behalf I would plead, and to whose wrongs I would wish to give a tongue, in hopes that the feeble remnant of a once happy and estimable people, may yet find some redress, or at least the comfort of public sympathy. I now proceed to give some account of the state of the Sutherlanders, on their martime " allotments," and how they got on in their new trade of fishing.

People accustomed to witness only the quiet friths and petty heavings of the sea, from the lowland shores, can form little conception of the gigantic workings of the Nothern sea, which, from a comparatively placid state, often rises suddenly without apparent cause, into mountainous billows ; and, when north winds prevail, its appearance becomes terrific beyond description. To this raging element, however, the poor people were now compelled to look for their subsistence, or starve, which was the only other alternative. It is hard to extinguish the love of life, and in was almost as hard to extinguish the love of country in a Highlandman in past times ; so that, though many of the vigorous and enterprising pursued their fortunes in other climes, and in various parts of Scotland and England, yet many remained, and struggled to accommodate them-selves to their new and appalling circumstances. The regular fishermen, who had hitherto pursued the finny race in the northern sea, were, from the extreme hazard of the trade, extremely few, and nothing could exceed the contempt and derision—mingled sometimes with pity, even in their rugged breasts—with which they viewed the awkward attempts and sad disasters of their new landward competitors. Nothing, indeed, could seem more helpless, than the attempt to draw subsistence from such a boisterous sea with such means as they possessed, and in the most complete ignorance of all sea-faring matters; but the attempt had to be made, and the success was as might be expected in such circumstances; while many—very many —lost their lives, some became in time, expert fishermen. Numerous as were the casualties, and of almost daily occurrence, yet the escapes, many of them extraordinary, were happily still more frequent; their disasters, on the whole, arose to a frightful aggregate of human misery. I shall proceed to notice a very few cases, to which I was a witness, or which occur to my recollection.

William M'Kay, a respectable man, shortly after settling in his allot-ment on the coast, went one day to explore his new possession, and in venturing to examine more nearly the ware growing within the flood mark, was suddenly swept away by a splash of the sea, from one of the adjoining creeks, and lost his life, before the eyes of his miserable wife, in the last month of her pregnancy, and three helpless children who were left to deplore his fate. James Campbell, a man also with a family, on attempt-ing to catch a peculiar kind of small fish among the rocks, was carried away by the sea and never seen afterwards. Bell M'Kay, a married woman, and mother of a family, while in the act of taking up salt water to make salt of, was carried away in a similar manner, and nothing more seen of her. Robert M'Kay, who with his family, were suffering extreme want, in endeavouring to procure some sea-fowls' eggs among the rocks, lost his hold, and falling from a prodigious height was dashed to pieces, leaving a wife, and five destitute children behind him. John M'Donald, while fishing, was swept off the rocks, and never seen more.

It is not my intention to swell my narrative, by reciting the "moving accidents " that befell individuals and boats' crews, in their new and hazardous occupation; suffice it to say, they were many and deplorable. Most of the boats were such as the regular fishermen had cast off as unservicable or unsafe, but which these poor creatures were obliged to purchase and go to sea with, at the hourly peril of their lives; yet they often not only escaped the death to which others became a prey, but were very successful. One instance of this kind, in which I bore a part myself, I will here relate. Five venturous young men, of whom I was one, having bought an old crazy boat, that had long been laid up as useless, and having procured lines of an inferior description, for haddock fishing, put to sea, without sail, helm or compass, with three patched oars; only one of the party ever having been on sea before. This apparently insane attempt gathered a crowd of spectators, some in derision cheering us on, and our friends imploring us to come back. However, Neptune being then in one of his placid moods, we boldly ventured on, human life having become reduced in value, and, after a night spent on the sea, in which we freshmen suffered severely from sea-sickness, to the great astonishment of the people on shore, the *Heather-boat*, as she was called, reached the land in the morning—all hands safe, with a very good take of fishes. In these and similar ways, did the young men serve a dangerous and painful apprenticeship to the sea, "urged on by fearless want," and in time became good fishermen, and were thereby enabled in some measure to support their families, and those dependent on them : but owing to peculiar circumstances, their utmost efforts were, in a great degree, abortive. The coast was, as I have said, extremely boisterous and destructive to their boats, tackle, &c. They had no harbours where they could land and secure their boats in safety, and little or no capital to procure sound boats, or to replace those which were lost. In one year on the coast, between Portskerra and Rabbit Island, (about 30 miles) upwards of one hundred boats had been either totally destroyed or materially injured, so as to render them unserviceable; and many of their crews had found a watery grave! It is lamentable to think, that while £210,000 were expended on the so-called improvements, besides £500 subscribed by the proprietors, for making a harbour, the most needful of all; not a *shilling* of the vast sum was ever expended for behoof of the small tenantry, nor the least pains taken to mitigate their lot! Roads, bridges, inns, and manses, to be sure, were provided for the accomodation of the new gentlemen tenantry and clergy, but those who spoke the Gaelic tongue were a proscribed race, and everything was done to get rid of them, by driving them into the forlorn hope of deriving subsistence from the sea, while squatting on their miserable allotments, where, in their wretched hovels, they lingered out an almost hopeless existence, and where none but such hardy "sons of the mountain and the flood" could have existed at all. Add to this, though at some seasons they procured abundance of fish, they had no market for the surplus; the few shepherds were soon supplied, and they had no means of conveying them to distant towns, so that very little money could be realised to pay rent, or procure orther necessaries, fishing tackle, &c., and when the finny race thought proper to desert their shores (as, in their caprice, they often do,) their misery was complete! Besides those located on the sea-shore, there was a portion of the people sent to the moors, and these were no better off. Here they could neither get fish nor fowl, and the scraps of land given them were good for nothing—white or reddish gravel, covered with a thin layer of moss, and for this they were to pay rent, and raise food from it to maintain their families! By immense labour they did improve some spots in these moors, and raise a little very inferior produce, but not unfrequently, after all their toil, if they displeased the factors, or the shepherds in the least, even by a word, or failed in paying the rent, they were unceremoniously turned out; hence, their state of bondage may be understood; they durst not even complain! The people on the property of Mr. Dempster, of Skibo, were little, if anything, better off. They were driven out though not by burning, and located on patches of moors, in a similar way to those on the Sutherland property, with the only difference that they had to pay higher than the latter for their wretched allotments. Mr. Dempster says "he has kept his tenantry;" but how has he treated them? This question will be solved, I hope, when the authorised inquiry into the state of the poor Highlanders takes place.

LETTER XII.

SIR,—Were it not that I am unwilling to occupy your valuable columns to a much greater extent, I could bring forward, in the history of many families, several interesting episodes to illustrate this narrative of my country's misfortunes. Numerous are the instances (some of the subjects of them could be produced even in this city) of persons, especially females whose mental and bodily sufferings, during the scenes I have described, have entailed on them diseases which baffle medical skill, and which death only can put an end to ; but I forbear to dwell on these at present, and pass on to the year 1827.

The depopulation of the county (with the exceptions I have described) was now complete. The land had passed into the hands of a few capitalists, and everything was done to promote their prosperity and convenience, while everything that had been promised to the small tenants, was, as regularly, left undone. But yet the latter were so stubborn that they could not be brought to rob or steal, to afford cause for hanging or transporting them ; nor were they even willing to beg, though many of them were gradually forced to submit to this last degradation to the feelings of the high-minded Gael. It was in this year that her ladyship, the proprietrix, and suite, made a visit to Dunrobin Castle. Previous to her arrival, the clergy and factors, and the new tenants, set about raising a subscription throughout the county, to provide a costly set of ornaments, with complimentary inscriptions, to be presented to her ladyship in name of her tenantry. Emissaries were dispatched for this purpose even to the small tenantry, located on the moors and barren cliffs, and every means used to wheedle or scare them into contributing. They were told that those who would subscribe would thereby secure her ladyship's and the factor's favour, and those who could not or would not, were given to understand, very significantly, what they had to expect, by plenty of menacing looks and ominous shakings of the head. This caused many of the poor creatures to part with their last shilling, to supply complimentary ornaments to honour this illustrious family, and which went to purchase additional favour for those who were enjoying the lands from which they had been so cruelly expelled.

These testimonials were presented at a splended entertainment, and many high-flown compliments passed between the givers and receiver: but, of course, none of the poor victims were present; no compliments were paid to them; and it is questionable if her ladyship ever knew that one of them subscribed—indeed, I am almost certain she never did. Three years after, she made a more lengthened visit, and this time she took a tour round the northern districts on the sea-shore, where the poor people were located, accompanied by a number of the clergy, the factors, &c. She was astonished and distressed at the destitution, nakedness, and extreme misery which met her eye in every direction, and made enquiries into their condition, and she ordered a general distribution of clothing to be made among the most destitute; but unfortunately she confined her inquiries to those who surrounded her, and made them the medium for distributing her bounty—the very parties who had been the main cause of this deplorable destitution, and whose interest it was to conceal the real state of the people, as it continues to be to this day.

At one place she stood upon an eminence, where she had about a hundred of those wretched dwellings in view; at least she could see the smoke of them ascending from the horrid places in which they were situated. She turned to the parish minister in the utmost astonishment, and asked "Is it possible that there are people living in yonder places?"—O yes, my lady," was the reply. "And can you tell me if they are any way comfortable?" "Quite comfortable, my lady." Now, sir, I can declare that at the very moment this reverend gentleman uttered these words, he was fully aware of the horrors of their situation; and besides that, some of the outcasts were then begging in the neighbouring county of Caithness, many of them carrying certificates from this very gentleman, attesting that they were objects of charity!

Her ladyship, however, was not quite satisfied with these answers. She caused a general warning to be issued, directing the people to meet her, at stated places as she proceeded, and wherever a body of them met her, she alighted from her carriage, and questioned them if they were comfortable, and how the factors were behaving to them? [N.B. The factors were always present on these occasions.] But they durst make little or no complaints. What they did say was in Gaelic, and, of course, as in other cases, left to the minister's interpretation; but their forlorn, haggard, and destitute appearance, sufficiently testified their real condition. I am quite certain, that had this great, and (I am willing to admit, when not misled) good woman remained on her estates, their situation would have been materially bettered, but as all her charity was left to be dispensed by those who were anxious to get rid of the people, root and branch, little benefit resulted from it, at least to those she meant to relieve. As I mentioned above, she ordered bed and body clothes to all who were in need of them, but, as usual, all was entrusted to the ministers and factors, and they managed this business with the same selfishness, injustice, and partiality, that had marked their conduct on former occasions. Many of the most needy got nothing, and others next to nothing. For an instance of the latter, several families, consisting of seven or eight, and in great distress got only a yard and a half of coarse blue flannel, each family. Those however, who were the favourites and toadies of the distributors, and their servants, got an ample supply of both bed and body clothes, but this was the exception; generally speaking the poor people were nothing benefitted by her ladyship's charitable intentions; though they afforded hay-making seasons to those who had enough already, and also furnished matter for glowing accounts in the newspapers, of her ladyship's extraordinary munificence. To a decent highland woman, who had interested her ladyship, she ordered a present of a gown-piece, and the gentleman factor who was entrusted to procure it, some time after sent six yards of cotton stuff not worth 2s. in the whole. The woman laid it aside, intending to show it to her ladyship on her next visit, but her own death occurred in the meantime. Thus, in every way were her ladyship's benevolent intentions frustrated or misapplied, and that ardent attachment to her family which had subsisted through so many generations, materially weakened, if not totally destroyed, by a mistaken policy towards her people, and an undue confidence in those to whose management she committed them, and who, in almost every instance, betrayed that confidence, and cruelly abused that delegated power. Hence, and hence only, the fearful misery and " destitution in Sutherlandshire."

LETTER XIII.

SIR,—In the year 1832, and soon after the events I have been describing, an order was issued by Mr. Loch, in the name of the Duke and Duchess of Sutherland, that all the small tenants, on both sides of the road from Bighouse to Melness (about thirty miles), where their cottages were thickly studded, must build new houses, with stone and mortar, according to a prescribed plan and specification. The poor people, finding their utter inability, in their present condition, to erect such houses (which, when finished, would cost £30 to £40 each), got up petitions to the proprietors, setting forth their distressed condition, and the impossibility of complying with the requisition at present. These petitions they supplicated and implored the ministers to sign, well knowing that otherwise they had little chance of being attended to; but these gentlemen could be moved by no entreaties, and answered all their applications by a contemptuous refusal. The petitions had, therefore, to be forwarded to London without ecclesiastical sanction, and, of course, effected nothing. The answer returned was, that if they did not immediately begin to build, they would be removed next term. The very word *removed* was enough; it brought back to their minds the recollection of former scenes, with all their attendant horrors. To escape was impossible, they had no where to go ; and in such circumstances they would have consented to any thing, even to the making " bricks without straw," like their oppressed proto- types of old.

In the midst of hopeless misery, then, and many of them without a shilling in their pockets, did they commence the task of building houses, such as I have mentioned, on the barren spots, and without any security of retaining them, even when they were built. The edict was law ; supplication or remonstrance was in vain; so to it they went, under circum- stances such as perhaps building was never carried on before, in a country called Christian and civilized. Plans and specifications were published, and estimates required by the factors, directing the whole proceedings, and, as usual, without consulting the feelings of the poor people, or in- quiring into the means they had for carrying them into effect. All was bustle and competition among masons and mechanics, of whom few resided in the country; most of them were strangers; and when they commenced work, the people were obliged to feed them, whether they had anything themselves to eat or not, and to pay them, even if they had to sell the last moveable for that purpose. Some of the masons, however, showed great lenity, and are still unpaid. Previous to this, in the year 1829, I and my family had been forced away like others, being particularly obnoxious to those in authority for sometimes showing an inclination to oppose their tyranny ; and therfore we had to be made examples of, to frighten the rest, but in 1833 I made a tour to the districts, when the building was going on, and shall endeavour to describe a small part of what met my eye on that occasion. In one district (and this was a fair specimen of all the rest), when the building was going on, I saw fourteen different squads of masons at work, with the natives attending them. Old grey-headed men, worn down by previous hardship and present want, were to be seen carrying stones, and wheeling them and other materials on bar- rows, or carrying them on their backs to the buildings, and, with their tottering limbs and trembling hands straining to raise the stones, &c., to the walls. The young men also, after toiling all night at sea, endeavour- ing for subsistence, instead of rest, were obliged to yield their exhausted frames to the labours of the day. Even female labour could not be dispensed with ; the strong as well as the weak, the delicate and sickly, and (shame to the nature of their oppressors !) even the pregnant, bare- footed, and scantily clothed and fed, were obliged to join in these rugged, unfeminine labours, carrying stones, clay, lime, wood, &c., on their backs or on barrows, their tracks often reddened with the blood from their hands and feet, and from hurts received by their awkwardness in handling the rude materials. In one instance I saw the husband quarrying stones, and the wife and children dragging them along in an old cart to the building. Such were the building scenes of that period. The poor people had often to give the last morsel of food they possessed to feed the masons, and subsist on shell-fish themselves when they could get them. The timber for their houses was furnished by the factors, and charged about a third higher than it could be purchased at in any of the neighbouring sea-ports. I spent two melancholy days witnessing these scenes, which are now present to my mind, and which I can never forget. This went on for several years, in the course of which, many hundreds of houses were erected on inhospitable spots, unfit for human residence. It might be thought that the design of forcing the people to build such houses, was to provide for their comfort and accommodation; but there was another object, which I believe was the only true motive, and that was, to hide the misery that prevailed. There had been a great sensation created in the public mind, by the cruelties exercised in these districts; and it was thought that a number of neat white houses, ranged on each side of the road, would take the eyes of strangers and visitors, and give a practical contradiction to the rumours afloat; hence the poor creatures were forced to resort to such means, and to endure such hardships and privations as I have described, to carry the scheme into effect. And after they had spent their all, and much more than their all, on the erection of these houses, and involved themselves in debt, for which they have been harassed and pursued ever since, they are still but whitened tombs; many of them now ten years in existence, and still without proper doors or windows, destitute of furniture, and of comfort; merely providing a lair for a heart-broken, squalid, and degenerated race.

LETTER XIV.

During the period in which the building was going on, I think in the year 1833, Lord Leveson Gower, the present Duke of Sutherland, visited the country, and remained a few weeks, during which he had an opportunity of witnessing the scenes I have described in my last; and such was the impression made on his mind, that he gave public orders that the people should not be forced to build according to the specific plan, but be allowed to erect such houses as suited themselves. These were glad tidings of mercy to the poor people, but they were soon turned to bitter disappointment; for no sooner had his lordship left the country, than Mr. Loch or his underlings issued fresh orders for the building to go on as before.

Shortly after this (in July, 1833) his Grace the first (and late) Duke of Sutherland, who had been some time in bad health, breathed his last in Dunrobin Castle, and was interred with great pomp in the family burying-place in the cathedral of Dornoch. The day of his funeral was ordered to be kept as a fast-day by all the tenantry, under penalty of the highest.

displeasure of those in authority, though it was just then herring-fishing season, when much depended on a day. Still this was a minor hardship. The next year a project was set on foot, by the same parties who formerly got up the expensive family ornaments presented to her Grace, to raise a monument to the late Duke. Exactly similiar measures were resorted to, to make the small tenantry subscribe, in the midst of all their distresses, and with similar results. All who could raise a shilling gave it, and those who could not, awaited in terror the consequences of their default. No doubt, the Duke deserved the highest posthumous honours from a portion of his tenantry—those who had benefitted by the large sums he and the Duchess had lavished for their accommodation ; but the poor small tenantry, what had been done for them? While the ministers, factors, and new tenantry, were rich and luxurious, basking in the sunshine of favour and prosperity, the miseries and oppressions of the natives remain unabated ; *they* were emphatically in the shade, and certainly had little for which to be grateful to those whose abuse of power had brought them to such a pass—who had drained their cup of every thing that could sweeten life, and left only

" A mass of sordid lees behind ! "

Passing the next two years, I now proceed to describe the failure of the harvest in 1836, and the consequences to the Highlands generally, and to Sutherland in particular. In this year the crops all over Britain were deficient, having had bad weather for growing and ripening, and still worse for gathering in. But in the Highlands they were an entire failure, and on the untoward spots occupied by the Sutherland small tenants there was literally nothing—at least nothing fit for human subsistence; and to add to the calamity, the weather had prevented them from securing the *peats*, their only fuel ; so that, to their exhausted state from their disproportionate exertions in building, cold and hunger were now to be superadded. The sufferings of the succeeding winter, endured by the poor Highlanders, truly beggar description. Even the herring-fishing had failed and consequently their credit in Caithness, which depended on its success was at an end. Any little provision they might be able to procure was of the most inferior and unwholesome description. It was no uncommon thing to see people searching among the snow for the frosted potatoes to eat, in order to preserve life. As the harvest had been disastrous, so the winter was uncommonly boisterous and severe, and consequently little could be obtained from the sea to mitigate the calamity. The distress rose to such a height as to cause a universal sensation all over the island, and a general cry for government interference to save the people from death by famine ; and the appeal backed by the clergy of all denominatious throughout the Highlands, (with the exception of Sutherland) was not made in vain.

Dr. M'Leod of Glasgow was particularly zealous on this occasion. He took reports from all the parish ministers in the destitute districts, and went personally to London to represent the case to government and implore aid, and the case was even laid before both houses of parliament.

C

In consequence of these applications and proceedings, money and provisions to a great amount were sent down, and the magistrates and ministers entrusted with the distribution of them : and in the ensuing summer, vessels were sent to take on board a number of those who were willing to emigrate to Australia. Besides this, private subscriptions were entered into, and money obtained to a very great amount. Public meetings were got up in all the principal cities and towns in Great Britain and Ireland, and large funds collected; so that effectual relief was afforded to every place that required it, with the single exception of that county which, of all others, was in the most deplorable state—the county of Sutherland! The reason of this I will explain presently; but first let me draw the reader's attention for a moment to the new circumstances in which the Highlands were placed. Failure in the crops in those northern and north-western parts of Scotland was a case of frequent and common occurrence; but famine, and solicitations for national aid and charitable relief, were something quite new. I will indeavour to account for the change. Previous to the ".change of tenancy," as the cruel spoliation and expatriation of the native inhabitants was denominated, when a failure occured in the grain and potato crops, they had recourse to their cattle. Selling a few additional head, or an extra score of sheep, enabled them to purchase at the sea-ports what grain was wanted. But now they had no cattle to sell ; and when the crops totally failed on their spots of barren ground, and when, at the same time, the fishing proved unprosperous, they were immediately reduced to a state of famine ; and hence the cry for relief, which as I have mentioned, was so generously responded to. But I would ask who were the authors of all this mass of distress? Surely the proprietors, who, unmindful that "property has its duties as well as its rights," brought about this state of things. They in common with other landed legislators, enacted the food taxes, causing a competition for land, and then encouraged strange adventurers to supersede the natives, and drive them out, in order that the whole of the Highlands should be turned into a manufactory to make beef and mutton for the English market. And when, by these means, they had reduced the natives to destitution and famine, they left it to the government and to charitable individuals to provide relief ! Language is scarcely adequate to characterize such conduct : yet these are the great, the noble, and right honourable of the land! However, with the exception of my unfortunate native county, relief was afforded, though not by those whose right it was to afford it. Large quantities of oatmeal, seed oats, and barley, potatoes, &c., were brought up and forwarded to the North and West Highlands, and distributed among all who were in need; but nothing of all this for the Sutherlanders. Even Dr. M'Leod, in all the zeal of his charitable mission, passed from Stornoway to the Shetland Islands without vouchsafeing a glance at Sutherland in his way. The reason of all this I will now explain. It was constantly asserted and reiterated in all places, that there was no occasion for government or other charitable aid to Sutherland, as the noble proprietors would themselves take in hand to afford their tenantry ample relief. This story was circulated through the newspapers, and repeated by the clergy and factors at all public meetings, till the public was quite satisfied on the subject. Meantime the wretched people were suffering the most unparalleled distress; famine had brought their misery to a frightful climax, and disease and death had commenced their work! In their agony they had recourse to the ministers, imploring them to represent their case to government, that they might partake of the relief afforded to other counties: but all in vain! I am aware that what I here assert is incredible, but not less true, that of the whole seventeen parish ministers, not one could be moved by the supplications and cries of the famishing wretches to take any steps for their relief! They answered all entreaties with a cold refusal, alleging that the proprietors would in their own good time, send the necessary relief; but, so far as I could ever learn, they took no means to hasten that relief. They said in their sermons "that the Lord had a controversy with the land for the people's wickedness; and that in his providence, and even in his mercy, he had sent this scourge to bring them to repentance," &c. Some people (wicked people, of course) may think such language, in such circumstances, savored more of blasphemy than of religious truth. Meantime, the newspapers were keeping up the public expectations of the munificent donations the proprietors were sending. One journal had it that £9,000 worth of provisions were on the way; others £8,000, and £7,000, &c. However, the other Highlanders had received relief at least two months before anything came to Sutherland. At last it did come : the amount of relief, and the manner of its appropriation shall be explained in my next.

LETTER XV.

Sir,—In my last I quoted an expression current among the clergy at the time of the famine "that God had a controversy with the people for their sins," but I contend—and I think my readers in general will agree with me—that the poor Sutherlanders were "more sinned against than sinning." To the aspersions cast upon them by Mr. Loch, in his book (written by an interested party, and evidently for a purpose) I beg the public to contrast the important work by General Stewart before mentioned, and draw their own conclusions. The truth is that the Sutherlanders were examples of almost all the humble virtues; a simple and uncorrupted, rural, and pastoral population : even the unexampled protracted cruelty with which they were treated, never stirred them to take wild or lawless revenge. During a period of 200 years, there had been only three capital convictions, and very few crimes of any description ; the few that did occur were chiefly against the excise laws. But those who coveted the lands, which in justice were their patrimony, like Queen Jezebel of old, got false witnesses to defame them (in order that a pretext might be afforded for expelling them from the possessions which had been defended with the blood of their forefathers). It was the factors, the capitalists, and the clergy, that had a controversy with the people, and not the Almighty, as they blasphemously asserted. The Sutherlanders had always been a religious, a devout, and a praying people, and now their oppressors, and not Divine Providence, had made them a *fasting people*. I proceed to give some account of that mockery of relief which was so ostentatiously paraded before the public in the newspapers, and at public meetings.

I have already observed that the relief afforded to the Highland districts generally, by the government, and by private charity, was not only effectual in meeting the exigency, but it was *bone fide* charity, and was forthcoming in time; while the pittance doled out to the Sutherlanders, was destitute of those characteristics. How the poor people passed the winter and spring under the circumstances before mentioned, I must leave to the reader's imagination; suffice it to say, that though worn to the bone by cold, hunger, and nakedness, the bulk of them still survived. The Highlanders are still proverbially tenacious of life. In the latter end of April, 1837, when news reached them that the long-promised relief, consisting of meal, barley, potatoes, and seed oats, had actually arrived, and was to be immediately distributed at Tongue and other stated places, the people at once flocked to those places, but were told that nothing would be given to any, till they produced a certificate from their parish minister that they were proper objects of charity. Here was a new obstacle. They had to return and implore those haughty priests for certificates, which were frequently withheld from mere caprice, or for some alleged offence or lack of homage in the applicant, who if not totally refused, had to be humbled in the dust, sickened by delay, and the boon only at last yielded to the intercession of some of the more humane of the shepherds. Those who were in the fishing trade were peremptorily refused. This is the way in which man, religious man, too! can trifle with the distress of his famishing brother.

The places appointed for distribution were distant from the homes of many of the sufferers, so that by the time they had waited on the ministers for the necessary qualification, and travelled again to places of distribution and back again, with what they could obtain, on their backs, several days were consumed, and in many cases from 50 to 100 miles traversed. And what amount of relief did they receive after all? From 7 to 28 lbs. of meal, and seed oats and potatoes in the same proportions; and this not for individuals, but for whole families! In the fields, and about the dykes adjoining the places where these pittances were doled out, groups of famishing creatures might be seen lying in the mornings (many of them having travelled the whole day and night previous), waiting the leisure of the factors or their clerks, and no attention was paid to them till those gentlemen had breakfasted and dressed, &c.; by which time the day was far advanced.

Several subsequent distributions of meal took place; but in every new case, fresh certificates of continued destitution had to be procured from the ministers and elders of the respective parishes. This was the kind, and quantity, of relief afforded, and the mode of dispensing it; different indeed from what was represented in the glozing falsehoods so industriously palmed on public credulity.

In the month of September, her Grace being then on a visit in the country, the following proceedings took place, as reported in the public papers of the day, which afforded a specimen of groundless assertions, clerical sycophancy, and fulsome adulation, for which it might be difficult to find a parallel :—

"The Presbytery of Tongue, at their last meeting, agreed to present the following address to the Duchess of Sutherland. Her Grace being then at Tongue, the Presbytery waited on her ; and the address being read by the moderator, she made a suitable reply :

"*May it please your Grace.*

"We, the Presbytery of Tongue, beg leave to approach your Grace with feelings of profound respect, and to express our joy at your safe arrival within our bounds.

"We have met here this day for the purpose of communicating to your Grace the deep sense which we entertain of your kindness during the past season to the people under our charge.

"When it pleased Providence by an unfavourable harvest to afflict the Highlands of Scotland with a scarcity of bread, and when the clergymen of other districts appealed to public charity in behalf of their parishoners, the confidence which we placed in your Grace's liberality led us to refrain from making a similar appeal.

"When we say that this confidence has been amply realised, we only express the feelings of our people ; and participating strongly in these feelings, as we do, to withold the expression of them from your Grace, would do injustice alike to ourselves and to them.

"In their name, therefore, as well as in our own, we beg to offer to your Grace our warmest gratitude. When other districts were left to the precarious supplies of a distant benevolence, your Grace took on yourself the charge of supporting your people ; by a constant supply of meal, you not only saved them from famine, but enabled them to live in comfort ; and by a seasonable provision of seed, you were the means, under God, of securing to them the blessing of the present abundant harvest.

"That Almighty God may bless your grace,—that he may long spare you to be a blessing to your people,--and that he may finally give you the inheritance which is incorruptible, undefiled, and that fadeth not away, is the prayer of

"May it please your Grace,

"THE MEMBERS OF THE PRESBYTERY OF TONGUE.

(Signed) "HUGH MACKENZIE, *Moderator.*"

The evident tendency of this document was to mislead her Grace, and by deluding the public, to allay anxiety, stifle inquiry, and conceal the truth. However, her Grace made a "suitable reply," and great favour was shown to the adulators. About a year before, the very clergyman whose signature is appended to this address exchanged part of his glebe for the lands of Dinsad and Inshverry; but in consenting to the change, he made an express condition that the present occupiers, amounting to eight families, should be "removed," and accordingly they were driven out in a body! To this gentleman, then, the honour is due of having consummated the Sutherland ejections; and hence he was admirably fitted for signing the address. I must not omit to notice "the abundant harvest" said to succeed the famine. The family "allotments" only afforded the sowing of from a half firlot to two or three firlots of oats, and a like quantity of barley, which, at an average in good seasons, yielded about three times the quantity sown; in bad years little or nothing; and even in the most favourable cases, along with their patches of potatoes, could not maintain the people more than three months in the year. The crop succeeding the famine was anything but an abundant one to the poor people; they had got the seed *too late,* and the season was not the most favourable for bringing it to even ordinary perfection. Hence, that "abundance" mentioned in the address was like all the rest of its groundless assumption. But I have still to add to the crowning iniquity —the provision distributed in charity had to be *paid for!* but this point I must postpone till my next.

LETTER XVI.

Sir,—It would require a closer acquaintance with the recent history of Sutherlandshire than I am able to communicate, and better abilities than mine, to convey to the reader an adequate idea of the mournful contrast between the former comfortable and independent state of the people and that presented in my last. They were now generally speaking, become a race of paupers, trembling at the very looks of their oppressors, objects of derision and mockery to the basest underlings, and fed by the scanty hand of those who had been the means of reducing them to their present state! To their capability of endurance must, in a great measure, be ascribed their surviving in any considerable numbers, the manifold inflictions they had to encounter. During the spring and summer many of the young and robust of both sexes left the country in quest of employment; some to the neighbouring county of Caithness, but most of them went to the Lowlands, and even into England, to serve as cattle drivers, labourers and in other menial occupations. No drudgery was too low for their acceptance, nor any means left untried, by which they could sustain life in the most frugal manner, and anything earned above this was carefully transmitted to their suffering relations at home. When harvest commenced they were rather better employed, and then the object was to save a little to pay the rent at the approaching term; but there was another use they had never thought of, to which their hard and scanty earnings had to be applied.

Not long after the termination of the Duchess' visit (during which the address given in my last was presented), I think just about two months after, the people were astonished at seeing placards posted up in all public places, warning them to prepare to pay their rents, and also the meal, potatoes, and seed oats and barley they had got during the spring and summer! This was done in the name of the Duchess, by the orders of Mr. Loch and his under-factors. Ground-officers were dispatched in all directions to explain and enforce this edict, and to inform the small tenants that their rents would not be received till the accounts for the provisions were first settled. This was news indeed!—astonishing intelligence this—that the pitiful mite of relief, obtained with so much labour and ceremony, and doled out by pampered · underlings with more than the usual insolence of charity, was after all to be paid for! After government aid and private charity, so effectually afforded to other Highland districts, had been intercepted by ostentatious promises of ample relief from the bounty of her Grace; after the clergy had lauded the Almighty, and her Grace no less, for that *bounty*; the poor creatures were to be concussed into paying for it, and at a rate too, considerably above the current prices. I know this, to persons unacquainted with Highland tyranny, extortion and opression, will appear incredible; but I am able to substantiate its truth by clouds of living witnesses.

The plan adopted deserves particular notice. The people were told, · "their rents would not be received till the provisions were first paid for." By this time those who had proeured a little money by labouring elsewhere, were returning with their savings to enable their relatives to meet the rents and this was thought a good time to get the "charity" paid up. Accordingly when the people, as usual, waited upon the factor with the rent, they were told distinctly that the meal. &c, must be paid first, and that if any lenity was shown, it would be for the rent, but none for the provisions! The meaning of this scheme seems to be, that by securing payment for the provisions in the first instance, they would avoid the odium of pursuing for what was given as charity, knowing that they could at any time enforce payment of the rent, by the usual summary means to which they were in the habit of resorting. Some laid down their money at once, and the price of all they had got was then deducted, and a receipt handed to them for the balance, in part of their rent. Others seeing this, remonstrated and insisted on paying their rent first, and the provisions afterwards, if they must be paid; but their pleading went for nothing, their money was taken in the same manner, (no receipts in any case being given for the payment of the "charity," and they were driven contemptuously from the counting-table.

A few refused to pay, especially unless receipts were granted for the "charity," and returned home with the money, but most of them were induced by the terror of their families to carry it back and submit like the rest. A smaller portion, however, still continued refractory, and alternate threats and wheedlings were used by the underlings to make these comply; so that gradually all were made to pay the last shilling it was possible for them to raise. Some who had got certificates of destitution being unable, from age or illness, to undergo the fatigue of waiting on the factors for their portion, or of carrying it home, had to obtain the charitable assistance of some of their abler fellow sufferers for that purpose, but when there was any difficulty about the payment, the carriers were made accountable the same as if they had been the receivers! Hitherto, the money collected at the church doors, had been divided among the poor, but this year it was withheld; in one parish to my personal knowledge (and as far as my information goes tho refusal was general), the parish minister telling them that they could not expect to get meal and money both, signifying that the deficient payments for the provisions had to be made up from the

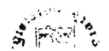

church collections. Whether this was the truth or not, it served for a pretext to deprive the poor of this slender resource; for, ever since—now four years—they have got nothing. This is one among many subjects of enquiry. Verily there is much need for light to be thrown on this corner of the land! A rev. gentleman from the west, whose failing it was to transgress the ten commandments, had, through some special favour, obtained a parish in Sutherlandshire, and thinking probably that charity should begin at home, had rather misapplied the poor's money which was left in his hand, for on his removal to another parish, there was none of it forthcoming. The elders of his new parish being aware of this, refused to entrust him with the treasurership, and had the collection-money kept in a locked box in the church, but when it amounted to some pounds, the box was broken up and the money was taken out. The minister had the key of the church.

Owing to the complete exhaustion of the poor people's means in the manner I have been describing, the succeeding year (1838) found them in circumstances little better than its predecessor. What any of them owed in Caithness and elsewhere, they had been unable to pay, and consequently their credit was at an end, and they were obliged to live from hand to mouth; besides, this year was unproductive in the fishing, as the years since have also been.

In the earlier part of this correspondence, I have treated of the large sums said to have been laid out on improvements, (roads, bridges, inns, churches, manses, and mansions for the new tenants); but I have yet to mention a poll-tax called road money, amounting to 4s. on every male of 18 years and upwards, which was laid on about the year 1810, most rigorously exacted, and continues to be levied on each individual in the most summary way, by seizure of any kind of moveables in or about the dwelling till the money is paid. To some poor families this tax come to £1 and upwards every year, and be it observed that the capitalist possessing 50,000 acres, only pays in the same proportion, and his shepherds are entirely exempt! Those of the small tenantry or their families, who may have been absent for two or three years, on their return are obliged to pay up their arrears of this tax, the same as if they had been all the time at home; and payment is enforced by seizure of the goods of any house in which they may reside. The reader will perceive that the laws of Sutherlandshire are different, and differently administered, from what they are in other parts of the country—in fact those in authority do just what they please, whether legal or otherwise, none daring to question what they do. Notwithstanding this burdensome tax, the roads, as far as the small tenants' interests are concerned, are shamefully neglected, while every attention is paid to suit the convenience and pleasure of the ruling parties and the new tenantry, by bringing roads to their very doors.

LETTER XVII.

Sir,—In my last letter I mentioned something about the withholding and misappropriation of the money collected at church doors for the poor; but let it be understood that notwithstanding the iniquitous conduct of persons so acting, the loss to the poor was not very great. The Highlander abhors to be thought a pauper, and the sum afforded to each of the few who were obliged to accept it, varied from 1s. 6d. to 5s. a year: the congregations being much diminished, as I had before occasion to observe. It is no wonder, then, that the poor, if at all able, flee from such a country and seek employment and relief in the various maritime towns in Scotland, where they arrive broken down and exhausted by previous hardship—meatless and moneyless; and when unable to labour, or unsuccessful in obtaining work, they become a burden to a community who have no right to bear it, while those who have reduced them to that state escape scot-free. Any person acquainted generally with the statistics of pauperism in Scotland will, I am sure, admit the correctness of these statments. The Highland landlords formerly counted their riches by the number of their vassals or tenants, and were anxious to retain them; hence the poem of Burns, addressed to the Highland lairds, and signed Beelzebub, by which the ever selfish policy of those gentlemen is celebrated in their endeavouring, by force, to restrain emigration to Canada. But since then the case is reversed. First the war, and then the food monopoly has made raising of cattle for the English markets, the more eligible speculation, against which the boasted feelings of clanship, as well as the claims of common humanity have entirely lost their force. Regarding the poll-tax or road money, it is also necessary to state, that in every case when it is not paid on the appointed day, expenses are arbitrarily added (though no legal process has been entered) which the defaulter is obliged to submit to without means of redress. There are no tolls in the county; the roads, &c., being kept up by this poll-tax, paid by the small tenants for the exclusive benefit of those who have superseded them. In this way very large sums are screwed out of the people, even the poorest, and from the absentees, if they ever return to reside. So that if the population are not extirpated by wholesale, a considerable portion of the sums laid out on improvements will ultimately return to the proprietors, from a source whence, of all others, they have no shadow of right to obtain it.

I have now arrived at an important event in my narrative; the death of an exalted personage to whom I have often had occasion to refer—tho Duchess-Countess of Sutherland.

This lady who had, during a long life, maintained a high position in courtly and aristocratic society, and who was possessed of many great qualities, was called to her account on the 29th of January, 1839, in the 74th year of her age. Her death took place in London, and her body was conveyed to Sutherland by way of Aberdeen, and finally interred with great pomp in the family vault, beside the late Duke, her husband, in the Cathedral of Dornoch. The funeral was attended to Blackwell by many of the first nobility in England, and afterwards by her two grandsons, Lord Edward Howard, and the Honourable Francis Egerton, and by her friend and confidential servant, Mr. Loch, with their respective suites. The procession was met by Mr. Sellar, Mr. Young, and many of her under-factors and subordinate retainers, together with the whole body of the new occupiers, while the small tenantry brought up the rear of the solemn cavalcade. She was buried with the rites of the Church of England. Mr. George Gunn, under-factor, was the only gentleman native of the county who took a prominent part in the management of the funeral and who certainly did not obtain that honour by the exercise of extraordinary virtues towards his poor countrymen : the rest were all those who had taken an active part in the scenes of injustice and cruelty which I have been endeavouring to represent to the reader, in the previous part of my narrative. The trump of fame has been seldom made to sound a louder blast, than that which echoed through the island, with the virtues of the Duchess; every periodical, especially in Scotland, was for a time literally crammed with them, but in those extravagent encomiums few or none of her native tenantry could honestly join. That she had many great and good qualities none will attempt to deny, but at the same time, under the sanction or guise of her name and authority, were continually perpetrated deeds of the most atrocious character, and her people's wrongs still remain unredressed. Her severity was felt, perhaps, far beyond her own intentions ; while her benevolence was intercepted by the instruments she employed, and who so unworthily enjoyed her favour and confidence. Her favours were showered on aliens and strangers ; while few, indeed, were the drops which came to the relief of those from whom she sprung, and whose coeval, though subordinate right to their native soil, had been recognised for centuries. Peace to her name! I am sorry it is not in my power to render unqualified praise to her character.

The same course of draining the small tenants, under one pretext or another, continued for some time after her Grace's decease; but exactions must terminate, when the means of meeting them are exhausted. You cannot starve a hen, and make her lay eggs at the same time. The factors, having taken all, had to make a virtue of necessity, and advise the Duke to an act of high-sounding generosity—to remit all the arrears due by the small tenantry. Due proclamation was made of his Grace's benevolent intentions, with an express condition annexed, that no future arrears would be allowed, and that all future defaulters should be instantly removed, and their holdings (not let to tenants, but) handed over to their next neighbour, and failing him, to the next again, and so on. This edict was proclaimed under the authority of his Grace and the factors, in the year 1840, about a twelvemonth after the Duchess's decease, and continues the law of the estate as regards the unfortunate natives, or small tenantry as they are generally called.

It will be perceived that I have now brought my narrative to an end : I may, however, with your permission, trouble you with a few remarks, in your next publication, by way of conclusion.

LETTER XVIII.

Sir,—In concluding my narrative, allow me to express—or rather to declare my inability to express—the deep sense I entertain of your kindness in permitting me to occupy so large a space of your columns, in an attempt to pourtray the wrongs of my country. I trust these feelings will be participated by those whose cause you have thus enabled me to bring before the public, as well as by all benovelent and enlightened minds, who abhor oppression, and sympathize with its victims. I am conscious that my attempt has been a feeble one. In many cases my powers of language fell short, and in others I abstained from going to the full extent, when I was not quite prepared with proof, or when the deeds of our oppressors were so horrible in their nature and consequence as to exceed belief.

Though nowhere in the North Highlands have such atrocities been practiced in the wholesale way they have been in Sutherland, yet the same causes are producing like effects, more or less generally in most, if not all, the surrounding counties. Sutherland has served as a model for successfully "clearing" the land of its aboriginal inhabitants, driving them to the sea-shore, or into the sea,—to spots of barren moors—to the wilds of Canada—and to Australia; or if unable to go so far, to spread themselves over Lowlands, in quest of menial employment among strangers, to whom their language seems barbarous, who are already overstocked with native labourers, besides those continually pouring in from Ireland. No wonder the Highland lairds combine to resist a government inquiry, which would lead to an exposure of their dark and daring deeds, and render a system of efficient poor laws (not sham, like those now existing) inevitable. Were all the paupers they have created, by "removing" the natives and substituting strangers and cattle in their places, enabled to claim that support from the soil they are justly entitled to, what would become of their estates?

Hence their alarm and anxiety to stifle all inquiry but that conducted by themselves, their favourites and retainers, and their ever-subservient auxiliaries, the parochial clergy. Will these parties expose themselves by tracing the true causes of Highland destitution? Oh, no! What they cannot ascribe to Providence, they will lay to the charge of the "indolent, improvident and intractible character," they endeavour to cover their own foul deeds by ascribing to their too passive victims. They say "the Highlanders would pay no rent." A falsehood on the very face of it. Were not the tenants' principal effects in cattle, the article of all others most convenient of arrest? "The Highlanders were unteachable, enemies to innovation or improvement, and incorrigibly opposed to the will of their superiors." Where are the proofs? What methods were taken to instruct them in improved husbandry, or any other improvements? None! They were driven out of the land of their fathers, causelessly, cruelly, and recklessly. Let their enemies say what have been their crimes of revenge under the most inhuman provocation? Where are the records in our courts of law, or in the statistics of crime, of the fell deeds laid to the charge of the expatriated Highlander? They are nowhere to be found, except in the groundless accusations of the oppressors, who calculating on their simplicity, their patient, moral, and religious character, which even the base conduct of their clergy could not pervert ; drove them unresisting, like sheep to the slaughter, or like mute fishes, unable to scream, on whom any violence could be practiced with impunity. It was thought an illiterate people, speaking a language almost unknown to the public press, could not make their wrongs be heard as they ought to be, through the length and breadth of the land. To give their wrongs a tongue—to implore inquiry by official, disinterested parties into the cause of mal-practices which have been so long going on, so as if possible to procure some remedy in future—has been my only motive for availing myself of your kindness to throw a gleam of light on Highland misery, its causes and its consequences. And I cannot too earnestly implore all those in any authority, who take an interest in the cause of humanity, to resist that partial and close-conducted, sham inquiry to which interested parties would have recourse to screen themselves from public odium, and save their pockets. Some of these parties are great, wealthy, and influential. Several of them have talent, education, and other facilities for perverting what they cannot altogether suppress, making "the worst appear the better reason," and white-washing their blackest deeds—therefore, I say, beware! They want now a government grant, forsooth, to take away the redundant population ! There is no redundant population but black cattle and sheep, and their owners, which the lairds have themselves introduced ; and do they want a grant to rid them of these? Verily, no! Their misdeeds are only equalled by their shameless impudence to propose such a thing. First, to ruin the people and make them paupers, and when their wrongs and miseries have made the very stones cry out, seek to get rid of them at the public expense! Insolent proposition ! "Contumelious their humanity." No doubt there have been some new churches built, but where are the congregations? Some schools erected, but how can the children of parents steeped in poverty profit by them? The clergy say they dispense the bread of life, but if they do so, do they give it freely—do they not *sell it* for as much as they can get, and do the dirty work of the proprietors, instead of the behests of him they pretend to serve? Did this precious article grow on any lands which the proprietors could turn into sheep walks, I verily believe they would do so, and the clergy would sanction the deed ! They and the proprietors think the natives have no right to any of God's mercies, but what they dole out in a stinted and miserable charity. Mr. Dempster of Skibo, the orator and apologist of the Highland lairds, says he "keeps two *permanent* soup-kitchens on his estate;" if this were true (as I have reason to believe it is not), what is to be inferred but that the wholesome ruin inflicted on the natives has rendered such a degrading expedient necessary. Their forefathers, a stalwart and athletic race needed no soup-kitchens, nor would their progeny, if they had not been inhumanely and unjustly treated. Mr. Loch says in his work, that the Sutherlanders were "in a state of nature." Well ; he and his coadjutors have done what they could to put them in an unnatural state—a state from which it would take an age to reclaim them. I admit there was great need of improvement in Sutherland fifty years ago, as there was at that time in the Lothians and elsewhere: but where, except in the Highlands, do we find general expulsion and degradation of the inhabitants resorted to by way of improvement? But Mr. Loch has improved—if not in virtue, at least in station—and become a great man and a legislator, from very small beginnings; he and his coadjutors have waxed fat on the miseries of their fellow-creatures, and on the animals they have substituted for human beings. Well, I would not incur their responsibility for all their grandeur and emoluments. Mr. Dempster has improved, and his factor from being a kitchen boy, has become a very thriving gentleman. These are the kind of improvements which have taken place, and all would go merrily if they could get entirely rid of the small tenents, "the redundant population," by a grant of public money. A redundant population in an extensively exporting country! This is *Irish* political economy. The same cause (the food taxes) is in operation in that unhappy country, and producing similar results; but the Irish do not always bear it so tamely; a little Lynch law, a few extra-judicial executions is now and then administered by way of example. This, however, is a wrong mode of proceeding, and one which I trust my countrymen will never imitate : better suffer than commit a crime. No system of poor law in the Highlands would be of any avail, but one that would confer SETTLEMENT ON EVERY PERSONS BORN IN THE PARISH. The lairds will evade every other, and to save their pockets would be quite unscrupulous as to the means. They could easily resort again to their burning and hunting, but a settlement on the English plan would oblige them either to support the paupers they have made, or send them away at their own expense. This would be bare justice, and in my humble opinion nothing short of it will be of any avail. Comparatively few of the sufferers would now claim the benefit of such settlements; the greater part of them have already emigrated, and located elsewhere, and would not fancy to come back as paupers whatever their right might be. But there are still too many groaning and pining away in helpless and hopeless destitution in Sutherland, and in the surrounding counties, and I have reason to know that the West Highlands are much in the same situation. There is much need, then, for official inquiry, to prevent this mass of human misery from accumulating, as well as to afford some hope of relief to present sufferers. I have now made an end for the present ; but should any contradiction appear, or any new event of importance to my countrymen occur, I shall claim your kind indulgence to resume the pen.

LETTER XIX.

Sir,—I am glad to find that some of my countrymen are coming forward with communications to your paper confirming my statements, and expressing that gratitude we ought all deeply to feel for the opportunity you have afforded of bringing our case before the public, by so humble an instrument as myself.

Nothing, I am convinced, but fear of further persecution, prevents many more from writing such letters, and hence you need not wonder if some of those you receive are anonymous. They express a wish, which from various sources of information, I am inclined to think general, that my narrative should appear, as it now does, in the form of a pamphlet, and that my own particular case should form an appendage to it. I had no intention originally of bringing my particular case and family sufferings before the public, but called on, as I am, it appears a duty to the public, as well as myself, to give a brief account of it, lest withholding it might lead to suspicion as to my motives and character.

I served an apprenticeship in the mason trade to my father, and on coming to man's estate I married my present wife, the partner of my fortunes, most of which have been adverse, and she, the weaker vessel, has largely partaken of my misfortunes in a life of suffering and a ruined constitution. Our marriage took place in 1818. My wife was the daughter of Charles Gordon, a man well known and highly esteemed in the parish of Farr, and indeed throughout the county, for his religious and moral character.

For some years I followed the practice of going south during the summer months for the purpose of improving in my trade and obtaining better wages, and returning in the winter to enjoy the society of my family and friends; and, also, to my grief, to witness the scenes of devastation that were going on, to which, in the year 1820, my worthy father-in-law fell a victim. He breathed his last amid the scenes I have described, leaving six orphans in a state of entire destitution to be provided for; for he had lost his all, in common with the other ejected inhabitants of the county.

This helpless family now fell to my care, and in order to discharge my duty to them more effectually, I wished to give up my summer excursions, and settle and pursue my business at home.

I, therefore, returned from Edinburgh in the year 1822, and soon began to find employment, undertaking mason work by estimate, &c., and had I possessed a less independent mind and a more crouching disposition, I might perhaps have remained. But stung with the oppression and injustice prevailing around me, and seeing the contrast my country exhibited to the state of the Lowlands, I could not always hold my peace; hence I soon became a marked man, and my words and actions were carefully watched for an opportunity to make an example of me. After I had baffled many attempts, knowing how they were set for me, my powerful enemies at last succeeded in effecting my ruin after seven years' labour in the pious work! If any chose to say I owed them money, they had no more to do than summon me to court, in which the factor was judge, a decreet, right or wrong, was sure to issue. Did any owe me money, it was quite optional whether they paid me or not, they well knew I could obtain no legal redress.

In the year 1827, I was summoned for £5 8s,, which I had previously paid [in this case the factor was both pursuer and judge!]: I defended, and produced receipts and other vouchers of payment having been made ; all went for nothing! The factor, pursuer and judge, commenced the following dialogue:—

Judge—Well, Donald, do you owe this money ?

Donald—I would like to see the pursuer before I would enter into any defences.

Judge—I'll pursue you.

Donald—I thought you were my judge, sir.

Judge—I'll both pursue and judge you—did you not promise me on a former occasion that you would pay this debt ?

Donald—No, sir.

Judge—John M'Kay (constable) seize the defender.

I was accordingly collared like a criminal, and kept a prisoner in an adjoining room for some hours, and afterwards placed again at the bar, when the conversation continued.

Judge—Well, Donald, what have you got to say now, will you pay the money ?

Donald—Just the same sir, as before you imprisoned me; I deny the debt.

Judge—Well, Donald, you are one of the damn'dest rascals in existence, but if you have the sum pursued for between heaven and hell, I'll make you pay it, *whatever receipts you may hold*, and I'll get you removed from the estate.

Donald—Mind, sir, you are in a magisterial capacity.

Judge—I'll let you know that—(with another volley of execrations.)

Donald—Sir, your conduct disqualifies you for your office, and under the protection of the law of the land, and in presence of this court, I put you to defiance.

I was then ordered from the bar, and the case continued undecided. Steps were, however, immediately taken to put the latter threat—my removal—my banishment !—into execution.

Determined to leave no means untried to obtain deliverance, I prepared an humble memorial in my own name, and that of the helpless orphans, whose protector I was, and had it transmitted to the Marquis and Marchioness of Stafford, praying for an investigation. In consequence of this on the very term day, on which I had been ordered to remove, I received a verbal message from one of the under-factors, that it was the noble proprietor's pleasure that I should retain possession, repair my houses and provide my fuel as usual, until Mr. Loch should come to Sutherlandshire, and then my case would be investigated. On this announcement becoming known to my opponent, he became alarmed, and the parish minister no less so, that the man he feasted with was in danger of being disgraced:

every iron was therefore put in the fire, to defeat and ruin Donald for his presumption in disputing the will of a factor, and to make him an example to deter others from a similar rebellion.

The result proved how weak a just cause must prove in Sutherland, or anywhere against cruel despotic factors and graceless ministers; my case was judged and decided before Mr. Loch left London! I, however, got Jeddart justice, for on that gentleman's arrival, I was brought before him for examination, though, I had good reason to know, my sentence had been pronounced in London six weeks before, and everything he said confirmed what I had been told. I produced the receipts and other documents, and evidence, which proved fully the statements in my memorial and vindicated my character apparently to his satisfaction. He dismissed me courteously, and in a soothing tone of voice bade me go home and make myself easy, and before he left the country he would let me know the result. I carried home the good news to my wife, but her fears, her dreams, and forebodings were not so easily got over, and the event proved that her apprehensions were too well founded, for on the 20th October, 1830, about a month after the investigation by Mr. Loch, the concluding scene took place.

On that day a messenger with a party of eight men following entered my dwelling (I being away about forty miles off at work), about 3 o'clock just as the family were rising from dinner; my wife was seized with a fearful panic at seeing the fulfilment of all her worst forebodings about to take place. The party allowed no time for parley, but having put out the family with violence, proceeded to fling out the furniture, bedding, and other effects in quick time, and after extinguishing the fire, proceeded to nail up the doors and windows in the face of the helpless woman, with a sucking infant at her breast, and three other children, the eldest under eight years of age, at her side. But how shall I describe the horrors of that scene? Wind, rain and sleet were ushering in a night of extraordinary darkness and violence, even in that inclement region. My wife and children, after remaining motionless a while in mute astonishment at the ruin which had so suddenly overtaken them, were compelled to seek refuge for the night under some neighbour's roof, but they found every door shut against them! Messengers had been dispatched warning all the surrounding inhabitants, at the peril of similar treatment, against affording shelter, or assistance, to wife, child, or animal belonging to Donald M'Leod. The poor people, well aware of the rigour with which such edicts were carried into execution, durst not afford my distressed family any assistance in such a night as even an "enemy's dog" might have expected shelter. After spending most part of the night in fruitless attempts to obtain the shelter of a roof or hovel, my wife at last returned to collect some of her scattered furniture, and erect with her own hands a temporary shelter against the walls of her late comfortable residence, but even this attempt proved in vain; the wind dispersed her materials as fast as she could collect them, and she was obliged to bide the pelting of the pitiless storm with no covering but the frowning heavens, and no sounds in her ears but the storm, and the cries of her famishing children.

Death seemed to be staring them in the face, for by remaining where they were till morning, it was next to impossible even the strongest of them could survive, and to travel any distance amid the wind, rain, and darkness, in that rugged district, seemed to afford no prospect but that of death by falling over some of the cliffs or precipices with which they were surrounded, or even into the sea, as many others had done before.

LETTER XX.

SIR,—Before proceeding to detail the occurrences of that memorable night in which my wife and children were driven from their dwelling, it seems necessary to guard against any misconception that might arise from my rather incredible statement, that the factor (whose name I omit for obvious reasons)was both pursuer and judge.

The pretended debt had been paid, for which payment I hold a receipt, but the person represented it as still due, and the factor advanced the amount, issued the summons, &c., and proceeded in court in the manner I described in my last. But to proceed with my narrative.

The only means left my wife seemed to be the choice of perishing with her children where she was, or of making some perilous attempt to reach distant human habitations where she might hope for shelter. Being a woman of some resolution, she determined on the latter course. Buckling up her children, *including the one she had hitherto held at her breast*, in the best manner she could, she left them in charge of the eldest (now a soldier in the 78th regiment), giving them such victuals as she could collect, and prepared to take the road for Caithness, fifteen miles off, in such a night and by such a road as might have appalled a stout heart of the other sex! And for a long while she had the cries of her children, whom she had slender hopes of seeing again alive, sounding in her ears. This was too much! No wonder she has never been the same person since. She had not proceeded many miles when she met with a good Samaritan, and acquaintance, of the name of Donald M'Donald, who disregarding the danger he incurred, opened his door to her, refreshed and consoled her, and (still under the cover of night) accompanied her to the dwelling of William Innes, Esq., of Sandside, Caithness, and through his influence, that gentleman took her under his protection, and gave her permission to occupy an empty house of his at Armidale (a sheep farm h held of the Sutherland family), only a few miles from the dwelling she h been turned out of the day before. On arriving there she was oblige take some rest for her exhausted frame, notwithstanding the hoi suspense she was in as to the fate of her children.

At this time I was working in Wick, and on that night had laglance under such great uneasiness and apprehension of something wrong of my that I could get no rest, and at last determined to set out and sent from fared with my family, and late in the evening overtook my wif benevolent conducter proceeding from Sandside. After a brief recital of the events of the previous night, she implored me to leave her and seek the children, of whose fate she was ignorant. At that moment I was in a fit mood for a deed that would have served as a future warning to Highland tyrants, but the situation of my imploring wife, who suspected my intention, and the hope of saving my children, stayed my hand, and delayed the execution of justice on the miscreants, till they shall have appeared at a higher tribunal.

I made the best of my way to the place near our dwelling where the children were left, and to my agreeable surprise, found them alive; the eldest boy in pursuance of his mother's instructions, had made great exertions, and succeeded in obtaining for them temporary shelter. He took the infant on his back, and the other two took hold 'of him by the *kilt*, and in this way they travelled in darkness, through rough and smooth, bog and mire, till they arrived at a grand-aunt's house, when, finding the door open they bolted in, and the boy advancing to his astonished aunt, laid his infant burden in her lap, without saying a word, and proceeding to unbuckle the other two, he placed them before the fire without waiting for invitation. The goodman here rose, and said he must leave the house and seek a lodging for himself, as he could not think of turning the children out, and yet dreaded the ruin threatened to any that would harbour or shelter them, and he had no doubt his house would be watched to see if he should transgress against the order. His wife, a pious woman, upbraided him with cowardice, and declared that if there was a legion of devils watching her she would not put out the children or leave the house either. So they got leave to remain till I found them next day, but the man impelled by his fears, did go and obtain a lodging two miles off. I now brought the children to their mother, and set about collecting my little furniture and other effects which had been damaged by exposure to the weather, and some of it lost or destroyed. I brought what I thought worth the trouble, to Armidale, and having thus secured them and seen the family under shelter, I began to cast about to see how they were to live, and here I found troubles and difficulties besetting us on every side.

I had no fear of being able by my work to maintain the family in common necessaries, if we could get them for money, but one important necessary, fuel, we could scarce at all obtain, as nobody would venture to sell or give us peats (the only fuel used), for fear of the factors; but at last it was contrived that they would allow us to take them by stealth, and under cover of night!

My employment obliging me to be often from home, this laborious ha..k fell to the lot of my poor wife. The winter came on with more atte.. its usual severity, and often amidst blinding, suffocating drifts, and to co.. ests unknown in the lowlands, had this poor, tenderly brought up a tem.. to toil through snow, wind, and rain, for miles, with a burden of but ev.. her back! Instances, however, were not few of the kind assisfast as s.. neighbours endeavouring by various ways to mitigate her hard the pitil.. gh, of course, all by stealth lest they should incur the vengeance sounds in.. tors.

During the winter and following spring, every means was used to induce Mr. Innes to withdraw his protection and turn us out of the house; so that I at last determined to take steps for removing myself and family for ever from those scenes of persecution and misery. With this view, in the latter end of spring I went to Edinburgh, and found employment, intending when I had saved as much as would cover the expenses, to bring the family away. As soon as it was known that I was away, our enemies recommenced their work. Mr. ———, a gentleman, who fattened on the spoils of the poor in Sutherland, and who is now pursuing the same course on the estates of Sir John Sinclair in Caithness; this manager and factor bounced into my house one day quite unexpectedly, and began abusing my wife, and threatened her if she did not instantly remove, he would take steps that would astonish her, the nature of which she would not know till they fell upon her, adding that he knew Donald M'Leod was now in Edinburgh, and could not assist her in making resistance. The poor woman, knowing she had no mercy to expect, and fearing even for her life, removed with her family and little effects to my mother's house which stood near the parish church, and was received kindly by her. There she hoped to find shelter and repose for a short time, till I should come and take her and the family away, and this being the week of the sacrament, she was anxious to partake of that ordinance in the house where her forefathers had worshipped, before she bade it farewell for ever. But on the Thursday previous to that solemn occasion, the factor again terrified her by his appearance, and alarmed my mother to such an extent that my poor family had again to turn out in the night, and had they not a more powerful friend, they would have been forced to spend that night in the open air. Next day she bade adieu to her native country and friends, leaving the sacrament to be received by her oppressors, from the hands of one no better than themselves, and after two days of incredible toil she arrived with the family at Thurso, a distance of nearly forty miles!

These protracted sufferings and alarms have made fatal inroads on the health of this once strong and healthy woman—one of the best of wives—so that instead of the cheerful and active helpmate she was formerly, she is now, except at short intervals, a burden to herself, with little or no hopes of recovery. She has been under medical treatment for years, and has used a great quantity of medicine with little effect; the injuries she received in body and mind, were too deep for even her good spirits and excellent constitution to overcome, and she remains a living monument of Highland oppression.

LETTER XXI.

Sir,—I beg leave, by way of conclusion, to take a retrospective glance of some of the occurrences that preceded the violent expulsion of my family, as described in my two last letters, and our final retirement from the country of our nativity.

For reasons before alleged, nothing could have given more satisfaction to the factors, clergy, and all the Jacks-in-office under them, than a final riddance of that troublesome man, Donald M'Leod; and hence their extreme eagerness to make an example of him, to deter others from calling their proceedings in question. I mentioned in letter XIX that on being unjustly and illegally imprisoned, and decerned to pay money I did not owe, I prepared and forwarded a memorial to the noble proprietors (the then Marquis and Marchioness of Stafford), setting forth the hardships of my case, and praying for investigation, alleging that I would answer any accusation of my enemies, by undeniable testimonials of honest and peaceful character. This memorial was returned with the deliverance that Mr. Loch, on his next visit to Sutherland, would examine into my case and decide. I then set about procuring my proposed certificate preparatory to the investigation, but here I found myself baffled and disappointed in a quarter from which I had no reason to expect such treatment. I waited on my parish minister, the Rev. Mr. M'Kenzie, requesting him to give me a certificate, and then, after him I could obtain the signatures of the elders and as many of the other parishoners as might be necessary. He made no objection at the time, but alleging that he was then engaged, said I could send my wife for it. I left directions with her accordingly, and returned to my work. The same night the factor (my pretended creditor and judge) *had the minister and his family to spend the evening with him*, and the consequence was that in the morning a messenger was dispatched from his reverence to my wife, to say, that she need not take the trouble of calling for the certificate, as he had changed his mind! Some days after, I returned and waited on the Rev. gentleman to inquire the cause of this change. I had great difficulty in obtaining an audience, and when at last I did, it was little to my satisfaction. His manner was contemptuous and forbidding; at last he told me that he could not give me a certificate as I was at variance with the factor; that my conduct was unscriptural, as I obeyed not those set in authority over me, &c. I excused and defended myself as well as I could, but all went for nothing, and at last he ordered me to be off, and shut the door in my face. This took place in June, 1830, and Mr. Loch was not expected till the September following, during which interval I had several re-encounters with the minister. Many of his elders and parishoners pleaded and remonstrated with him on my behalf, well knowing that little attention would be paid in high quarters to my complaints however just, without his sanction; and considerable excitement prevailed in the parish about this dispute, but the minister remained immoveable. Meantime the parish schoolmaster mentioned in confidence to one of the elders (who was a relation of my wife, and communicated it to us) that my case was already decided by Mr. Loch, though a sham trial would take place; that he had been told this, and he had it from good authority, and that the best thing I could do was to leave the place entirely. I could not believe this, but the result proved the truth of it. Matters continued in the same way till Mr. Loch's arrival, when I ventured to repeat my request to the minister, but found him still more determined, and I was dismissed with more than usual contempt. I then got a certificate prepared myself, and readily obtained the signatures of the elders and neighbouring parishoners to the amount of several hundreds, which I presented to Mr. Loch, along with the before mentioned memorial, when the following dialogue took place between that gentleman and me in presence of the factors, &c.

Mr. Loch.—Well, Mr. M'Leod, why don't you pay this £5 8s. you were summoned for?

Donald.—Just, Sir, because I don't consider myself entitled to pay it. I hold legal receipts to show that I paid it two years ago; besides, that is a case to be legally decided before a competent court, and has no connexion with my memorial.

Mr. L.— Will you pay it altogether or by instalments, if you are allowed to remain on the estate?

D.—Let the case be withdrawn from the civil court or decided by the civil magistrate, before I answer that question.

Mr. L.—Well, can you produce the certificate of character mentioned in this memorial?

I handed over to him the certificate mentioned above, with three or four sheets full of names attached to it. He look at it for some time (perhaps surprised at the number of signatures) and then said,—

Mr. L.—I cannot see the minister's name here, how is this?

D.—I applied to the minister and he would not sign it.

Mr. L.—Why?

D.—He stated as his reason that I was at variance with the factors.

One of the factors.—That is a falsehood.

Mr. L.—I will wait upon Mr. M'Kenzie on the subject.

D.—Will you allow me, sir, to meet you and Mr. M'Kenzie face to face, when he is asked to give his reasons?

Mr. L.—Why will you not believe what he says?

D.—I have got too much reason to doubt it; but if he attempts to deny what I have stated, I hope you will allow him to be examined on oath?

Mr. L.—By no means, we must surely believe the minister.

After asking me some further questions which had nothing to do with the matter in hand, he dismissed me in seeming good humour.

I pressed to know his decision in my case, but he said, you will get to know it before I leave the country; make yourself easy, I will write to your parish minister in a few days. The result was the cruel expulsion of my family and the spoliation of my goods, as detailed in my two last letters.

Mr. Loch in his judgement on my case, alleged as his principal reason for punishing me that Mr. M'Kenzie denied my assertions in regard to himself, and represented me as a turbulent character.

During our temporary residence at Armidale, I took an opportunity of again waiting on the Rev. gentleman when he was catechising in a neighbouring fishing village with several of his elders in company, and asked to speak with him in their presence. He attempted to meet me outside the door, but I pushed in when the elders were sitting at breakfast; saying, "no sir, I wish what passes between you and me to be before witnesses.

I want a certificate of my moral character, or an explanation from you before your elders why it is withheld." Here my worthy friend Donald M'Donald (the preserver of my wife's life on the memorable night of her expulsion) interfered and expostulated with his reverence, who driven into a corner, found no excuse for refusal, except that he had not writing materials convenient. I directly met this objection by producing the articles required, yet, strange to say, he found means to shuffle the business over by a solemn promise, in presence of his elders, to do it on a certain mentioned day. I waited on him that day, and after long delay was admitted into his parlour and accosted with, "Well M'Leod, I am not intending to give you a certificate." "Why so, sir?" Because you have told falsehoods of me to Mr. Loch, and I cannot certify for a man that I know to be a liar:" adding "Donald, I would favour you on your father's account, and much more on your father-in-law's account, but after what you have said of me, I cannot." I repelled the charge of being a liar, and said "I do believe that if my father and father-in-law, whom you have mentioned with so much respect, stood at the gate of Heaven seeking admittance, and nothing to prevent them but a false accusation on the part of some of the factors, you woud join in refusing their entrance to all eternity." He rose up and said, "you are a Satan and not fit for human society." I retired for that time; but ultimately forced him, by incessant applications, to write and sign the following:—

"This certifies that the bearer, DONALD M'LEOD, is a native of this parish a married man, free from church censure; therefore he, his wife and family may be *admitted as Gospel hearers* wherever Providence may order their lot.
Given at Farr Manse. (Signed)

Previous to granting this certificate the minister proposed to bind me up not to use it to the prejudice of the Marquis of Stafford, or any of his factors! This point, however, he did not carry, for when he submitted it to the session he was overruled by their votes.

This concludes the narrative of what I have myself suffered at the hands of the petty tyrants whom I had enraged by denouncing their barbarous treatment of my countrymen, and whose infamous deeds I have had the satisfaction of exposing to public reprobation. I shall not resume the pen on this subject unless I see that what I have written requires to be followed up to prevent a 'continuation of such atrocities as are already recorded. I am a Highlander, and must have revenge for the wrongs I have suffered. The revenge I desire is that these letters may be preserved for many a day in my native country, to keep up the remembrance of the evil that was done to many an innocent individual, and among others to

DONALD M'LEOD.

THE LATE RIOTS IN DURNESS.

LETTER XXII.

When concluding that series of letters, descriptive of the woes of Sutherlandshire, which I now republish in the form of a pamphlet, I was not expecting so soon to find occasion to add important new matter to the sad detail. Another portion of my native county has fallen under the oppressor, and got into the fangs of law, which being administered by those interested, little mercy can be expected by the wretched defaulters.

All those conversant with the public papers will have seen an article, copied from the *Inverness Courier*, entitled " Riot in Durness, Sutherlandshire," in which as usual a partial and one-sided account of the affair is given, and the whole blame laid on the unfortunate inhabitants. The violation of law, committed by the poor people driven to desperation, and for which they will no doubt have to pay dear, is exaggerated, while their inhuman oppression and provocation are carefully left out of sight. The following facts of the cases are a combination of my own knowledge, and that of trustworthy correspondents who were eye-witnesses of this unfortunate occurrence, which will yet be productive of much misery to the victims—perhaps end in causing their blood to be shed !

Mr. Anderson, the tacksman of Keenabin, and other farms under Lord Reay, which were the scene of the riot, was one of the earliest of that unhallowed crew of new tenants, or middlemen, who came in over the heads of the native farmers. He, with several others I could name, some of whom have come to an unhappy end, counting the natives as their slaves and their prey, disposed without scruple of them and all that they had, just as it suited their own interest or convenience, reckless of the wrongs and misery they inflicted on these simple unresisting people. They were removed from their comfortable houses and farms in the interior, to spots on the sea shore, to make room for the new-comers with their flocks and herds, and to get their living, and pay exorbitant rents, by cultivating kelp, and deep-sea fishing. In these pursuits their persevering courage and industry enabled them to surmount appalling difficulties, though with much suffering and waste of health and life. The tacksman set up for a fish curer and *rented the sea to them* at his own pleasure, furnishing boats and implements at an exorbitant price, *while he took their fish at his own price*, and thus got them drowned in debt and consequent bondage, from which, by failures both in the kelp and fishing trades, they have never been able to relieve themselves. Seeing this, and thinking he could, after taking their all for thirty years, put their little holdings, improved by their exertions, to a more profitable use, this gentleman *humanely* resolved to extirpate them, root and branch, after he had sucked their blood and peeled their flesh, till nothing more could be got by them, and regardless of the misery to which he doomed them, how they might fare, or which way they were to turn to procure a subsistence. To emigrate they were unable, and to repair to the manufacturing towns in quest of employment, when such multitudes are in destitution already, would afford no hope of relief. Where, then, were they to find refuge? To this question, so often urged by the poor out-casts in Sutherlandshire, the general answer of their tyrants was, "let them go to hell, but they must leave our boundaries."

Human patience and endurance have limits, and is it to be wondered at that poor creatures driven to such extremities should be tempted to turn on their oppressors, and violate the letter of the law? Hence it is true that the poor people gathered, and seized and burned the paper which appeared as a death warrant to them (and may in one way or other prove so to them) and did their utmost, though without much personal violence, to scare away their enemies, and though law may punish, will humanity not sympathize with them? The story, as represented in the papers, of severe beating and maltreatment of the officers is, to say the least, a gross exaggeration, The intention, however indefensible on the score of law, was merely to intimidate, not to injure. The military, it seems, is now to be called upon to wind up the drama in the way of their profession, I pray it may not end tragically. If the sword be unsheathed at Cape Wrath, let the southrons look out! If the poor and destitute—made so by injustice —are to be cut down in Sutherland, it may only be the beginning; there are plenty of poor and destitute elsewhere, whose numbers the landlords, to save their monopoly, might find it convenient to curtail; and to do which they only want a colourable pretext. Meanwhile, I shall watch the progress of the affair at Durness, and beg to call on all rightly constituted minds, to sympathize with the distress of the unfortunate people.

LETTER XXIII.

SIR,—Having lately exposed the partial and exaggerated statements in the *Inverness Courier*, (the organ of the oppressors of Sutherlandshire,) my attention is again called to subsequent paragraphs in that paper, and which I feel it my duty to notice.

Since my last, I have received communications from correspondents on whom I can rely, which, I need scarcely say, give a very different colour to the proceedings from what appears in the *Courier*, emanating, as it evidently does, from the party inflicting the injury. The first notice in that paper represents the conduct of the poor natives in the blackest aspect, while the latter, that of the 27th October, is calculated to mislead the public in another way, by representing them as sensible of their errors, and acknowledging the justice of the severities practiced upon them.

The *Courier* says, "We are happy to learn that the excitement that led to the disturbance by Mr. Anderson's tenants in Durness has subsided, and that the people are quiet, peaceful, and fully sensible of the illegality and unjustifiable nature of their proceedings. The Sheriff addressed the people in a powerful speech, with an effect which had the best conse-quences. They soon made written communications to the Sheriff and Mr. Anderson, stating their contrition, and soliciting forgiveness ; promising to remove voluntarily in May next, if permitted in the meantime to remain and occupy their houses. An agreement on this footing was then happily accomplished, which, while it vindicates the law, tempers justice with mercy. Subsequently, Mr. Napier, Advocate-Depute, arrived at the place to conduct the investigation," &c.

Latterly the *Courier* says,

" The clergyman of the parish convinced the people, and Mr. Lumsden, the Sheriff, addressed them on the serious nature of their late proceedings; this induced them to petition Mr. Anderson, their landlord, asking his forgiveness ; and he has allowed them to remain till May next. We trust something will be done in the interval for the poor homeless *Mountaineers*." This is the subdued, though contemptuous tone of the *Courier*, owing doubtless to the noble and impartial conduct of the Advocate-Depute, Mr. Napier, who in conducting the investigation, found, notwithstanding the virulent and railing accusations brought by those who had driven the poor people to madness, that their conduct was very different from what it had been represented. The *Courier*, in his first article, called for the military "to vindicate the law" by shedding the blood of the Sutherland rebels ; but now calls them "poor homeless mountaineers." His crocodile tears accord ill with the former virulence of him and his employers, and we have to thank Mr. Napier for the change. The local authorities who assisted at the precognition did the utmost that malice could suggest to exasperate that gentleman against the people, but he went through the case in his own way, probing it to the bottom, and qualifying their rage by his coolness and impartiality.

Notwithstanding a series of injuries and provocations unparalleled, this is the first time the poor Sutherlanders, so famous in their happier days for defending their country and its laws, have been led to transgress; and I hope when the day of trial comes, the very worst of them will be found "more sinned against than sinning." It is to be lamented that the law has been violated, but still more to be lamented that all the best attributes of our common nature—all the principles of justice, mercy, and religion, have been violated by the oppressors of this people, under colour of law ! The poor victims, simple, ignorant, and heart-broken, have men of wealth, talent, and influence, for their opponents and accusers—the very individu-als who have been the authors of all their woes, are now their vindictive persecutors—against the combination of landlords, factors, and other officials, there is none to espouse their cause. One of my correspondents says, the only gentleman who seemed to take any interest in the people's cause was ordered by the Sheriff Lumsden out of his presence. Another says, no wonder the Sheriff was so disposed, for when he arrived in Dor-noch, the officials represented the people as savages in a state of rebellion, so that he at first declined proceeding without military protection, and in consequence, a detachment of the 53rd Regiment in Edinburgh Castle received orders to march ; and could a steamboat have been procured at the time, which providence prevented, one hundred rank and file would have been landed on the shores of Sutherlandshire, and, under the direction of the people's enemies, would probably have stained their arms with innocent blood ! But before a proper conveyance could be obtained, the order was countermanded, the Sheriff having found cause to alter his opinion; the people, though goaded into momentary error, became immediately amenable to his advice. The clergyman of the parish, also, made himself useful on this occasion, threatening the people with punishment here and hereafter, if they refused to bow their necks to the oppressor. According to him, all the evils inflicted upon them were ordained of God, and for their good, where-as any opposition on their part proceeded from the devil, and subjected them to just punishment here, and eternal torment hereafter. Christ says " Of how much more value is a man than a sheep ?" The Sutherland clergy never preached this doctrine, but practically the reverse. They literally prefer flocks of sheep to their human flocks, and lend their aid to every scheme for extirpating the latter to make room for the former. They find their account in leaguing with the oppressors, following up the threatenings of fire and sword by the Sheriff, with the terrors of the bottomless pit. They gained their end; the people prostrated themselves at the feet of their oppressors, "whose tender mercies are cruel." The *Courier* says, "the law has thus been vindicated." Is it not rather injustice and tyranny that have been vindicated, and the people make a prey? When they were ordered, in the manner prescribed, to put themselves entirely in the wrong, and beg mercy, they were led to believe this would procure a full pardon and kinder treatment. But their submission was immediately followed up by the precognition, in which, as I said before, every means was used to criminate them, and exaggerate their offence, and it depends on the view the Lord Advocate may be induced to take, what is to be their fate. One thing is certain, Mr. Anderson and his colleagues will be content with nothing short of their expatriation, either to Van Dieman's Land or the place the clergy consigned them to, he cares not which. For the mercy which, as the *Courier* says, has been tempered with justice, of allowing the people to possess their houses till May, while their crop had been lost by the bad weather, or destroyed by neglect during the disturbance, they are mainly indebted to Mr. Napier. Anderson found himself shamed into a consent, which he would otherwise never have given. God knows, their miserable allotments, notwithstanding the toil and money they have expended on them, are not worth contending for, did the poor creatures know where to go when banished, but this with their attachment to the soil, makes them feel it like death, to think of removing. Anderson craftily turned this feeling to his advantage, for, though he obtained the degrees of ejectment in April,' *he postponed their execution till the herring fishery was over*, in order to drain every shilling the poor people had earned, exciting the hope, that if they paid up, they would be allowed to remain ! The *Courier* hopes " something will be done for the poor *mountaineers*." O my late happy, highminded countrymen is it come to this? Represented as wild animals or savages, and hunted accordingly in your own native straths, so often defended by the sinews and blood of your vigorous ancestors!

Surely, your case must arouse the sympathy of generous Britons, otherwise the very stones will cry out! Surely, there is still so much virtue remaining in the country that your wrongs will be made to ring in the ears of your oppressors, till they are obliged to hide their heads for very shame, and tardy justice at length overtake them in the shape of public indignation.

LETTER XXIV.

Sir,—Since my last communication was written, I have received letters from several correspondents in the north, and, as I intimated, now proceed to lay a portion of their contents before the public. Much of the information I have received must be suppressed from prudential considerations. Utter ruin would instantly overtake the individual, especially if an official, who should dare to throw a gleam of light on the black deeds going on, or give a tongue to the people's wrongs; besides, the language of some of the letters is too strong and justly indignant, to venture its publication, lest I might involve myself and others in the toils of law, with the meshes of which I am but little acquainted; hence my correspondence must generally speaking, be suppressed or emasculated. From the mass of evidence received, I am fully satisfied that the feeble resistance to the instruments of cruelty and oppressions at Durness, and which was but a solitary and momentary outbreak of feeling, owes it importance as a *riot* entirely to the inventive and colouring talents of the correspondent of the *Inverness Courier*. One of my correspondents says, "this affray must be a preconcerted one on the part of the authorities;" another says "the Advocate-Depute asked me, why did the Duke of Sutherland's tenants join Mr. Andersons's tenants; my reply was (which he allowed to be true) that when Anderson would remove his, he and his either hand neighbours would directly use their influenc to get the duke's small tenants removed likewise, as they hate now to see a poor man at all, and if any of the tenants would offer to say so much, they would not be believed; this is the way the offspring of the once valiant M'Kay's are now used, their condition is beyond what a pen can describe, but we are here afraid to correspond with such a character as you: if it was known, we would be ruined at once." Another says "there was not a pane of glass, a door, or railing, or any article of furniture broken within or without the inn at Durine, nor as much as a hair of the head of a Sheriff, Fiscal, or Constable, touched. If it was the Sheriff or Fiscal Fraser who published the first article, titled Durness Riot, in the *Inverness Courier*, indeed they should be ashamed of their unpardonable conduct;" another says "after all their ingenuity it was only one Judas they made in Durness, and if there was any one guilty of endeavouring to create disturbance it was himself. Therefore, we may call him Donald Judas *Mac an Diobhail fear-casaid nam breugan*, and the authorities should consider what credence his evidence deserved in criminating the people he was trying to mislead." Another correspondent says "Fraser the Fiscal (a countryman himself, but an enemy as all renegades are) inserted a most glaring and highly coloured mis-statement in the *Inverness Courier*, and is ever on the alert to publish anything that might serve his employers and injure his poor countrymen;" another says "The Fiscal and Sheriff Lumsden were very severe on the people before the Advocate-Depute, but after he had gone through the business they found it prudent to alter their tone a good deal," he adds "I incurred the Fiscal's displeasure *for not giving the evidence he wanted for condemning the people*, and to punish me, he would pay me only 10s. for attending the precognition five days and a night. But when the Duke comes I will lay the case before him and tell him how Fraser was so anxious to get the people into a scrape. He is a little worth gentleman." The conduct of the Fiscal requires no comment, and his, it is said, is the *Courier's* authority for its mis-statements. The plan of the persecutors is not only to ruin and expel the natives, by any and every means, but to deprive them of public sympathy, by slandering their character, belying their actions, and harassing them in every possible way, so as to make them willing to leave their native soil before a regular authorised enquiry takes place, which would (in case their victims remain on the spot, not only expose their nefarious deeds, but also lead the way to a regular law for obliging them to provide in some way for the poor they have made.

These are now the two objects of their fears. first, lest they should be shown up, and secondly, that a real—and not, as hitherto, a sham—poor-law should be established, to make them contribute to relieve the misery they have so recklessly and wickedly created. With these preliminaries. I present you a large extract *verbatim*, from the letter of a gentleman, with whom, though I know his highly respectable connexions, I am personally unacquainted. Coming evidently from a person of education and character, it seems justly entitled to the consideration of all who are pleased to interest themselves in the woes and wrongs of Sutherland, and the outrages there offered to our common humanity :—

"You are aware that Anderson was a pretty considerable speculator in his time, (but not so great a speculator as * * *,) extensively engaged in the white and herring fishings, at the time he held out the greatest inducements to the poor natives who were expelled from other places in the parish, who came and built little huts on his farm and were entirely dependent on their fishings and earnings with him. In this humble sphere they were maintaining themselves and families, until God in just retribution turned the scales upon Anderson; his speculations proved unsuccessful, he lost his shipping, and his cash was fast following; he broke down his herring establishments, and so the poor fishermen had to make the best of it they could with other curers. Anderson now began to turn his attention to sheep farming, and removed a great many of his former tenants and fishermen : however, he knew little or nothing of the details of sheep farming, and was entirely guided by the advices of his either hand neighbours, Alex. Clark of Erriboll and John Seobe of Koldale (both sheep farmers); and it is notorious that it was at the instigation of these creatures that he adopted such severe measures against those remaining of his tenants—but, be this as it may, this last summer when the whole male adult population were away at the fishing in Wick, he employed a fellow of the name of C———l to summon and frighten the poor women in the absence of their husbands. The proceeding was both cowardly and illegal; however, the women (acting as it can be proved upon C———l's own suggestion!) congregated, lighted a fire, laid hands on C———l and compelled him to consign his papers to the flames! Anderson immediately reported the case to the Dornoch law-mongers, who smelling a job, dispatched their officer;—off he set to Durness as big as a mountain, and together with one of Anderson's shepherds proceeded to finish what C———l had begun: however, he 'reckoned without his host,' for ere he got half through, the women fell in hot love with him also—and embraced him so cordially, that he left with them his waterproof Mackintosh, and 'cut' to the tune of "Caberfeidh." No sooner had he arrived in Dornoch, than the gentlemen there concluded that they themselves had been insulted and ill-used by proxy in Durness. Shortly afterwards they dispatched the same officer and a messenger-at-arms, with instructions to raise a trusty party by the way to aid them. They came by Tongue, went down to Farr on the Saturday evening, raised Donald M'Kay, pensioner, and other two old veterans, whom they sent off before them on the Sabbath *incog.*; however, they only advanced to the ferry at Hope when they were told that the Durness people were fully prepared to give them a warm reception, so they went no further, but returned to Dornoch, and told there a doleful Don Quixote tale. Immediately thereafter, a 'council of war' was held, and the Sheriff-substitute, together with the fiscal and a band of fourteen special constables marched off to Durness. Before they arrived the people heard of their approach, and consulted among themselves what had best be done (the men were by this time all returned home.) They allowed the whole party to pass through the parish till they reached the inn; this was on a Saturday evening about eight or nine o'clock;—the men of the parish to the amount of four dozen called at the inn, and wanted to have a conference with the Sheriff, this was refused to them. They then respectfully requested an assurance from the sheriff that they would not be interfered with during the Sabbath, this was likewise refused. Then the people got a little exasperated, and, determined in the first place on depriving the sheriff of his sting, they took his constables one by one, and turned them out of the house *minus* their batons. There was not the least injury done, or violence shewn to the persons of any of the party. The natives now made their way to the sheriff's room and began to dictate (!) to him; however, as they could not get him to accede to their terms, they ordered him to march off; which, after some persuasion he did; they laid no hands on him or the fiscal. And, to show their civility, they actually harnessed the horses for them, and escorted them beyond the precincts of the parish!!! The affair now assumed rather an alarming aspect. The glaring and highly coloured statement referred to, appeared in the *Inverness Courier*, and soon found its way into all the provincial and metropolitan prints; the parties referred to were threatened with a military force. The Duke of Sutherland was stormed on all hands with letters and petitions. The matter came to the ears of the Lord Advocate. Mr. Napier, the Depute-Advocate, was sent from Auld Reekie, and the whole affair investigated before him and the Sheriff, and Clerk and Fiscal of the County. How this may ultimately terminate I cannot yet say, but one thing is certain, the investigators have discovered some informality in the proceedings on the part of the petty lawyers, which has for the present suspended all further procedure! ·I am glad to understand that the Duke of Sutherland expresses great sympathy with the poor people. Indeed I am inclined to give his Grace credit for good intentions, if he but knew how his people are harassed, but this is religiously concealed from him.

I live at some distance from Tongue, but I made myself sure of the certainty of the following extraordinary case which could have occurred nowhere but in Sutherland.

The present factor in Tongue is from Edinburgh.—This harvest, a brother of his who is a clerk, or something in that city, came down to pay him a visit; they went out a-shooting one day in September, but could kill no birds. They, however, determined to have some sport before returning home; so, falling in with a flock of goats belonging to a man of the name of Manson, and within a few hundred yards of the man's own house, they set two, and after firing a number of ineffectual shots, succeeded at length in taking down two of the goats, which they left on the ground! Satisfied and delighted with this manly sport they returned to Tongue. And next day when called upon by the poor man who owned the goats, and told they were all he had to pay his rent with, this exemplary factor said to him, 'he did not care should he never pay his rent,'—'he was only sorry he had not proper ammunition at the time,'—as 'he would not have left one of them alive!!!' Think you, would the Duke tolerate such conduct as this, or what would he say did the fact come to his ears? As Burns says :—

> " This is a sketch of H————h's way,
> Thus does he slaughter, kill, and slay,
> And 's weel paid for 't."

The poor man durst not whisper a complaint for this act of brutal despotism; but I respectfully ask, will the Duke of Sutherland tolerate such conduct? I ask will such conduct be tolerated by the legislature? Will Fiscal Fraser and the Dornoch law-mongers smell this job?

LETTER XXV.

SIR,—Having done my best to bring the wrongs of the Sutherlanders in general, and, latterly, those of Mr. Anderson's tenantry in particular, under the public eye in your valuable columns, I beg leave to close my correspondence for the present, with a few additional facts and observations. Before doing so, however, 1 must repeat my sense—in which I am confident my countrymen will participate—of your great kindness in allowing me such a vehicle as your excellent paper through which to vent our complaints and proclaim our wrongs. I also gratefully acknowledge the disinterested kindness of another individual, whose name it is not now necessary to mention, who has assisted me in revising and preparing my letters for the press. I hope such friends will have their reward.

It is unnecessary to spin out the story of the Durness Riot (as it is called) any longer. It evidently turns out what I believed it to be from the beginning—a humbug scheme for further oppressing and destroying the people ; carrying out, by the most wicked and reckless means, the long prevailing system of expatriation, and, at the same time, by gross misrepresentations, depriving them of that public sympathy to which their protracted sufferings and present misery give them such strong claims. In my latest correspondence from that quarter the following facts are contained, which further justify the previous remarks, viz :—

A gentleman who makes a conspicuous figure in the proceedings against the people, is *law-agent* of Mr. Anderson, the lessee, from whose property the poor *crofters* were to be ejected ; and C———l, the first officer sent to Durness, was employed by them. This C———l was an unqualified officer, but used as a convenient tool by his employers, and it was actually, as I am assured, this man who advised or suggested to the poor women and boys, in absence of the male adults, to kindle the fire, and lay hold on him, and compel him to consign his papers to the flames !—acting doubtless under the directions of his employers.

The next emissary sent was an qualified officer ; qualified by having served an apprenticeship as a thief-catcher and w——— chaser in the police establishment of Edinburgh, who, when he came in contact with the virtuous Durness women, behaved as he was wont to do among those of Anchor Close and Halkerston's Wynd ; and I am sorry to say some of the former were inhumanly and shamefully dealt with by him.—See *Inverness Courier* of 17th November. And here I am happy to be able in a great degree to exonerate that journal from the charge brought against it in former letters. The Editor has at last put the saddle on the right horse —namely, his first informers, the advisers and actors in the cruel and vindictive proceedings against the poor victims of oppression.

It is lamentable to think that the Sheriff-substitute of Sutherland should arrive in Durness, with a formidable party and a train of carts, to carry off to Dornoch Jail the prisoners he intended to make, *on the Sabbath-day !* If this was not his intention, what was the cause of the resistance and defeat he and his party met with ? Just this (according to the *Courier* and my own correspondents), that he would not consent to give his word

that he would not execute his warrant on the Sabbath-day, although they
. were willing to give him every assurance of peaceably surrendering on the
Monday following. Provoked by his refusal, the men of Durness, noted
for piety as well as forbearance, chose rather to break the laws of man on
the Saturday, than see the laws of God violated in such a manner on the
Sabbath. He and his party, who had bagpipes playing before them on
leaving Dornoch, told inquirers, that "they were going to a wedding in
Durness." It was rather a divorce to tear the people away from their
dearly-loved, though barren, hills. Under all the circumstances, many, I
doubt not, will think with me that these willing emissaries of mischief got
better treatment than they deserved. It is high time the law-breaking
and law-wresting petifoggers of Sutherlandshire were looked after. This
brings again to my mind the goat-shooting scene, described in my last,
which was the more aggravated and diabolical from having been perpetrated during the late troubles, and while a military force was hourly
expected to cut down such as should dare to move a finger against those
in authority ; knowing that, under these circumstances, no complaints of
the people would be hearkened to. But this was not the only atrocity of
the kind that took place in the country at this time. I have seen a letter
from a respectable widow woman residing in Blairmore, parish of Rogart;
to her son in Edinburgh, which, after detailing the harassment and misery
to which the country is subject, says—"I had only seven sheep, and one
of Mr. Sellar's shepherds *drowned* five af them in Lochsalchie, along with
other five belonging to Donald M'Kenzie ; and many more, the property
of other neighbours, shared the same fate. We could not get so much as
the skins of them." But they durst not say one word about it, or if they
did, no one would hearken to their complaints. God alone knows how
they are used in that unfortunate country, and he will avenge it in his own
time.

A correspondent of mine says—"At an early period of your narrative,
you stated that the natives were refused employment at public works, even
at reduced wages; but, if you believe me, sir, in the last and present
year, masons, carpenters, &c., were brought here from Aberdeenshire, and
employed at those works, while equally good, if not better native trades-
men were refused, and obliged to go idle. This, however, was not
admitted as an excuse when house-rent, poll-tax, or road-money was
demanded, but the most summary and oppressive means were used for
recovery. They have been paying these strangers four or five shillings
a-day, when equally good workmen among the natives would be glad of
eighteen-pence !"

In this way, the money drained from the natives in the most rigorous
manner, is paid away to strangers before their eyes, while they themselves
are refused permission to earn a share of it ! My correspondent adds—
" We know the late Duchess, some years before her demise, gave orders
(and we cannot think the present Duke of Sutherland has annulled these
orders) that no stranger should be employed, while natives could be found
to execute the work. But it seems the officials, and their under-strappers,
can do what they please, without being called to account, and this is but

one instance among the many in which their tyranny and injustice is manifested." Every means, direct and indirect, are used to discourage the aborigines, to make them willing to fly the country, or be content to starve in it.

May I not ask, will the Duke of Sutherland never look into the state of his country? Will he continue to suffer such treatment of the people to whom he owes his greatness; proceedings so hazardous to his own real interest and safety? Is it not high time that that illustrious family should institute a searching inquiry into the past and present conduct of those who have wielded their power only to abuse it?

Their extensive domains are now, generally speaking, in the hands of a few selfish, ambitious strangers, who would laugh at any calamity that might befall them, as they do at the miseries of those faithful subjects whom they have supplanted. Many of these new tenants have risen from running about with hobnails in their shoes, and a colly-dog behind them, their whole wardrobe being on their back, and all their other appointments and equipage bearing the same proportion—to be Esquires, Justices of the Peace, and gentleman riding in carriages, or on blood-horses, and living in splendid mansions, all at the expense of his Grace's family, and of those whom they have despoiled of their inheritance. · The time may come—I see it approaching already, when these gentlemen will say to his Grace "if you do not let your land to us on our own terms, you may take it and make the best of it; who can compete with us?" This will be the case, especially when the natives are driven away, and the competition for land, caused by the food taxes, comes to an end. Let his Grace consider these things, and no longer be entirely guided by the counsels of his Ahithophel, nor adopt the system of Rehoboam towards the race of the devoted vassals of his ancestors, a portion of whose blood runs in his veins.

" Woe is me? the possessors of my people slay them, and hold themselves not guilty;" and they that sell them say, "blessed be the Lord, for I am rich; and their own shepherds pity them not." "Let me mourn and howl" for the pride of Sutherland is spoiled!

In a former letter I put the question to the Sutherland clergy, "of how much more value is a man than a sheep?" No reply has been made.

I ask again, "you that have a thousand scores of sheep feeding on the straths that formerly reared tens of thousands of as brave and virtuous men as Britain could boast of, ready to shed their blood for their country or their chief; were these not of more value than your animals, your shepherds, or yourselves? You that spend your ill-gotten gains in riotous living, in hunting, gaming, and debauchery, of how much more value were the men you have dispersed, ruined, and tortured out of existence, than you and your base companions?" But I now cease to unpack my heart with words, and take leave of the subject for the present; assuring my kind correspondents, that their names will never be divulged by me, and pledging myself to continue exposing oppression so long as it exists in my native country.

In conclusion, I implore the Government to make inquiry into the con-

E

dition of this part of the empire, and not look lightly over the outrooting of a brave and loyal people, and the razing to the ground of that important portion of the national bulwarks, to gratify the cupidity of a few, to whose character neither bravery nor good feeling can be attributed.

Yours, &c.,

DONALD M‘LEOD.

APPENDIX.

During the publication of the foregoing series of letters in the *Chronicle*, I have received a very great number of letters, all tending to establish and illustrate, and in no instance to contradict, the facts adduced. Much of this correspondence is valuable from being well written, and containing the graphic descriptions of eye witnesses. I regret, therefore, that the limits to which I had resolved and arranged to confine the size of this pamphlet, will admit of my giving at present but a very small selection of this large and daily increasing mass of corroborative evidence. This is also partly caused by the space unavoidably occupied in the recent case of the so-called Durness riots, as well as by my personal narrative, on neither of which I had originally calculated.

Should the present publication be favourably received, I may, however, soon follow it up with some supplementary matter, especially if the course of proceedings in that devoted county should continue. In this case the correspondence would be an interesting and appropriate adjunct. I have in the previous pages repeatedly pledged myself to keep watch and ward, and bring the wrongs of Sutherland before the public so long as I can hold a pen, or obtain a medium for the publication of them, and, with God's help, I will not shrink from the engagement.

I am quite aware that great allowances must be made, by readers of education and literary taste, should these pages be honoured with a perusal by any such. I am not capable of writing to please critics; I had a higher aim, and my success in bringing out the case of my countrymen must now stand the ordeal of public opinion. For my own part, zeal and faithfulness are all I lay claim to, and if my conscience tells me true, I deserve to have these conceded to me, by both friends and enemies.

There are three remarkable cases in the correspondence which I cannot think to postpone; the first is that of Angus Campbell, who possessed a small lot of land in the parish of Rogart, in the immediate neighbourhood of the parish minister, the Rev. Mr. M'Kenzie. This Rev. Divine, it seems, had, like King Ahab, coveted this poor man's small possession, in addition to his own extensive glebe, and obtained a grant of it from the factor. Agus Campbell, besides his own numerous family, was the only support of his elder brother, who had laboured for many years under a painful and lingering disease, and had spent his all upon physicians.

Angus having got notice of the rev. gentleman's designs, had a memorial drawn up and presented to her Grace the late Duchess, who, in answer, gave orders to the factor to the effect that, if Angus Campbell was to be removed for the convenience of Mr. M'Kenzie, he should be provided with another lot of land equally as good as the one he possessed. But, like all the other good promised by her Grace, this was disregarded as soon as she turned her back; the process of removal was carried on, and to punish Angus for having applied to her, he was dealt with in the following manner, as stated in a memorial to his Grace the present Duke, dated 30th March, 1840.

In his absence, a messenger-at-arms with a party, came from Dornoch to his house, and ejected his wife and family; and having flung out their effects, locked the doors of the dwelling house, offices, &c., and carried the keys to the safe keeping of the rev. Mr. M‘Kenzie, for his own behoof. These proceedings were a sufficient warning to all neighbours not to afford shelter or relief to the victims; hence the poor woman had to wander about, sheltering her family as well as she could in severe weather, till her husband's arrival. When Angus came home, he had recourse to an expedient which annoyed his reverence very much; he erected a booth on his own ground in the church-yard *and on the tomb of his father*, and in this solitary abode he kindled a fire, endeavouring to shelter and comfort his distressed family, and showing a determination to remain, notwithstanding the wrath and threatenings of the minister and factors. But as they did not think it prudent to expel him thence by force, they thought of a stratagem which succeeded. They spoke him fair, and agreed to allow him to resume his former possession, if he would pay the expenses (£4 13s) incurred in ejecting him. The poor man consented, but no sooner had he paid the money than he was turned out again, and good care taken this time to keep him out of the church-yard. He had then to betake himself to the open fields, where he remained with his family, till his wife was seized with an alarming trouble, when some charitable friend at last ventured to afford him a temporary covering; but no distress could soften the heart of his reverence, so as to make *him* relent.

This Campbell is a man of good and inoffensive character, to attest which he forwarded a certificate numerously signed, along with his memorial to the Duke, but received for answer, that as the case was settled by his factor, his Grace could not interfere !

The second case is that of an aged women of four score—Isabella Graham, of the parish of Lairg, who was also ejected with great cruelty. She too sought redress at the hands of his Grace, but with no better success. A copy of the substance of her memorial, which was backed by a host of certificates, I here subjoin :—

"That your Grace's humble applicant, who has resided with her husland on the lands of Toroball for upwards of fifty-years, has been removed from her possession for no other reason than that Robert Murray, holding an adjoining lot, coveted her's in addition. That she is nothing in arrears of her rent, and hopes from your Grace's generosity and charitable disposition, that she will be permitted to remain in one of the houses belonging to her lot, till by some means or other she may obtain another place previous to the coming winter, and may be able to get her bed removed from the open field, where she has had her abode during the last *fifteen weeks !* Your Grace's humane interposition most earnestly but respectfully implored on the present occasion, and your granting immediate relief will confirm a debt of never-ending gratitude, and your memorialist shall ever pray, &c."

[The following letter will explain the third case without any comment.]

December 8, 1841.

DEAR SIR,—In your descriptions of the inhuman treatment to which the poor Sutherlanders have been, and are still exposed, you have not hitherto represented the unhallowed proceedings which took place between five and six years ago, in the "Episcopal City of Dornoch," when the parish church underwent an extensive repair, and considerable additions were made to it solely for the *private* convenience of the *great* Sutherland family, who defrayed the whole expense.

During the progress of these works, the church-yard, in which the inhabitants had buried their dead for time immemorial, presented the most revolting spectacle imaginable, being strewed with human bones, skulls, and pieces of coffins, &c., exhumed by the workmen employed in digging for the foundations of the new additions to the church, in levelling the church-yard, and forming new and enlarged walks.

These relics of mortality were permitted to remain exposed to view long after the mason-work was completed, and an entire coffin was actually suffered to remain on the surface for a fortnight; while the tomb-stones which indicated their resting place, bearing the endearing inscriptions of parents and children, were rudely thrown aside, and afterwards not replaced nor preserved, but used, it is said, in the formation of a new enclosure wall. It is true indeed, that one or two families of the aristocracy there threatened resistance, but their anger was appeased, if not their vanity gratified, by having their family tomb-stones fixed inside one of the entrance porches. The resident inhabitants of Dornoch, however, whose progenitors had been buried there for ages, were denied even the privilege of re-interring the remains exhumed by workmen brought from a distance who felt no sympathy for the lacerated feelings of the community, and refused to re-inter the human bones; alleging that their instructions were limited to be careful in preserving and delivering to the agent of the Duke, at Golspie, any ancient coins or other relics of antiquity that might be discovered in the course of the excavations. Matters continued in this painful position till a new church-yard was formed at a distance from the town, and where, ultimately, the surplus earth, &c., was removed from the old church-yard.

Whether it was that the inhabitants disliked the idea of being buried beyond the sound of the church bell, or apart from their relatives, or from whatever other cause, it is certain the dying made it a last special request that they should be buried in some of the neighbouring parishes,—and thus the *new* church-yard was likely to be so only *in name*. Ultimately, however, the death of a poor person at a distance presented an opportunity of providing at least one tenant, and since that period the objections to the new burying ground are not now so frequently made.

A stranger to the Sutherland tyrannical system of management may well exclaim in wonder and horror,—Why did the inhabitants tolerate such unhallowed proceedings?—and why did the clergyman of the parish silently witness the barbarous treatment of the remains of his late parishioners? Those, however, who have perused your graphic account of the dreadful sufferings of the people, will be at no loss to discover from whence arises their apparent apathy.

I am, &c.,

A DORNOCH CORRESPONDENT.

To Mr. Donald M'Leod.

[The following letter appeared in the Edinburgh Weekly Chronicle of the 18th Dec., 1841.]

MR. Editor,—Sir, the publication of Donald M'Leod's Letters, while it adds to your high reputation for independence, reflects in a double sense on a brother contemporary in the *North*; and I must say with Donald M'Leod, that the Editor recently alluded to by him is ever to be found with "the powers that be." He catches at any circumstance that affords an opportunity of lauding a lord or a laird, and he is always laying his blarney on their *doors* with a trowel; while his negative praise of the poorer natives is disgusting to those who really know them.

The subject of Donald's letters leads me now to notice a *removing*, which I fear is too truly apprehended at the term of Whitsunday, in one of the remote glens of Ross-shire: and though not very extensive, it is of a very aggravated nature, inasmuch as the victims are not only able to keep their holdings, but are men of the most spotless character. These are chiefly the M'Crie's of Corryvuik, in Strathconan, a county now possessed by one of the wealthiest men in Scotland, but who, it would seem, feels but little solicitude about this portion of the dependants over whom Providence has placed him as guardian. The farm has been occupied for time immemorial by the progenitors of the present tenants, all of whom have lived upon it from infancy. They maintained their means and credit in the worst of times, and are fully stocked;—they have never been in arrears to the laird;—and it is believed that their names were never called in a court of law, either as suitors or defenders. They are known as the quiet, unobtrusive, primitive people of Corryvuik; and at a happier period of their lives, they were the pride of their proprietors (the ancient family of Fairburn), though they now feel, that the chain which bound them to their native soil and chiefs is snapped assunder for ever.

MRS. H. BEECHER STOWE.

MADAM,—I would wish to address you as inoffensively as our present position before the public can admit of. Without any provocation on my part, you have assailed my character most shamefully, and I must tell you, that though a humble individual who has devoted much of his time and means in advocating the cause and righteous claims of the poor, remonstrating with, and exposing the ungodly dealings of the rich towards them, unaided as I am by classical education, or the smiles of fortune; yet I consider my reputation and character as a narrator of unvarnished facts, equally as sacred, and as dear to me, as you can consider your own as an accomplished novelist and sophistical adulator of the oppressors of the poor. Taking the advantage of your auspicious position in society; surrounded by the beauties of English aristocracy, golden diamond, ducal braclets, glittering gold soverigns, fame, favour and fortune, thinking the whole world was bound to believe whatever you would say or write—yes Madam, dreaming in these paradises of grandeur, wealth, dignity and luxury, you, in the greatness of your soul, thought to demolish me for ever, by making me out as a ridiculous fabricator of falsehood. Against whom? The fascinating, angelic, and spotless Duchess of Sutherland. I do acknowledge to you, and before the world, to be the legitimate parent and author of the accusations against the House of Sutherland, which found their way to the American public prints, of which you gave a specimen in your "Sunny Memories," to convince the American people of how ridiculous, and execssively absurd they were. I know that it was reported, and circulated through the public press in England and Scotland, that I was dead; but even if dead, it would be very unlady-like of you to attack even a dead man's character, at least until you made a searching enquiry into the veracity or falsehood of his statements. If you believed this report, they have deceived you, and as sure as I am a living Scotchman my motto is, *nemo me impune lacessete.* I do really sympathize with you, for I know it is a humiliating reflection for you, that for the sake of aristocratic adulation and admiration, which you could well spare, that you have exposed yourself to be publicly chastised by an old Highland Scotch broken down stone mason; yet you have done it and I am sorry for it, and to do you justice, to do my own character justice, but above all to do the public justice, I consider it my bounden duty to bring you to the test, that the public may judge aright who is the greatest fabricator of false stories—you or me—expecting the public judgment will be based upon the evidence we advance to confirm the veracity of our opposed statements, and the source from which we obtain our evidence. I deny the charge of fabricating falsehood against the Duchess of Sutherland, or against the House of Sutherland, nor against any other despotic depopu-

lating house in the highlands of Scotland; neither had I need to exaggerate nor to colour the truth; indeed I have taken more pains to modify
the truth than I should have done, so that people could believe me. I
challenge, yea, I court contradiction, or a combatant upon fair ground.

"No favour—honour bright."

Then at it. In prefacing your "Sunny Memories" you say—"This book
will be found to be really what its name denotes, Sunny Memories." I
admit this to be an indisputable fact, for I believe you never basked in the
sunshine of favour more luxuriously than you did while in England. You
had no doubt a pecuniary object in view in going to England, and you
have realized it to your heart's desire. The ladies of England had also a
particular object in view in inviting you there, and you satisfied them,
Their fame as the greatest philanthropists under heaven—their superiority
in accomplishments and gorgeous sublimity to any other nation on earth,
are now established for ever, and for ever, (as they and you think). Next
you say—"The writer has been decided to issue these letters principally,
however, by the persevering and deliberate attempt in certain quarters to
misrepresent the circumstances which are here given. So long as these
misrepresentations affected those who were predetermined to believe
unfavourably, they were not regarded; but as they have had some influence in certain cases upon really excellent and honest people, it was desirable that the truth be plainly told." * * * Now Madam had you
kept up to the principle of telling the plain truth, you would have saved
me the disagreeable task of correcting you, and of pointing out to yourself, and to the public, where you have failed to ascertain or tell the plain
truth. Truth and Justice, Madam, are Heaven-begotten twin sisters, but
if they had not, nor have not any other place of abode upon earth but the
palaces of English dukes and duchesses, lords, primates, and bishops, and
the mansions of money-mongers, manufacturers, commissioners and factors
such people, by your own confession, with whom you associated, and corresponded while in England, I say that long since the *heavenly pair*
would perish homeless, houseless, friendless, unpitied, and persecuted
among snow and frost on the streets of England, Ireland, and Scotland;
but being immortal, they will ultimately prevail and triumph over falsehood, sophistry and injustice.

Your lavishing of praise and admiration of English feminine beauty
and virtue, of mansions, scenery, institutions, aristocratic manners and
arrangements, I will let you go with it by merely offering a short but an
earnest prayer up to Heaven, that the Lord of Heaven and earth may
preserve the American ladies from being smitten or infected by the fatal
contagion with which your Sunny Memories are pregnant, and that they
may not adopt the English system of grinding down the people upon
whom they depend for protection in the time of need, and for supplying
them with all the necessaries of life at all times, to starvation and beggary,
to crime and punishment, and then separate themselves from them as
unclean animals, in railway cars, in churches, in schools, in streets,
theatres, and assemblies, considering their very breath to pollute the

atmosphere, and exceedingly dangerous to their refined constitutions. This is my prayer, and for the sake of the American ladies and the American people, I hope I will be heard and answered. The Americans should have sad recollection of what their fathers told them of the English systems and manners among themselves in the days of yore, and should watch well and guard themselves against being beguiled to adopt any more of the English systems than what is consistent with humanity, nature and true godliness. None will deny, but English ladies in general are beautiful women (yet there are some, no but many, ugly exceptions,) and can assume affability to a most coaxing and deceptive extent when they have an object in view to gain ; but any one less or more acquainted with their history, or with themselves personally, for any length of time, may discern with many of them *souls* so much chocked up with pride and ambition, that all which can be admired about them is only skin deep, especially among the majority of your bosom favourites while in England.

It is likewise well known throughout the whole world that the British aristocracy, such as landocracy, priestocracy, moneyocracy, cottonocracy, and many other robbingocracies, do enjoy all the luxuries, grandeur, amusement, and pleasure, that *seared* consciences can enjoy, that art can produce, and that *ill gotten* wealth can purchase. But how many thousands, yea millions of as valuable human beings as they are, are toiling and languishing in misery and want all their life time, to keep up this unnecessary grandeur and dignity? Ah! Madam, this is an enquiry you should have made, if you are really what you say you are,—a sympathiser with suffering humanity,—before spending so much of your valuable time and talents, praising and admiring English grandeur and dignity. The majority of these dignitaries and nobles never did anything to benefit society ; so that all you have seen about them must be the production of plunder, and the *price of blood.* Yes, I say, for one instance, you ought to ascertain how many slaves his grace the Duke of Sutherland, himself alone, would require to build, and to furnish, and keep up his establishment in London, viz. Stafford House, (of notoriety) which you have so elaborately described in letter 16 of your "Sunny Memories." But as you have neglected to inform the American ladies how this magnificent establishment is supplied, I must inform them. You say in letter 17, "That the total population of the Sutherland estate is twenty-one thousand seven hundred and eighty-four." Correct, or incorrect as this statement may be, I leave it to you; but if correct, his Grace's people must have increased most *wickedly* since his Grace permitted them to *marry*, and since I left Scotland four years ago. Likewise, if correct, I can tell you Madam, without hesitation, that three-fourths of that immense population are living in poverty and incredible penury. I will risk my reputation, yes my life, that sixteen thousand of them do not consume, upon an average, half-a-pound of animal food of any description through the whole year, and that they have to live upon the scantiest and poorest allowances of all other food that human beings can exist upon. Yes, all that they can scrape and save is needed at Stafford House. Then I will allow that three thousand of them live a little better, but who are not to be envied; then take one thousand seven hundred who live comfortable, but not in affluence. Add to those a score or two of sheep farmers, who occupy three-fourths of Sutherlandshire, paying heavy rents, and live sumptuously,—in short all proceeds are sent up to supply the *needs* of Stafford House, and this is but one of its many streams of wealth. No wonder, Madam, that you have seen such wonderful splendour, and been so delightfully entertained at Stafford House—especially invited there to vindicate their character from the accusations brought against them by Donald M'Leod, and others of the plebian order. There is still a balance of one thousand and forty-four of the population yet unaccounted for,—these are of the unproductives. They consist of factors, sub-factors, established (by law) ministers, school-masters, sheriffs, police, constables, fiscals, lawyers, pettifoggers, gamekeep-ers, foresters, shepherds ground officers, water and mussel bailiffs, and an host of blood-sucking subordinates, vermin, who pick up every cent that can be concealed or saved from Stafford House. It is well known and easily believed, where poverty prevails, there is strife, and where strife is, there is a field for plunder to suit these low vermin inquisitors. Now, Madam, I grant that the Duke of Sutherland and his predecessors were, and are, the most humane and liberal of all other Highland, Scotch, Irish, or English plun-dering depopulators. But if it was possible or practicable to try the ex-periment, that is, to bring nineteen thousand of the American slaves to Sutherlandshire, and give them all the indulgence, all the privileges, and comforts the aborigines of that county do enjoy, I would risk all that is sacred and dear to me, that they would *rend the Heavens*, praying to be restored to their old American slave owners, and former position. I con-sider this but a small tribute or compliment to the slave owners; yet I know that there is nothing bad but what can be worse, for there are many more painful ways of killing a dog than to hang him. I would respect-fully ask who are the greatest objects of commisseration and sympathy,— a brave, moral, intelligent and enterprising race of people, who were born free, who were nurtured in the school of freedom, and defenders of free-dom in all the ages of time; against whom there was no priestly denunci-ations to be traced in sacred, ancient, moral, or modern history; and who were robbed and deprived of all the liberties and rights they were told and taught by their fathers to be their indisputable inheritance, and enthralled to the lowest degree of degradation, submission, and poverty. I say are they not much more to be pitied, than an unfortunate race, who at an early period of time became the victims of cruel priestcraft, taking the ad-vantage of a curse, said to be pronounced by a drunken father, very likely in delirium tremens; or to the misrepresentation of that *curse* left on sa-cred record, which left that race denounced, consigned, and designated to be slaves and the servant of servants—consequently despised, left untold, untaught in the science of enterprise, progress, or civilization and totally ignorant of the rights and privileges of human beings. Both cases are to pitied and lamented, but I hold the latter case to be far more tolerable to endure than the former. The child who has been born blind is not so helpless, nor so much to be pitied when he comes to manhood, as the poor fellow who has been deprived of his sight after arriving at manhood; the former never knew what light or the use of it was, and will not pine and lament over the loss of it; besides, in most cases natural instincts will, to a certain extent, make up for the deficiency. Whereas, the latter poor fellow who knew what light is and the use of that inestimable gift of God, when he stumbles, or falls, or strikes his head against a post, it is not the personal injury he sustained, that is the principal cause of his bewailing and sufferings, no, but the loss of his sight, and that he had none to lead him past danger.

It is a melancholy, undeniable *fact* that Republic Americans do breed, sell, and buy slaves; that they chase them with blood hounds when they run away; that they flog them; that they shoot and hang them for dis-obedience; that they separate husbands and wives, parents and children. But will any one prove to me that the condition of the unfortunate people would be better or more tolerable should the Americans, like High-land Scotch and English dukes, marquises, earls, and lairds, make and take as many slaves as they choose for nothing. Methinks it would be more consistent to admit, that buying and selling, and the higher the price of slaves are, is a sure guarantee that they will be taken care of, (leaving humanity out of sight.) If a man purchases a horse at a high price, he will take care of that animal; but if he knew that he could get as many horses as he choosed for nothing, and that when one horse died or was lamed, that he had nothing to do but to go and take another, you could not expect that man to care much whether his horses were well fed or housed.

The American slave owners themselves are to be pitied, for they are the dupes or victims of false doctrine, or rather say, of the misinterpretation of sacred records. They believe to have a divine right to sell and buy African slaves; to flog, hang and shoot them for disobedience; and to chase them with blood hounds and Methodist ministers, if they run away. But the English aristocracy maintains to still higher prerogatives, in di-rect opposition to sacred records,—they believe to have divine right to monopolise the whole creation of *God* in Britian for their own private use, to the exclusion of all the rest of His creatures. They have enacted laws to establish these rights, and they blush not to declare these laws sacred. And it is to be lamented that these laws and doctrines are generally be-lieved. Let any one peruse their Parchment Rights of Property, and he will find that they include the surface of the earth, all the minerals, &c. below the surface to the centre, all that is above it up to the heavens, rivers of waters, bays, and creeks, of mixed salt water and fresh water, for one and one-fourth leagues out to the sea, with all the fishes of every des-cription which spawn or feed therein, and all fowls who lay and are raised on land,—a right to deprive the people of the least pretention of right to the creation of *God* but what they choose to give them,—a right to compel the people to defend their properties from invaders; to *press* and *ballot* as many of them as they choose; hand-cuff them if they are unwilling, and force them to *swear by God* to be true and faithful slaves,—a right to im-prison them, to flog, to hang, and shoot them if refractory, or for the least disobedience. Yes, a right to force them away to foreign and unhealthy climes, to fight nations who never did them any injury, where they perish in thousands by disease, fatigue and starvation, like brute beasts; to hang, shoot, or flog them to death for even taking a morsel of food when dying for want of it : all for to gain more possessions and power for British aristocracy. Only read the history of the East and West Indies ; of the Peninsula, Crimea, and China Wars.

Slavery is *damnable*, and the most disgusting word in the English or any other language; and it is to be hoped that the Americans will soon discern its deformity, pollution and iniquity, and wipe away that old English polluted stain from their character. But there is not the least shadow of hope that ever the British aristocracy will think shame, or give up their system of slavery ; for it is the most profitable now under heaven, and the most admired, and adopted by all other nations of the earth ; at least until the promised Millenium will arrive, whatever time that blessed era will take in coming—unless the people in their might will rise some morning early, and demand their rights and liberties with the united voice of *thunder* which will make the most hardened and stubborn of the aristocratic adamant hearts tremble and ache. British ocracy's sympathy with American slaves is, in reality, a burlesque; for I do assure you, Madam, they care no more for the emancipation of the American slaves than they do for the emancipation of Greenland *whales* and *seals* from their captors. Self-interest and fame was their object in jumping at your "Uncle Tom's Cabin" and in their adulation of the authoress, and has been their object since ever I began to take notice of their sophistical movements, and long before it. Much to their praise (though it cost them twenty-one million pounds sterling) the British people abolished slavery in the West India British Colonies. But who were their bitter and inveterate opponents ?—English Bishops, and aristocracy ; but now they take all the praise to themselves. Their principal cause for denouncing American slavery is, if properly searched out, that their West Indian estates does not make such lucrative returns to them now as they used to do, and not their sympathy for the African race. However, it is an admitted fact, that it is characteristic of British aristocracy to be the most liberal sympathisers with foreign victims of oppression, injustice and barbarous, ungodly laws ; but with me their motives are very questionable, they having reverse qualifications at home. But they know that their foreign sympathy, liberality, and abhorrence of foreign slavery will find a conspicuous place in the public press, magazines, school books, reports and tracts, and that their praise will reach the utmost corner of the earth—that their fame, as the most humane, the most benevolent and blessed, will be *ballooned* up to Heaven by bishops, priests, ministers, that (reverently speaking) *God* might approve of it. At home they are the most liberal contributors to Bible and Missionary Societies, especially to the publication and circulation of missionary reports, where the donors and donations are sure to be magnified and praised up to heaven ; and the recipients represented as the most ignorant of the plan of salvation and of the Christian religion—denying not but they had the image of God on them, yet not (in intellect) much above the condition of the brute creation. These hired emmissaries have contributed on a large scale, and assisted greatly the calumniators of the Highlands of Scotland. I know many of them going about *preaching, praying, circulating Gaelic Bibles* and religious tracts, at the same time surveying the country and collecting information of the districts more susceptible and profitable for sheep-farming, and publishing the most gross, unfounded and inconsistent falsehoods regarding the character and intelligence of the people, that could be *coined* by the arch-enemy of mankind—(you know who that is.) However, all this had the desired consummation or effect. The benevolence of aristo-cratic donors and liberal donations were praised in every sublime term that the English language could supply; and to magnify their liberal and benevolent dispositions still more, the demerits, undeservedness, the barbarianism and sloth of the recipients were described in the grossest Billingsgate language that could be collected. But follow those over-praised and admired aristocratic personages home to these palaces, which cost you, *Madam,* so much time and labour to describe to your American friends, (although you were supplied with catalogues and invoices of their interior, and a plan or map of their pleasure grounds), and ask them the few following questions :—In the name of wonder how did you manage to get these splendid edifices built and furnished so gorgeously, when I know you yourselves never put a hand to any work? The reply would be—We employ men to do it for us. Still more surprised, you ask—How have you got the enormous sums of money required to pay them? The truthful reply should be—Oh, we have large, extensive landed estates, and we can tax the people who occupy and labour them as we please. Others would reply, we employ so many thousands of people, and we pay them as we please; for every shilling they work for, or get, we have three shillings, and were it not for the tricks you Yankees play on us at times, we might be a great deal richer than we are, even richer than the landlords.

But halt a little until you see a poor industrious tenant of one of these landed aristocracy, approaching the gate of this palace with a humble petition, shewing a most grevions complaint, for an outrage committed by one of his graces or lordship's factors or underlings, and prevented to enter any farther by a bulldog at full chain length; if he got past the dog, met another bull in human shape, dressed in livery, from whom there was no escaping, and had to stand still until his grace or lordship thought it proper to take an airing walk for his health after breakfast or dinner, and after waiting for days in this humiliating position, ultimately told that nothing could be done for him, or ordered back to the tyrant underling against whom he complained for redress, and you may easily guess what kind of redress or reception the poor fellow would get. Shift then to the palace of a church-ocracy, cotton-ocracy, or any other ocracy you please, and see a poor fellow in rags, exhausted in frame, with trembling limbs, leaning on his staff, coming up to the gate soliciting a crumb of bread or a morsel of broken meat from the table which he was supplying all his lifetime. There you will see the broken meat thrown away to feed useless dogs, and the poor fellow collared by a police constable, and next day sentenced to thirty days' imprisonment in Bridewell, breaking stones or teasing oakum, for his impudence; but two blacks will never make a white —if you, Madam, and I were sitting side by side for six months, I would bet you a dollar my side of the leaf would be the darkest—hence we must turn up the most *ridiculous bright* side of the question. Did you, Madam, enquire while in England, how this noble institution called the Poor Man's Church, in England and Ireland, whose bishops, structure, and constitution you admired so much, and laboured so much in recommending to others, is maintained? I know you did not. That such questions were entirely out of your way. This is another of the costly and pernicious aristocratic institutions of the country, self styled the "Poor Man's Church." It is not difficult to make you understand how it is so called. Church revenues were at one period, yes for ages, divided into three parts,—the first part for the maintenance of the priesthood—the second for the maintenance and repair of the *fabric* of the Church, and the third for the relief and support of the poor. But the Clergy, aided by their patrons, the aristocracy, have contrived and enacted laws to saddle the maintenance of the fabric on the people, in the form of Church Rates, the maintenance of the poor on the people in the form of Poor Rates, while the Apostolic priesthood, descended from the poor fishermen of Galilee, swallowed up both their own and the poor people's share. Not satisfied with this, the Church does not disdain to seize the poor man's pots and pans, and even the bed that he rests his weary limbs on, to sell them by public auction to raise funds to wash the priests' surplices, and to ring the bells. The twenty-five State Bishops of England divide among themselves incredible sums of money. By a late Parliamentary return, it will be seen the sums they leave behind them at their death are enormous. From another Parliamentary return it is proved, as stated in the House of Commons by Captain Osborn, that eleven Irish State Bishops left behind them at their death, the sum of one million eight hundred and seventy-five thousand pounds sterling, accumulated within a period of from forty to fifty years. The Bishop of Cashel during a single life, saved £400,000 from the tributes levied on the poorest, worst fed, worst clad, of all the nations of the earth. How much charity and spirit of christianity dwelt in his palace, or occupied his bosom, may be guessed? How much piety and christian virtue must the prelates of Dublin, Tuam, Armagh, and Clogher have excercised to enable them to hoard up fortunes of from £250,000 to £600,000 a piece during their lives. This is a sample of the Bishops of the English Church in Ireland, for which the British nation are keeping up an army of 34,000 soldiers, besides an army of mounted police, to watch over its safety. Surely these are expected to be serious and strenuous sympathisers with American slaves. Now you must know Madam, that there was only £151,127 12s. 4d. of hard cash divided by the bishops among themselves; but this only represents but a small proportion of their actual gains; we have to add to this the rents and profits of 670,000 acres of the Irish land which, in 1845, amounted to £92,000; tithe composition, £531,781 14s 7d.; minister money, £10,000; then what is termed Deans and Chapter, £22,624 5s. 5d., besides other perquisites, makes a total of £807,533 12s. 4d. What work is done for all this expenditure? According to report, out of 2364 parishes in Ireland, 155 have no churches, and not a single protestant inhabitant; 45 parishes, having under 50 protestants, including men, women and children, they are not on that account however, relieved from paying tithes to the English Church which are still compulsory exacted—of 300 dignities, and prebends 75 of them have no duties to perform, and 96 other sinecures. The Archdeacon of Meath has £731, and not one protestant to attend him or a soul to cure. I find seven benefices, with 62 protestants, without one church or a clergyman, who pays £2869 11s. of tithe. I find eight parishes with only 173 members of the State Church who pay £4860 of tithe composition. Need we be surprised that such a system as this should have issued in beggary and wretchedness and crime to the Irish people, and kept that nation hanging on the brink of rebellion since they became subject to the English Government. This is the church, which Babington Macauly describes the "most ridiculous, and indefensible of all the institutions now existing in the civilized world." and by Mr. Roebuck as the "greatest ecclesiastical enormity in Europe." Space will not permit me to dwell on these cases, which could be multiplied almost without end. Indeed the rapacity of the clergy is almost proverbial. They are not satisfied with one living, they would grasp at ten if they could get them. What do they care about duties, it is the money they want. They are in reality what Milton styled them in his day, "non resident, and plurality gaping prelates, the gulphs and whirlpools of benefices, but the dry pits of all sound doctrine who engross many pluralities under a non-resident and slumbering dispatching of souls, who let hundreds of parishes famish in one diocese, while they, the prelates, are mute, and yet enjoy that wealth which would furnish all those dark places with able supply; and yet they eat, and yet they live at the rate of lords, and yet hoard up; consuming and purloining even that which by their foundation is allowed and left to the poor and to the reparation of the church."

The English people who believe in the Episcopalian creed and doctrine are entitled to support this apostolic institution named after them and they do it sweetly. It is a difficult thing to get exact estimates of the total revenue of this institution in England. Churchmen have always been exceedingly loath to give information on this subject. When the Government in 1835 had made enquiries on the subject, the ecclesiastical commission was called on to make a return of the income of the clergy to Parliament, they then gave in the net revenue of the church at only £3,436,851; but since then the tithe commutation act has come into operation, then it became the interest of the church to claim as much as possible, forgetting their previous return. What has been the consequences? The tithes commuted swelling up at once to six millions and a half sterling, and they found out that if the tithes yet uncommuted be rated at the same value as those commuted, the annual income of the clergy from tithes alone will at least amount to £8,000,000 a year. Besides the tithes, there are the charitable foundations of England, most of which they have got into their hands. These are the professorships, fellowships, tutorships. masterships, &c , in the universities, and the revenues of Oxford and Cambridge amounts to no less than £741,000. Then the surplice fees for the consecration of burial grounds, preacherships, lectureships, chaplainships, chapel of ease, easter dues, christening fees, marriage fees, burial fees, episcopal revenues from land and other sources, when added together, will form a total of not less than ten millions sterling per year. Then Madam, I will give you a brief sketch of how the British people are taxed for other aristocratic purposes; the process is simple indeed. They don't ask the consent of those whom they tax—they take particular care to keep them out of their counsels as much as possible : they merely tax us and make us pay, having at all times at hand, and under their command a strong body of police, soldiers, and diabolical agencies of all sorts, and pay the people must. See how they manage to get it,—so much on sugar, so much on tea, coffee, tobacco, malt, hops, cocoa, soap, spirits, window light, &c. &c. "We are quarrelling about an income tax of seven-pence the pound sterling," said Mr. Cobden, in his speech in the House of Commons, March 13th, 1852. What amount do the people pay on articles consumed by them ? For every 20s. they expend on tea, they pay 10s. of duty; for every 20s. on sugar, they pay 6s.; on coffee, 8s.; on soap, £s.; on beer, 4s.; on tobacco, 16s.; on spirits, 14s.; on every 20s. they expend upon these articles, and other articles in proportion, you cannot but see that this amounts to an income tax, not 7d. the pound, but sometimes of 12s., 15s., or 16s. per pound ; while men of thousands a year expend their money upon luxuries, with comparatively little tax." It is really wonderful how the aristocratic classes have contrived to evade the payment of their due share of the taxation of the country. According to their own Parliamentary Report, the land tax of Great Britian amounts to £1,183,-000, which is only one pound in every thirty-three pounds raised by taxation in Britain. The taxes are mainly extorted from the working classes, who are the least able to bear the imposition, while the rich both exempt themselves, and spend the taxes so raised in the most riotous, reckless, extravagance. The land tax, so far as I can trace, has not been increased ' since 1688, though other taxes during that period have nearly twenty fold. Yet from the beginning of George the Third's reign to 1834, the aristocracy had seized upon and enclosed not less than 6,840,540 acres of common land, but the taxes were not increased one cent. This is not all, they have enacted laws to exempt the landed and agricultural classes from taxes imposed on the rest of the community. The landlord laws enact that all shall pay the stamp duties but themselves. The assessed taxes have been removed down to the farm-house, and the shepherd's dog. The laws authorize entail, by which real estates are preserved to a series of heirs, unattachable by the claims of creditors. They have specially exempted lands from the heavy probate and legacy duty, imposed on all other kinds of property descending by inheritance or *Will.* By these means alone, according to calculation, they saved themselves the enormous sum of £3,-000,000 annually. I say, for instance, that a poor labouring man, by dint of hard industry and economy, has saved two hundred pounds, which he leaves to a relative at his death. The amount is taxed at the rate of one to ten per cent., according to the nearest of kin. But say that a lord, duke, or earl dies, and leaves an estate of from one to forty thousand pounds a year, not one penny is in this case paid in the shape of tax. They managed that the industrious, and all other classes but their own, should pay sweetly for public misrule. To help themselves still further, they have saddled eight hundred and forty-one of their order upon the nation, under the lucrative title of State Pensioners, whose pensions average £1,876, total, £1,638,371 per annum, not speaking of the thousands of lower grades of pensioners. I shall conclude this portion of my address to you, by briefly informing you of the expenses of the aristocratic fighting establishment of Great Britian, during thirty years of peace, (both military and naval),—£549,083,112 ; average per annum, £16,150,000, including the expenses of putting down the Canadian Liberals, and of the Opium War in China. (See Lord John Russell's speech in the House of Commons, on the 18th of July, 1848.) In short, Madam, if I was to enumerate what I know myself of the extravagant expenditure of the British Aristocratic Government, and of the monopolising systems of Great Britain, you would be astonished how the producers of all the wealth and splendour you have seen in England could exist at all. The Duke of Wellington alone cost the nation £2,762,563, since he entered the army, up to 1818. No wonder that the magnificent edifices, the sumptuous furnishings and embellishments, the beauties of art and nature within and without these edifices, and the amiable demeanour of the crafty ladies of England, have dazzled your eyes, so much so as to throw all republic grandeur, liberty, beauty, and arrangements, completely in the shade of insignificaney. But, Madam, had you made proper enquiry and research, you would have found that all these magnificent superstructures and splendour which rivetted your attention, and brought forth your admiration and superfluity of praise, were founded on American and West Indian slavery, and East Indian plunder, embellished and supplied by home plunder ; then you have a fair specimen, rather an ocular demonstration of the *sublime* and *ridiculous*—somewhat like what you will find in Spain, Portugal and Italy. There you will find superb mansions, and churches which will surpass any you have seen in England, connected with an institution they call The Holy Inquisition. But in the rear and basement, you may find racks, gags, wheels, and other instruments of punishment; helpless, hopeless victims going through various ordeals of lingering death, and a charnel house to receive them. Let no one suppose that I include the English people in this black catalogue; no, I respect them, for they are the real victims of unnecessary dignity and grandeur.

In your perambulation in Scotland, you have seen only one church worthy of your notice, and that same one was faulty, and not one living literary, scientific, or theological gentleman met you, even in Edinburgh, (modern Athens) that was worth mentioning his name, but Doctor Guthrie, a Free Church minister, and Doctor Henderson, a homœpathic physician. Of all the letters you found waiting you in Edinburgh, there were only five of them worthy of your notice, viz: "A very kind and beautiful one from the Duchess of Sutherland, another from her brother

F

the Earl of Carlisle, making an appointment for meeting you as soon as you arrived in London; another from the Rev. Mr. Kingsley and his lady. Letters from Mr. Binney, and Mr. Sherman—all containing invitations to visit them in London." You say, in writing to your dear sister upon this subject, "As to all engagements, I am in a happy state of acquiescence, having resigned myself as a very tame lion into the hands of my keepers. Whenever the time comes for me to do anything, I will try to behave myself as well as I can,—which, as Dr. Young says, is all an *angel* can do in the same circumstances." Oh, Madam, what presumptive comparisons. When God appoints and commissions men or angels to advocate the cause of the oppressed, and preach deliverance to the captive and slave. The oppressors of the people will not be (nor were not) their admired, bosom' friends and only associates; they would not be embarrassed, nor would hearken to the flattering correspondence and invitation of Dukes, Duchesses, Earls, nor of such as those who accumulated immense wealth and grandeur by grinding down the faces of the poor and industrious ; nor yet would they be coaxed from performing their mission faithfully, by presents of platefulls of glittering gold—long purses, containing unaccounted large amounts of the same precious metal, and boxes of jewelry and diamond bracelets—yes, and costly dresses, not knowing their number. We have an ocular demonstration of this in the behaviour and conduct of men (not speaking of angels), down from Moses to Luther, Calvin and John Knox—men who despised that which you admired—who did not hesitate to proclaim the messages they received from their master to the different Pharoah's they had to contend with in the world, and chose rather to associate with the captives—partake of their suffering and afflictions, than to share in the festivities, sumptuousness, and luxuries of the oppressors. None who will peruse your "Sunny Memories" carefully, but must come to the conclusion, that if ever you received any injunctions from heaven regarding the American slaves, that you have merchandised them. Mr. Gough, the great teetotal advocate and abstainer, hearing of your success, soon followed you to Britain; but what would you think of him yourself, had he made the distillers and brewers of Britain his only bosom associates and co-operators in putting down the vices of intemperance in America or anywhere else, which brought thousands, yea, millions of the people to a premature grave, crime, and condign punishment. I say what would you think of him should these gentlemen load him with many thousand sovereigns for praising their mansions, and extensive establishments for manufacturing crime and woe to an extent which would throw the American establishment of the same character into the shade of insignificance; would you yourself consider him worthy the name of a teetotal advocate, or a sympathiser with the victims. I am sorry to say that my view of your movements and manœuvers in Britian, is a *fac simile*; only this, that you have received many thousand sovereigns (yes, to an unknown amount), for the express purpose and conditions of emancipating American slaves. What have you done with these immense sums?—not a single dollar of it can be traced to where it was intended, and should be found.

I was present at the great meeting or soiree you had in the Music Hall, Edinburgh, (the seat of learning,) I know that you have been well received there, and almost every body thought you were worthy of it, (I among the rest); a great deal of merited eulogy, and a great deal of what I consider fulsome, blasphemous adulation, were poured out upon you that evening, but all seemed to go down well with you; you were held up by the orators of the evening to the immense assembly as the *Angel of Freedom*, the *Angel of* LIGHT, *&c.* But among the flattering orators there were none worthy of your notice, (as I said before) but Doctor Guthrie! Why? because he spoke highly of the Duchess of Sutherland. This pays the Doctor well, for when the Duchess comes to Edinburgh, she attends divine worship in the Doctor's church, the only Free church she ever entered, and she graces the offering plate with two or three sovereigns; she will call upon the Doctor at his house and take him out for an afternoon's drive in her carriage, and send her compliments to him when in Sutherland (her Highland deer stalking and game preserve estate) in cart loads and hurly loads of deer carcases and fowl. Her daughters, viz: Duchess of Argyle, and Lady Blantyre, will follow the example of their mother, and the Proprietrix of Cromarty, who is married to her son, Marquis of Stafford, will not be behind any of them. I assure you the Doctor has fine times of it between them all, and bound to praise them well.

But the only portion of his speech on this great eventful, and never-to-be-forgotten occasion, which amused you most was, "In allusion to the retorts which had been made in Mrs. Tyler's letter to the ladies of England, on the defects in the old country." You introduced the Doctor to your readers of the Sunny Memories as "a tall thin man, with a kind of quaintness in his mode of expressing himself, which sometimes gives an air of drollery to his speaking." (True indeed, but a good man, and a man I admired much, though he befooled himself that night.) "I do not deny," he said "but there are defects in our country, what I say of them is this,—that they are incidental very much to an old country like our own, as Dr. Simpson knows very well and so does every medical man, that when a man gets old he gets infirm, his blood vessels get ossified. What is true of an old country is true of old men, and old women too. I am very much disposed to say of this young nation of America, that their teasing with our defects, might just get the answer which a worthy member of the Church of Scotland gave to his son, who was so dissatisfied with the defects in the church, that he was determined to go over to a younger communion—"Ah Sandy, Sandy, man, when your lum reeks as lang as ours, it will maybe need sweeping too." Now, I do not deny but we need sweeping; every one knows that I have been singing out about sweeping for the last five years. Let me tell my good friends in Edinburgh and in the country, that the sooner you sweep the better, for the chimney may catch fire and reduce your noble fabric to ashes. He continued and said, "They tell us in that letter about the poor needle-woman that had to work sixteen hours a day," (but the doctor forgot to say for eight pence per day). 'Tis true, exclaimed the doctor; but does our law compel them to work sixteen hours a day; may they not go where they like and get better wages, and better work—can the slaves do that!" Then the doctor went on to detail about ragged children and his own sympathy towards them, and what he had done for them. Now, the doctor was invited to this meeting to speak of the incompatabilty of American slavery with Christianity ; but he knew better how to please his favourable Duchess than to speak consistently to his text—praising English ladies and justifying the Duchess of Sutherland from charges brought against her and others in the liberal public press of the nation, was his sole object in speaking at the meeting. I really felt sorry for the poor misguided "thin tall" doctor, yet I could not allow him to escape with impunity for his reckless, inconsistent and uncalled-for conduct that night. A few days afterwards, I addressed the following letter to him through the Edinburgh *Guardian.* You will observe there was some peculiar cause for inviting the doctor to this meeting, and that he was invited at the request of some great personage or another, or he would not be there. He was the only one of that reverend body who was invited, or took any part in the proceedings that night, for this cause : the meeting was got up by the Anti-Slavery Society, who raised such a hue and cry against the Free Church ministers for years before this, for taking money from the American slave-holders to build churches, and Dr. Guthrie was then the Free Church champion—defending their conduct, who, at every meeting, would pin up his opponents to the wall ; however, the *Anties* managed to break down the good and friendly feeling between the Free Church body and the Americans, which I believe, if allowed to continue undisturbed, would have ten times more effect for the emancipation of the slaves, at least of ameliorating their condition, than all the agitation, excitement and novels which have been displayed upon the subject.

To the Editor of the Edinburgh Guardian.

SIR,—You are already aware that the higher a man's position is in society, and in the estimation of the people, the more dangerous he is when he errs. It is a singular anamoly that the ecclesiastical orators of. the platform in our day cannot praise one party enough without calumniating other parties. This I deplore, and gentlemen guilty of such practice should be ashamed of themselves, however much they may be applauded, and whatever amount of merriment they may create at the time ; it is passing strange that the Rev. Dr. Guthrie could not praise Mrs. Beecher Stowe enough, a lady who understood so well that she could not serve God in a more acceptable way than to help those who could not help themselves, hence, who merited for herself the gratitude of every sympathiser with suffering humanity ; nor yet could he praise *God* enough, "for (as he saith) giving us in our day (in the person of that lady) one in whom the *finest genius* is associated with the *purest* and *truest Piety,*" without attacking the memory of *Byron and of Burns,* two shining men to whom the world are so much indebted, with a view to deteriorate their memory in the estimation of his hearers in the Music Hall on the 19th ultimo. Be ashamed, Doctor, for your hyperbolic assertions ; both these valuable men are dead, but still speaking, and their memory is associated with truth, though not with whining hypocrisy, falsifying philosophy, and perverting truth, *a trade which pays well in our day*,—besides, you have not been long acquainted with Mrs. B. Stowe yet, and you should be more cautious and sparing of praise. In like manner, the Doctor could not praise and make manifest his love to the American people as the greatest and noblest on earth (ourselves excepted) for their *pure faith, many Bibles, Family Altars, Free Press, Flags,* and peaceable liberty, especially for their *soil* and *air*, which, he says, makes extraordinary changes on men, though he never was there, and is not sure what change they would make on him if he went,—I say, he could not do all this without putting his religious iron bull upon the neck of unfortunate people (whose position in life is not their crime, but their misfortune), with a view to sink them lower in the estimation of the world than even Highland and Irish tyrannical landlords and their tools placed them. "Take (said the humane Doctor) an *Indolent Celt*, let him go to to America, he becomes active,—take a wild Irishman, he becomes civilized,— a blind bigoted Papist, his eyes are opened, and he turns his back on Rome. These are facts extraordinary; we pour with many good elements a singular amount of impurity across the Antlantic, but America does not cast it off, it merges, changes, and reforms it like the sea that receives many muddy rivers, but keeps it own bosom clean." Now, Sir, the Doctor was requested to speak at this meeting to the incompatibility of American Slavery with Christianity, and I tell him that all this unfounded foulsome calumny which he poured out against Highland and Irish Celts, is as incompatible with Christianity as is falsehood with truth, and as American Slavery is with Christianity ; and should it be true, it is uncalled for, and out of order, and that it would be more like a minister and expounder of the gospel of truth, if he had said,—take the poor oppressed trodden down Hgihland *Celts* who have been ejected from every portion of their fatherland, created by *God* susceptible to rear food for man, and who were cast upon sterile moors and barren by-corners, to whom every inducement or encouragement for activity and industry in their native land was sternly denied,—let them go to America, where such are cheerfully held out to them, and they will soon become active trustworthy members of society, respected, prosper like other men, and bely their *lay* and *clerical* calumniators. He should continue, and say,—take the poor Irish, who could not submit so tamely to oppression, who were often driven to madnes by legalised plunderers,—let them go to America, where they are not subject to such ungodly exactions and persecution as in Ireland, and they will soon become as civil, as peaceable, as honest, as easily dealt with, and as industrious as other men (independent of the miraculous efficacy of the soil and air). But the Doctor says their eyes are opened, and they turn their back on Rome,—that is to say, on their father's religion. I much doubt this applauded assertion. No, Doctor, but their eyes are open, and they turn their backs on the insatiable Erastian Church of England in Ireland, and see themselves out of the reach of her cruel Tithe and Tax Collectors, and *far far* away from her Rathcormack sabre and batten abettors, where they are not annoyed day and night by her licensed emissaries of discord, who have for centuries kept them and brother Protestants in each other's throats about religion, and they now find themselves living among people worthy of the name, where every man may believe what he pleases, worship as he pleases; where, if he is a good citizen, none will dispute his right, where every man pays priest or parson, as he pays his tailor and shoemaker, where they can live in harmony among Protestants, Jews, Greeks, Mahometans, Shakers, Jumpers, Latter-Day Saints, &c., and where churches of all denominations are as free as the Doctor's and mine are. This would be more like Doctor Guthrie, for it is the only cause which he or any one else can assign for the *indolent* Celt becoming active, and the *wild* Irishman becoming civilized, and not the mysterious efficacy of the American *soil* and *air*.— Where, Doctor, under heaven, will you find better soil and air than in Ireland and the Highlands of Scotland. The doctor would have us to believe that he would fight for the American Slaves if he would see any of them set up for sale—(not so fast, Doctor);—but, strange to tell, that he is aware that a Highland landlord, a very few years ago, employed constables, policemen and other minions, to apprehend a great number of Highlanders among the rocks and hills, where they fled for safety, to handcuff them, and force them on board an old rotten ship which he hired to carry them away from the land of their birth, and should be aware that the majority of this people perished, houseless, homeless, among snow and frost on the frozen *soil*, and among the *biting air* of North America. I never heard that the Doctor found fault with him for this, far less fight with him, although he had only to step over from his own house, with a good cudgel, to St Andrew's Square, to meet him; but these were Highlanders, and had no claim on the Doctor's sympathy or interposition; yet, there is no doubt the Doctor will fight, but the Atlantic must be between him and the adversary; he will fight none at home. The slave and pauper *makers* in Ireland and Scotland, yea, those who dispersed the brave *sons* of the mountains and valleys of Caledonia, and of Green Erin, to the four winds of heaven, the Doctor will stroke their honourable heads, and clap them gently, exclaiming, you are the blessed, graceful humane *ones* who are purging our nation from the impure Irish and Scottish Celts, may you be spared to see the consummation of your desire. Hearken to his sorrow for the pitiless storm of unmerited abuse which was poured on the head of a certain noble lady of the Stafford-House meeting, viz: Duchess of Sutherland, and he cries aloud, shame to them who did it. And who would confound the incidental defects of this country, which, he says, are becoming so old and infirm, that her blood-vessels are *ossified* with the deep-stained sins of America. Dear me, Doctor, I thought a little ago that the Americans were most pious; what has become of their *pure faith*, *Bibles*, and *Family Altars?* Be that as it may, I am neither ashamed nor afraid to tell you, Doctor, in the face, that if the number could be computed and compared, that Highland and Irish landlords sent more human beings to a premature grave, and caused a greater amount of pining and grief than ever the slave lords of America did since America became a Republic, and that if it was not for America, they would triple the number. Now, hearken to the Doctor's sympathy with the poor needle woman. He exultingly bawls out at this meeting,—but does our law compel them to work 16 hours a-day. True, Oh, Doctor! it does not but the law of nature does, for they would rather do it than starve, and there is no other alternative; but does that lessen their pain? The Doctor says—can they not go elsewhere and get better wages?—*miscalled humanity*—how far can penniless, helpless, and unprotected women go in search of work, or of better wages? and where would they go, Doctor? The Doctor says that liberty speaks no tongue but Saxon, and only found among Saxon people. What has become of the *Tongues* of Hungarian, Italian, and Polish patriots? Oh, Doctor, Doctor, you are away with it now, but with all your fawning and pandering in quest of Aristocratic adulation and honour, the Saxons themselves can scarcely believe you. At present I will leave you by merely advising you not to go to America, especially in an impaired state of health, for fear you may lose your notion of *Rags* and *Soup-Kitchens* among the slaves and slave lords of America, and on the Queen's first visit to Edinburgh, decline to be created Bishop of the Ragged Schools of Scotland, for you really merit the honour. While I join with you in your quotation from the Poet, viz.—

> We but ask our rocky strand,
> Freedom's true and brother band—
> Freedom's strong and honest band;
> Valleys by the slave untrod,
> And the pilgrim's mountain sod,
> Blessed by our Father's God.

I pray that their numbers may be few, who will be so unfortunate as to come within the bounds of of the Docter's sympathy. Yours, &c,

DONALD McLEOD.

Doctor Guthrie did err in some expressions he made use of at that meeting, and he erred more so in going to the meeting at all, yet I love him and respect him as a Christian minister and sympathiser with suffering humanity. You would have left him unmentioned as you left the other orators, were it not for his praise of Duchesses and English ladies, and his sarcasm and retorts upon Mrs. Tyler, and you only held his name up for his quaintness and drollery, fearing to offend the English ladies by letting them know that there was any talent in Scotland; but I tell you that it would take all the bishops in England to compose and deliver an address or speech any thing equal to the other more sublime portions of his speech that night. But I will leave the worthy Rev. Doctor; he caught grief enough from his own brethren in the church, and from other quarters, for being at the meeting, and it is a great pity he was there. And I ask you what has become of this money, and what have you done with it—not with this £1,000, but with the many thousands you have got in Scotland and England. Here is the express conditions upon which you got it, from the mouth of Mr. Ballantine, Secretary for the anti-Slavery Society, after detailing the progress of the penny offering at this meeting, he says:—"It was accordingly proposed to appeal to the readers of Uncle Tom's Cabin in

Scotland to contribute one penny each to create a fund to be placed in the hands of Mrs. Stowe to be distributed by her for the benefit of the slave, and for the cause of emancipation. That appeal was made, and it has been promptly and cordially responded to. The result of that appeal is now before you—(cheers). I cannot state precisely what amount of money has been collected, as sums are still daily coming in, but up to this hour it presents itself in the form of 1000 sovereigns"—(loud cheering.) I have all their speeches here before me, and in case my readers may think that I am exaggerating the adulation of Mrs. Stowe in Edinburgh, you have a verse here, which, along with other seven verses of the composition, was sung before her by one of the speakers :—

> Freedom's angel now's come,
> Mercy's sister now's come :
> Grim oppression drees his doom :
> Harriet Beecher Stowe's come.

Would you meet such a reception in Scotland now ? No. You have let the veil of deception drop unawares. Now you will excuse me, Madam, for directing your attention to chapter 17 of your Sunny Memories, where you have attacked me individually, though clandestinely, in order to justify the House and Duchess of Sutherland from the charges brought against them in the American prints. You say—"My Dear C.—As to the ridiculous stories about the Duchess of Sutherland, which found their way into many of the American prints, one has only to be here moving in society to see how excessively absurd they are. In all these circles I have heard the great and noble of the land spoken of and canvassed, and if there had been the shadow of a foundation for any such accusation, I certainly should have heard it recognised in some manner. As I have before intimated, the Howard family, to which the Duchess belongs, is one which has always been on the side of popular rights and popular reform. Lord Carlisle, her brother, has been a leader of the people during the time of the Corn Law reformation, and she has been known to take a wide and generous interest in all these subjects." Heavens! by whom was she known to be so, Madam,—you have discovered mysteries that were never known before, none under heaven heard it before.

> " Go ! if your ancient but ignoble blood,
> Has crept through scoundrels ever since the flood—
> Go ! and pretend your family is young ;
> Nor own your fathers have been fools so long.
> What can ennoble sots, or slaves, or cowards;
> Not all the blood of all the Howards."—*Pope.*

You say, " Imagine, then, what people must think when they find in respectable American prints the absurd stories of her turning her tenants out into the snow, and ordering the cottages to be set on fire over their heads, because they would not go out." " But, if you ask how such an absurd story could ever have been made up, whether there is the least foundation to make it on, I answer that it is the exaggerated report of a movement made by the present duke of Sutherland's father, in the year 1811, and which was a part of a great movement that passed through the Highlands of Scotland, when the advancing progress of civilization began to make it necessary to change the estates from military to agricultural establishments." You go on then detailing the results of the union of England and Scotland, the situation of the Sutherland estate in the map of the Highlands. You say, "The general agent of the estate of Sutherland is Mr. Loch." You are right, he was, and you provided a place for his whole speech before the House of Commons, on the second reading of the Scotch Poor Law Bill, June 12th, 1845, where he strenuously endeavoured to vindicate and exonerate himself and His Grace of Sutherland from the charges of cruelty and injustice to the people, brought against them in that House on that occasion by Mr. Crawford. No wonder that he exerted himself that day to silence his opponents, and to dupe the House. He was 21 years a member in the House for the Northern Boroughs, and this is the only speech of his which found its way to the public prints, or considered worthy of being borrowed or copied by any other print. (The honour of it was left for you alone Madam.) If I am not mistaken the very day this speech was delivered in the House of Commons, the case of a poor cripple woman, from the parish of Farr, Sutherlandshire, was decided against His Grace, in the Court of Session, Edinburgh, and I had 71 more cases from his estate at the same time, in the hands of a solicitor, all pursuing his Grace for the support the law of the land provided for them, but denied them. Yet I find in your quotations from Mr. Loch's speech, this—" Therefore the statements that have been made, so far from being correct, are in every way an exaggeration of what is the fact. No portion of the kingdom has advanced in prosperity so much; and if the honourable member, Mr. S. Crawford, will go down there, I will give him every facility to see the state of the people, and he shall judge with his own eyes whether my representation be not correct * * * But I will not trouble the House * * * the statements I have made are accurate, and I am quite ready to prove them, any way that is necessary." To follow this *trumpeted up speech* of Mr. Loch in your "Sunny Memories," would be lost time, and abuse of ink, paper, and type. Every Highlander over which he had any control, or had the least transaction with him, experimentally knew him to be the greatest deceiver, and the most avowed enemy of the Celtic race that ever existed ; hence I will confine myself to a few remarks which will be corroborated by hundreds of living witnesses. " In the years 1812-13 and 1816-17, so great was their misery, that it was necessary to send down oatmeal for their supply, to the amount of £2,200, and that given to them." (The phrase given signifies gratis.) I know meal was sent these years to the amount of nearly one third of the stated amount ; but I know for a certainty that the people had to pay this trumpeted-up charity at the rate of £2 8s. sterling per boll. I knew my own father to pay it with cattle, and on the least calculation he handed over to his Grace, or his factor, eight pounds of good Highland beef for every pound of course oatmeal he received three months prior ; and so did every one, who paid for that meal in *kind.* His Grace's liberality to kirk sessions, and the poor viz. " £450-a-year ;" to say the least, this is monstrous exaggeration. He says, "before 1812 there were no bakers, and only two shops in the county, and two blacksmiths." Now Madam, I can tell you, (and hundreds will back me) that before 1812 there were thousands of bakers in Sutherlandshire, and had plenty to bake, and that for time immemorial prior to that date, they never needed charity or supply of oatmeal from their chiefs or any one else. Prior to 1812, and as long as I can remember, there were 26 shops in the county, and 31 blacksmiths. There was scarcely a parish in the county but there were two blacksmiths employed. The Sutherland people never knew what want was, until they became subjected to Loch's iron sway. You go on and say, "What led me more particularly to inquire into these facts was, that I received by mail while in London, an account containing some of these stories which had been so industriously circulated in America: these were dreadful accounts of cruelties practised, in the process of inducing the tenants to change their places of residences." The following is a specimen of these stories :

" I was present at the pulling down and burning of the house of William Chisholm, Badinloskin, in which was lying his wife's mother, an old bedridden woman, of near one hundred years of age, none of the family being at home. I informed the party about to set fire to the house of the circumstance, and prevailed on them to stop till Mr. Sellar would come; on his arrival, I told him of the poor old woman being in a condition unfit for removal. He replied, ' D——n her, she has lived too long, let her burn.' Fire was immediately set to the house, and the blankets in which she was carried were in flames before she could be got out. She was placed in a little shed, and it was with great difficulty they were prevented from firing that also. The old woman's daughter arrived while the house was on fire, and assisted the neighbours in removing her out of the flames and smoke, presenting a picture of horror which I shall never forget, but cannot attempt to describe : she died in five days."

"With regard to this story, Mr. Loch the agent says. 'I must notice the ` only thing like a fact stated in the newspaper extract which you sent me, wherein Mr. Sellar is accused of acts of cruelty toward some of the people. This Mr. Sellar tested by bringing an action against the then sheriff-substitute of the county. He obtained a verdict for heavy damages. The sheriff, by whom the slander was propogated, left the county. Both are since dead."

Having, through Lord Shaftesbury's kindness, received the benefit of Mr. Loch's corrections to this statement, I am permitted to make a little further extract from his reply. He says—

"In addition to what I was able to say in my former paper, I can now state that the Duke of Sutherland has received from one of the most determined opposers of the measure, who travelled to the north of Scotland as editor of a newspaper, a letter regretting all he had written on the subject, being convinced that he was entirely misinformed. As you take so much interest in the subject, I will conclude by saying that nothing could exceed the prosperity of the county during the past year; their stock, sheep, and other things sold at high prices; their crops of grain and turnips were never so good, and the potatoes were free from all disease : rents have been paid better than was ever known . . . . As an instance of the improved habits of the farmers, no house is now built for them that they do not require a hot-bath and water-closets."

From this long epitome you can gather the following results: first, if the system was a bad one, the Duchess of Sutherland had nothing to do with it, since it was first introduced in 1806, the same year her grace was born; and the accusation against Mr. Sellar dates in 1811, when her grace was five or six years old. The Sutherland arrangements were completed in 1819, and her Grace was not married to the duke till 1823, so that, had the arrangement been the worst in the world, it is nothing to the purpose so far as she is concerned.

As to whether the arrangement *is* a bad one, the facts which have been stated speak for themselves. To my view, it is an almost sublime instance of the benevolent employment of superior wealth and power in shortening the struggles of advancing civilization, and elevating in a few years a whole community to a point of education and material prosperity which, unassisted, they might never have obtained."

Yes, Madam, a "sublime instance," you say, "of the benevolent employment of superior wealth and power in shortening the struggles of advancing civilization." I say yes, indeed, the shortest process of civilization we have recorded in the history of nations. (*Oh marvellous !*) From the year 1812 to 1820, the whole interior of the county of Sutherland, whose inhabitants were advancing rapidly in the science of agriculture and education, who by nature and exemplary training were the bravest, the most moral, and patriotic people that ever existed,—even admitting a few of them did violate the excise laws, (the only sin which Mr. Loch and all the rest of their avowed enemies could bring against them,)—where a body of men could be raised on the shortest possible notice, that *kings* and *empeiors* might and would be proud of; and the whole fertile valleys, and straths which gave them birth, were in due season waving with corn; their mountains and hill sides studded with sheep and cattle; when rejoicing, felicity, happiness, and true piety prevailed; where the marshal notes of the bagpipes sounded and reverberated from mountain to glen, from glen to mountain: I say *marvellous!* in eight years converted to a solitary wilderness, where the voice of man praising God is not to be heard, nor the image of God upon man not to be seen; where you can set a compass with twenty miles of a radius upon it, and go round with it full stretched and not find one acre of land within the circumference, which came under the plough for the last thirty years, except a few in the parishes of Lairg and Tongue,—all under mute brute animals. This is the advancement of civilization, is it not Madam? Return now, with me, to the beginning of your elaborate *eulogy* on the Duchess of Sutherland, and if you are open to conviction, I think you should be convinced that I never published, nor circulated in the American, English, or Scotch public prints any ridiculous absurd stories about her grace of Sutherland. An abridgement of my lucubrations are now in the hands of the public, and you may peruse them. I stand by them as facts, (*stubborn cheils*,) I can prove them to be so even in this country, by a cloud of living witnesses, and my readers will find that, instead of bringing excessive absurd accusations against her Grace, that I have endeavoured, in some instances, to screen her and her predecessors from the public odium their own policy, and the doings of their servants, merited. Moreover, there is thirty years since I began to expostulate with the house of Sutherland for their shortsighted policy in dealing with their people as they were doing, and it is twenty years since I began to expose them publicly, with my real plain name, Donald M'Leod attached to each letter, and a copy of the public paper where it appeared, directed and sent by post to the Duke of Sutherland. These exposing and remonstrating letters were published in the Edinburgh papers where the Duke and his predecessors had their principal Scotch law agent, and you may easily believe that I was closely watched, so as to find one false accusation in my letters, but they were baffled. I am well aware that every *one* letter I have written on the subject would constitute a *true libel*, and I knew the editors, printers, and publishers of these papers were as liable or responsible for true libel as I was. But the House of Sutherland could never venture to raise an action of damages against either of us. In 1841, when I published my first pamphlet, I paid $4 50, for binding one of them in splendid style, which I sent by mail to his grace the present Duke of Sutherland with a complimentary note, requesting him to peruse it, and let me know if it contained anything offensive or untrue. I never received a reply, nor did I expect it, yet I am satisfied that his grace perused it. I posted a copy of it to Mr. Loch, his chief commissioner; to Mr. W. Mackenzie, his chief lawyer, Edinburgh; and to every one of their underlings, and sheep farmers, and ministers in the county of Sutherland who abbetted the depopulators, and I challenge the whole of them and other literary scourges who aided and justified their unhallowed doings, to gainsay one statement I have made. Can you, or any other believe, that a poor sinner like Donald M'Leod would be allowed for so many years to escape with impunity, had he been circulating and publishing calumnious absurd falsehoods against such personages as the House of Sutherland. No, I tell you, if money could secure my punishment, without establishing their own shame and guilt, that it would be considered well spent long ere now,—they would eat me in penny pies if they could get me cooked for them.

I agree with you that the Duchess of Sutherland is a beautiful accomplished lady, who would shudder at the idea of taking a faggot or a burning torch in her hand, to set fire to the cottages of her tenants, and so would her predecessor, the first Duchess of Sutherland, her good mother; likewise would the late and present Dukes of Sutherland, at least I am willing to believe that they would. Yet is was done in their name, under their authority, to their knowledge, and with their sanction. The Dukes and Duchesses of Sutherland, and those of their depopulating order, had not, nor has any call to defile their pure hands in milder work than to burn people's houses; no, no, they had, and have plenty of willing tools at their beck to perform their dirty work. Whatever amount of humanity and purity of heart the late or the present duke and duchess may possess or be ascribed to them, we know the class of men from whom they selected their commissioners, factors and underlings. I knew every one of these wicked servants who ruled the Sutherland estate for the last fifty years, and I am justified in saying that the most skilful phrenologist and physi. ognomist that ever existed could not discern one spark of humanity in the whole of them, from Mr. Loch down to Donald *Sgrios*, or in other words, damnable Donald, the name by which he was known. The most part of those vile executors of the atrocities I have been describing are now dead, and to be feared but not lamented. But it seems the chief were left to give you all the information you required about British slavery and oppres. sion. I have read from speeches delivered by Mr. Loch at public dinners among his own party, " that he would never be satisfied until the Gaelic language and the Gaelic people would be extirpated root and branch from the Sutherland estate; yes, from the highlands of Scotland." He published a book, where he stated as a positive fact, that "when he got the manage. ment of the Sutherland estate, that he found 408 families on the estate who never heard the name of Jesus,"—whereas I could make an oath that there were not at that time, and for ages prior to it, above two families within the limits of the county who did not worship that name, and holy Being every morning and evening. I know there are hundreds in the Canadas who will bear me out in this assertion. I was at the pulling down and burning of the house of William Chisholm, I got my hands burnt taking out the poor old woman from amidst the flames of her once comfortable though humble dwelling, and a more horrifying and lamenta. ble scene could scarcely be witnessed. I may say the skeleton of once a tall, robust high-cheek-boned respectable woman, who had seen better days, who could neither hear, see, nor speak, without a tooth in her mouth, her cheek skin meeting in the centre, her eyes sunk out of sight in their sockets, her mouth wide open, her nose standing upright among smoke and flames, uttering piercing moans of distress and agony, in articulations from which could be only understood, Oh, *Dhia, Dhia, tein'!, tein'!*—oh God, God, fire, fire! When she came to the pure air her bosom heaved to a most extraordinary degree, accompanied by a deep hollow sound from the lungs, comparable to the sound of thunder at a distance. When laid down upon the bare, soft, moss floor of the roofless shed, I will never forget the foam of perspiration which emitted and covered the pallid death. looking countenance. This was a scene, Madam, worthy of an artist's pencil, and of a conspicuous place on the stages of tragedy. Yet you call this a specimen of the ridiculous stories which found their way into respectable prints, because Mr. Loch, the chief actor, told you that Sellar, the head executive, brought an action against the sheriff and obtained a verdict for heavy damages. What a subterfuge ; but it will not answer the purpose, "*the bed is too short to stretch yourself, and the covering too narrow and short to cover you.*" If you took your information and evidence upon which you founded your Uncle Tom's cabin from such dis. creditable sources, (as I said before), who can believe the one-tenth of your novel ? *I cannot.* I have at my hand here the grand-child of the murdered old woman, who recollects well of the circumstance. I have not far from me a respectable man, an elder in the Free Church, who was examined as a witness at Sellar's trial, at the spring assizes of Inverness, 1816, which you will find narrated in letters four and five of my work. I think, Madam, had you the opportunity of seeing the scenes which I, and hundreds more, have seen, and see the ferocious appearance of the infamous *gang*, who constituted the burning party, covered over face and hands with soot and ashes of the burning houses, cemented by torch grease and their own sweat, kept continually drunk or half drunk, while at work; and to observe the hellish amusements some of them would get up for themselves and for an additional pleasure to their leaders. The people's houses were generally built upon declivities, and in many cases not far from pretty steep precipices, they preserved their meal in tight made boxes, or chests, as they were called; when this fiendish party found any quantity of meal, they would carry it between them to the brink, and dispatch it down the precipice amidst shrieks and yells; this was considered grand sport to see the box breaking to atoms and the meal mixed with the air. When they would set fire to a house, they would watch any of the domestic animals making their escape from the flames, such as dogs, cats, hens or any poultry, these were caught and thrown back to the flames; grand sport for demons in human form. I assure you the Dukes and Duchesses of Sutherland had no need to try their hand at burning houses while James Loch, William Young, Patrick Sellar, Francis Suther, John Horseburgh, Captain Kenneth M'Kay, and Angus Leslie were alive, nor while George Loch, George Gunn, and Robt. Horseburgh, &c., is alive. Mr. Seller (as I said before) was brought to trial for culpable homicide and fire-raising; and those dog, cat, and hen murderers who acted under him and took act and part with him were the exculpatory witnesses, who saved his neck from a sudden jerk, or himself from teasing oakum in the hulks for many years. As to this vaunted letter his " Grace received from one of the most determined opposers of the measures, who travelled in the north of Scotland as editor of a newspaper regretting all that he had written on the subject, being convinced that he was misinformed." I may tell you, Madam, that this man did not travel to the north, or in the north of Scotland as editor; his name was Thomas Mullock, he came to Scotland a fanatic speculator in literature in search of money, or a lucrative situation, vainly thinking that he would be a dictator to every editor in Scotland, he first attacked the immortal Hugh Miller of the *Witness*, Edinburgh, but in him he met more than his match. He then went to the north, got hold of my first pamphlet, and by setting it up in a literary style, and in better English than I did, he made a splendid and promising appearance in the northern papers for some time, but he found out that the money expected was not coming in, and he found that the hotels, head inns, and taverns, would not keep him up any longer without the prospect of being paid for the past or for the future. I found out that he was hard up, and a few of the highlanders in Edinburgh and myself, sent him from twenty to thirty pounds sterling. When he saw that that was all he was to get, he at once turned tail upon us, and instead of expressing his gratitude, he abused us unsparingly, and regretted that ever he wrote in behalf of such a hungry, moneyless class. He smelled (like others we suspect) where the gold was hoarded up for hypocrites, and flatterers, and that one apologizing letter to his grace would be worth ten times as much as he could expect from the highlanders all his lifetime, and I doubt not but it was, for his apology for the sin of mis-information got wide circulation.

He then went to France and started an English paper in Paris, and for the service he rendered Napoleon in crushing republicanism during the besieging of Rome, &c., the Emperor presented him with a *Gold Pin*, and in a few days afterwards sent a *Gendarme* to Mullock with a brief notice that his service was not any longer required, and a warning to quit France in a few days, which he had to do. What became of him after I know not, but very likely he is dictating to young Loch, or some other *Metternich.*

No feelings of hostile vindictiveness, no desire to inflict chastisement, no desire to make riches, influenced my mind, pourtraying the scenes of havoc and misery which in those past days darkened the annals of Suther-land, I write in my own humble style with higher aims, wishing to prepare the way for demonstrating to the Dukes of Sutherland, and all other High-land proprietors, great and small, that the path of selfish aggrandisement and oppression, leads by sure and inevitable results, yea to the ruin and destruction of the blind and misguided oppressors themselves. I consider the Duke himself victimised on a large scale by an incurable wrong system and by being enthralled by wicked counsellors, and servants. I have no hesitation in saying, had his Grace and his predecessors, bestowed one half of the encouragement they had bestowed upon strangers, upon the aborigines, a hardy, healthy, abstemious people, who lived peaceably in their primative habitations, unaffected with the vices of a subtle civiliza-tion, possessing little, but enjoying much; a race devoted to their heredi-tary chief, ready to abide by his counsels, a race profitable in peace, and loyal available in war; I say his Grace, the present Duke of Sutherland, and his beautiful Duchess, would be without compeers in the British dominions their rents at least doubled, would be as secure from invasion and annoyance in Dunrobin Castle as Queen Victoria could, or can be, in her Highland residence, Balmoral, and far safer than she is in her English home, Buckingham Palace ; every man and son of Sutherland would be ready, as in the days of yore, to shed the last drop of blood in defence of their patron, if required. Congratulations, rejoicings, dancing to the marshal notes of the pipes, would meet them at the entrance to every Glen and Strath in Sutherlandshire, accompanied, surrounded, and greeted as they proceeded, by the most grateful, devotedly attached, happy, and bravest peasantry, that ever existed; yes, but alas! where there is nothing now but desolation and the cries of famine and want to meet the noble pair, the ruins of once comfortable dwellings, will be seen the land marks of the furrows and ridges which yielded food to thousands, the footprints of the arch enemy of human happiness, and ravager before, after, and on each side, solitude, stillness, and quiet of the grave, disturbed only at intervals by the yells of a shepherd, or fox-hunter, and the bark of a collie dog. Surely we must admit the Marquises and Dukes of the house of Sutherland have been duped, and victimized to a most extraordinary and increditable extent, and we have Mr. Loch's own words for it in his speech in the House of Commons, June 21st, 1845, " I can state, as from facts, that from 1811 to 1833, not one sixpence of rent has been received from that county; but on the contrary, there has been sent there for the benefit and improvement of the people, a sum exceeding sixty thousand pounds, sterling." Now think you of this immense wealth which has been expended, I am not certain, but I think the rental of the county would exceed £60,000 a year, you have then from 1811 to 1833, twenty-two years, leaving them at the above figures, and the sum total will amount to £1,320,000 expended upon the self styled Sutherland improvements, add to this £60,000 sent down to preserve the lives of the victims of those improvements from death by famine, and the sum total will turn out in the shape of £1,380,-000 ; it surely cost the heads of the house of Sutherland an immense sum of money to convert the county into the state I have described it, in a former part of this work, (and I challenge contradiction), I say the expelling of the people from their Glens and Straths, and huddling them in motely groups on the sea-shores, and barren moors, and to keep them alive there, and to make them willing to be banished from the nation, when they thought proper, or when they could get a *haul* of the public money, to pay their passage to America or Australia, cost them a great deal. This fabulous incredible munificence of their Graces to the people, I will leave the explanation of what it was, how it was distributed, and the manner in which payment and refunding of the whole of it was exacted off the people, to my former description of it in this work; yet I am willing to admit that a very small portion, if any, of the *refunding* of the amount sent down, ever reach the Duke's or the Marquis's coffers, which is easily understood by not granting receipts for it. Whatever particle of good the present Duke might feel inclined to do, will be ever frustrated by the counteracting energy of a prominent evil principle; I knew the adopting ' and operations of the Loch policy towards the Sutherland peasantry, cost the present Duke and his father many thousands of pounds, and, I predict, will continue to cost them on a large scale while a Loch is at the head of their affairs, and principal adviser. Besides how may they endanger what is far more valuable than gold and silver ; for those who are advised by men who never sought counsel or advice from God, all their lifetime, as their work will testify, do hazard much, and are trifling with omniscience,

You should be surprised to hear and learn, Madam, for what purposes the most of the money drained from the Duke's coffers yearly are expended, since he became the Duke and proprietor of Sutherland, and upholding the Loch policy. There are no fewer than seventeen who are known by the name of Water Bailiffs, in the county, who receive yearly salaries, what doing, think you ? protecting the operations of the Loch policy, watching day and night the fresh water lakes, rivers, and creeks, teeming with the finest salmon and trout fish in the world, guarding from the famishing people, even during the years of famine and dire distress, when many had to subsist upon weeds, sea ware, and shellfish, yet guarded and preserved for the amusement of English anglers; and what is still more heart-rending, to prevent the dying by hunger to pick up any of the dead fish left by the sporting anglers, rotting on the lake, creek, and river sides, when the smallest of them, or a morsel, would be considered by hundreds, I may say thousands of the needy natives, a treat, but durst not touch them, or if they did and found out, to jail they were conducted, or removed summarily from his Grace's domains; (let me be understood, these gentlemen had no use of the fish, only killing them for amusement, only what they required for their own use, and complimented to the factors, they were not permitted to cure them).

You will find, Madam, that about three miles from Dunrobin Castle there if a branch of the sea which extends up the county about six miles, where shellfish called mussels, abounds; here you will find there are two sturdy men, called mussel bailiffs, supplied with rifles and ammunition and as many Newfoundland dogs as assistants, watching the mussel scalp, or beds, to preserve them from the people in the surrounding parishes of Dornoch, Rogart, and Golspie, and keep them to supply the fishermen on the opposite side of the Moray Firth with bait, who come there every year and take away thousands of tons of this nutritive shellfish, when many hundreds of the people would be thankful for a diet per day of them, to pacify the cravings of nature. You will find the unfortunate native fisherman who pays a yearly rent to his Grace for bait, that they are only permitted theirs from the refuse left by the strangers of the other side of the Moray Firth, and if they violate the *iron* rule laid down to them, they are entirely at the mercy of the underlings : there has been an instance of two of the fishermen's wives going on a snowy, frosty, day, to gather bait, but on account of the boisterous sea, could not reach the place appointed by the factors; and one took what they required from the forbidden ground, and was observed by some of the bailiffs in ambush, who pursued them like tigers, one came up to her unobserved, took out his knife and cut the straps by which the basket or creel on her back was suspended, the weight on her back fell to the ground, and she, poor woman, big in the family way, fell her whole length forward in the snow and frost, another turned round to see what happened, and he pushed her back with such force that she fell her whole length; he then trampled their baskets and mussels to atoms, and took them both prisioners, ordered one to go and call his superior bailiff to assist him, and kept the other for two hours standing wet as she was, among frost and snow until the superior came a distance of three miles. After a short consultation upon the enormity of the crime, the two poor women were led like convicted criminals to Golspie, to appear before Licurgus Gunn, and in that deplorable condition were left standing before their own doors in the snow, until Marshal Gunn found it convenient to appear to pronounce judgment,—verdict; You are allowed to go into your houses this night, this day week you must leave this village for ever, and the whole of the fishermen fo the village are strictly prohibited from taking bait from the Little Ferry until you leave;

G

my bailiffs are requested to see this my decree strictly attended to. Being the middle of winter and heavy snow, they delayed a week longer: ulti-mately the villagers had to expel the two families from among them, so as they would get bait, having nothing to depend upon for subsistence but the fishing, and fish they could not without bait. This is a specimen of the injustice and subjugation of the Golspie fishermen, and of the peo-ple at large; likewise of the purposes for which the duke's money is ex-pended in that quarter. If you go then, to the other side of the domain, you will find another kyle, or a branch of the sea which abounds in cockles and other shellfish, which, fortunately for the poor people, are not forbidden by a Loch Ukase. But in the years of distress, when the people were principally living upon vegetables, sea weeds and shellfish, various diseases made their appearance among them, hitherto unknown. The ab-sence of meal of any kind being considered the primary cause; some of the people thought they would be permitted to exchange shellfish for meal with their more fortunate neighbours in Caithness, to whom such shell-fish were a rarity, and so far the understanding went between them, that the Caithness boats came up loaded with meal, but the Loch embargo, through his underling in Tongue, who was watching their movements, were at once placed upon it, and the Caithness boats had to return home with the meal, and the duke's people might die or live, as they best could. Now, Madam, you have steeped your brains, and ransacked the English language to find refined terms for your panegyric on the duke, duchess, and family of Sutherland. (I find no fault with you, knowing you have been well paid for it.) But I would briefly ask you (and others who de-voted much of their time and talent in the same strain,) would it not be more like a noble pair, who, (if they did) merit such noble praise as you have bestowed upon them, if they had, especially during years of famine and distress, freely opened up all these bountiful resources which God in his eternal wisdom and goodness prepared for his people, and which should never be intercepted nor restricted by man or men. You and others have composed hymns of praise, which it is questionable if there is a tune in heaven to sing them to.

So I returned, and considered all the oppressions that are done under the sun: and behold the tears of such as were oppressed, and they had no comforter; and on the side of their oppressors there was power; but they had no comforter—Ec-CLES. iv.1.

> "The wretch that works and weeps without relief
> Has one that notices his silent grief.
> He, from whose hands alone all pow'r proceeds,
> Ranks its abuse among the foulest deeds,
> Considers *all* injustice with a frown,
> But *marks* the man that treads his fellow down.
> Remember Heav'n has an avenging rod—
> To smite the poor is treason against God."—COWPER.

But you shall find the duke's money is expended for most astonishing purposes; not a little of it goes to *hire* hypocrites and *renowned literary* flatterers. to vindicate the mal-administration of those to whom he en-trusted the management of his affairs, and make his grace, (who is by nature a simple-minded man) believe his servants are innocent of all the charges brought against them, and doing justice to himself and to his people, when they are doing the greatest injustice to both; so that instead of calling his servants to account at any time, and enquiring into the broad charges brought against them—as every wise landlord should do—it seems the greater the enormities of foul deeds they commit, and the louder their accusation may sound through the land, the farther they are received into his favour. The fact is, that James Loch was Duke of Sutherland, and not the "tall, slender man with rather a thin face, light brown hair, and mild blue eyes" who armed you up the extraordinary elegant staircase in Stafford House: and Geordy Loch, his son, succeeded his father, and the duke will have no more control over him than he had over the old fox. The Duke of Sutherland would neither need foreign or home eulogisers, were it not for the unhallowed crew he has chosen to manage his affairs. Read the following humble appeal of his grace for a certificate of character. In the year 1848, "Duke of Sutherland, and those entrusted with the management of his vast possessions, preferred a somewhat queer request to the Highland Distribution Committee, viz. for 'the service of the Committee's staff' to report whether he, [his grace] had adequately fulfilled his self-imposed responsibilities." That the Duke should require a certificate of good behaviour towards his people is undoubtedly a little odd indeed, and at the expense of a public charity; but such was the case, and Captain Elliot, Inspector General of the Board, received orders "to attend to the duke's wishes." The result of the Captain's mission to Sutherland was a high-flown report, extolling the ducal bounty towards his Sutherlanders, which utterly excluded the necessity of any aid from the Committee, although he knew well that hundreds of bolls of the charity meal were there at that time, but which was studiously kept out of view, that the duke might have the honour and praise of supporting his people. But what was my surprise to find in the next published proceedings of the Committee, a correspondence with Mr. Loch, M.P., the duke's premier, who put the Committee in mind that his grace had formerly subscribed £1000 to the fund, and conjoined with this reminiscence, a supplication to the committee to grant his noble employer the sum of £3500 to help towards the relief of the poor people of Sutherland. Subsequently the duke's petition was acceded to, with this preconcerted modification, namely, that the money was not to be expended for the relief of the poor Sutherlanders, but "on the formation of a road bisecting his grace's territory in the most favourable direction," (Mr. Loch's own words.) The premier goes then to prove the vast utility of the road in question, (planned by himself, and to be executed by the Committee,) it being designed to stretch from Inchnadamp in Assyut, to the boundary of the county of Caithness. Now, Madam, I can tell you, and hundreds of my countrymen in Canada, and thousands of them at home can tell you, (as I have said before) that not one single native of Sutherland will ever reap any benefit of this road, every inch of it going through a solitary wilderness, and deer forests, where men are forbidden to travel,—

exclusively for the benefit of his grace's deer stalkers, game keepers, and shepherds.

It is evident from the above correspondence between the dishonourable *Celtic* hater aud destroyer, Mr. Loch, and the audacious *trust betraying, base, Edinburgh Committee,* that there was pre-arrangement between the unprincipled parties to increase his graee's riches, with £3500 of poor famishing people's money. Yes, with a sum which would make 3400 destitute families sing for joy by the distribution of this amount among them. (Another report which was latterly published in the Edinburgh papers, states that his grace got £6000.) These are undeniable facts; but who can believe that it could be endured in christianised Scotland; that an owner of such large possessions should be so unscrupulously voted such a sum, out of the funds gathered from the benevolent in every quarter of the globe. Did Scotch private soldiers under the tropics subscribe out of their scanty pay, to enable the notorious Mr. Skene, and his committee, to take the free gift of £6000, or even £3500 of the relief distribution money to make a road from Inchnadamp, in Assynt, to Caithness, exclusively for his own use, or to any other Highland proprietor; yet according to the reports of the infamous committee, obscure as they were studiously kept, they show that after the ducal and lordly gifts were granted, the net balance at the credit of the Treasurer was £38,000, and the bulk of this balance in hand was dedicated to the relief of Highland distressed proprietors, leaving a discretionary power with themselves [the committee] to hand it over to those who they in their judgment considered most needful and deserving : (but the short of it is, to their own nearest relations and greatest favourites.) Of this sum we find in their own reports that Dundonnell, a Rosshire proprietor, got £1756 : we have Mr. Skene's (a distant relative of Dundonnell) own words for it as "bonus on account of the great outlay as an individual proprietor had made, and £1500 for road making." Then pleasingly writes the accomodating Secretary, Skene, to the Highland road requiring proprietors, "The broad offer to contribute one third of the expenses in meal, although I doubt not if money would be preferred this would be no obstacle." That roads were and are needed in the Highlands none will deny, and that able bodied men in want, and could not get employment should work at these roads none should oppose. But I strenuously contend that if men were required to render a full amount of labour, they were entitled to an equitable proportion of wages. It was monstrous to administer a fund unconditionally subscribed for the relief of the destitute, upon the principle that the poor creatures were to be fully worked, and in requittal, were to be only half fed. Never was there a more fatal failure, than in the mal-administration of that magnificent fund intended for the relief and welfare of the afflicted Highland population. Never were the malversation of Highland proprietors and underlings, more odiously discerned and exhibited to the world than in this case, Not being satisfied plundering the people by every system and plan that the *Satanic* council could devise, against which the people contended for at least this last seventy years, struggling against

many adverse circumstances, casualties of the season, and tyrannical exactions, often in want, but not repining or complaining, until ultimately they
became helpless, and as it were, fell into the slough of despondency, *en
masse*; when their long endurance came to an end, despair took hold of
their souls, and clamour for food was the result; appeal after appeal was
made to the public in their behalf, which was responded to; yet when
a christian world came in a glorious manner to their rescue from death
by famine, we find a set of rapacious Highland proprietors coming forward and placing their unhallowed hands upon the world's gift, and as
if they in audible terms or words *swore* by heaven, we shall not allow
this. Neither they did, for by examining minutely the distribution of
the fund you will find that they pocketed two-thirds of the whole : in the
first place, they got three-fourths of the meal bought for the people, to
improve their estates, and they exacted (agreeable to the Trevellyan test
scheme) ten hours labour for every pound of adulterated meal. Now,
taking able bodied men's wages at the lowest figure, 1s. 6d. per day, you
find the lairds gained 1s. 6d. per day of every man they employed, besides reaping the benefits of the improvements. Then the road-making
gifts, which they let to the competition of needy and greedy unfeeling
contractors, where men were not much better paid nor dealt with than
they were with the lairds—just a bare subsistence. Ah! what a fortunate famine this was for the Highland proprietors, especially to those
of extensive domains, and favourites of Mr. Skene and his committee.
I assure you they should pray for a return of it every seven years.

Now, Madam, I am about done with you at this time, but before closing
I would ask you, can you believe that the proprietor of Stafford House,
which you have so elaborately pourtrayed. whose elegance and sumptuousness threw all the grandeur which ever you have seen in America
into insignificance, and which threw yourself into a nervous rapture of
admiration, which you could not withstand, until the proprietrix mistress
of the robe conveyed you to a private room, and eased you by whisper-
ing in your ear, "Dear me, Mrs. Stowe, be not concerned so much or so
much embarrassed in your mind, at the sight of this select company and
of the splendour of the house; I assure you, though beautiful, we are not
angels, we are all mortal beings; and though the house is splendid it is
not heaven, but earthly materials," or some soothing words to that effect,
that brought you back again to your senses. I say could, or can you
believe that if there was the least speak of the *grace of God* in the *soul*
of His Grace the Duke of Sutherland, and his Duchess, or yet of humanity and common honesty, would they lower and degrade their position
in society, their name and titles among the nobles, so as to become the
most conspicuous among these villainous Highland plunderers of the
poor, and receive double the amount of any of the rest, of the booty ?
No, Madam, neither could I believe it myself, were it not that I knew
the simple minded duke, in all his affairs is advised by the vilest of the
vile, and the lowest of the low in principle.

These are stern facts, I must allow, but they are beyond contradiction,
and should not be concealed, but merit universal reprobation and public

censure. Public confidence has been shamefully abused, the poor have been cheated, degraded, and I may say demoralised; the funds intended and provided for the indigent poor have been squandered upon a needless useless staff of pampered officials, and Highland proprietors. You may praise them, and admire them and their palaces as much as you please, but the denunciations of the sacred volume condemn the oppressors of the poor, their abettors and apologisers, to their faces, and you cannot silence them. Should such a calamity overtake the Highlanders again, where will they look for commiseration or aid after this iniquitious abuse? I answer, let them trust in God, as Cromwell used to say, and keep their powder dry; I say let them take what they can get, and where they can get it. Let them not leave a bull, cow, or bullock; ram, sheep, or lamb; deer, or roe; blackcock, hen, or pheasant; moor-cock, hen, or snipe, &c., feeding and fattening upon the straths and glens which should be rearing corn and cattle for them and families: and take all the salmon and trout which is provided for them in the rivers and lakes upon which they can lay hands on, muscles and cockles to boot, (" Hunger," say a Highland proverb, has "long arms," and Bacon says "rebellion of the belly is worst,") and then their spoilers and monopolizers of every provision God has provided for the Celtic race in the Highlands of Scotland, will soon come to their right senses. I see no other alternative, unless the nation will step in and demand retribution for past wrongs, and secure even-handed justice for the people in future. What did I say, retribution for past wrongs, and secure justice for the people in future? hundreds will confer upon me a derisive laugh, and bawl out Utopianism. But allow me to allude to an historical parallel. After the conquest, the Norman kings afforested a large portion of the soil of conquered England, in much the same way as the landlords are now doing in the Highlands of Scotland. To such an extent was this practice carried on, that an historian informs us, that in the reign of King John, "the greater part of the kingdom" was turned into forest, and that so multiform and oppressive were the forest laws, that it was impossible for any man who lived within the boundaries to escape falling a victim to them. To prepare the land for these forests, the people were required to be driven, in many cases, as in the Highlands, at the point of the bayonet; and notwithstanding what Voltaire has said to the contrary, cultivated lands were laid waste, villages were destroyed, and the inhabitants extirpated. Distress ensued, and discontent followed as natural consequences. But observe, the Norman kings did all this in virtue of their feudal supremacy; and in point of law and right, were better entitled to do it than the Highland lairds are to imitate their example in the present day. Was it, however, to be tolerated? were the people to groan for ever under his oppression? No. The English Barons gave a practical reply to these questions at Runneymede, which it is unnecessary to detail. King John did cry out *utopian* at first, but was compelled to disafforest the land, and restore it to its natural and appropriate use; and the records of that great day's proceedings are universally esteemed as one of the brightest pages in English history.

With this great example before their eyes, let the most conservative pause before they yield implicit faith in the doctrine that every one of them may do with his land as he pleases. The fundamental principle of land tenure are unchanged since the days of Magna Charta; and however much the tendency of modern ideas may have cast these principles into oblivion, they are still deeply graven in the constitution, and if necessity called, would be found as strong and operative in the present day as they were five centuries ago. If the barons could compel the sovereign to open his forests, surely the sovereign may more orderly compel the barons to open theirs, and restore them to their natural and appropriate use; and there is a power behind the throne which impels and governs all. These are deep questions that should be stirred in the country, in the midst of extremities and abuse of power. For it is impossible for any one to travel in the Highlands of Scotland, and cast his eyes about him without feeling inwardly that such a crisis is approaching, and indeed consider it should arrive long ago. Sufferings have been inflicted in the Highlands as severe as occasioned by the policy of the brutal Norman kings in England; deer have extended ranges, while men have been hunted within a narrower and still narrower circle. The strong has fainted in the race for life; the old have been left to die. One after another of their liberties have been cloven down. To kill a fish in the stream, or a wild beast in the hill is a transportable crime, even in the time of famine. Even to travel through the fenceless forest is a crime; paths which at one time linked hamlet to hamlet for ages have been shut and barred. These oppressions are daily on the increase, and if pushed much further, (I should say if not speedily and timely pushed back) it is obvious that the sufferings of the people will reach a pitch, when action will be the plainest duty, and the most sacred instinct. To prevent such forbidden calamity, permit me to address a few lines to Her Majesty.

Come Victoria, Queen of Great Britain, Berwick-upon-Tweed, and Ireland; thou, the most beloved of all Sovereigns upon earth, in whose bosom and veins the blood of the Stuarts, the legitimate Sovereigns of Scotland is freely circulating; who hath endeared thyself to thy Celtic lieges in a peculiar manner, stretch forth thy Royal hand to preserve that noble race from extirpation, and becoming extinct, and to protect them from the violence, oppression, and spoilation to which they have been subjected for many years. Bear in mind, that this is the race in whom your forefathers confided, entrusted and depended so much at all times, especially when a foreign invader threatened and attempted to take possession of the Scotch throne; and never trusted to them in vain. And though they unfortunately divided, upon which of the Stuart family was to rule over them, and much valuable blood shed on that account; yet the impartial investigator into that affair will find the zeal, patriotism and loyalty of each party meriting equal praise and admiration, though the *butchers*, and literary scourges of the defeated party converted the praise and loyalty due to them, into calumny and abuse. But these gloomy days of strife and murder are over, and the defeated consider that they sustained no loss but that they gained much; and I assure your majesty that your name is now imprinted upon every Scotch Highlander's *heart* in letters more valuable than gold, and that the remnant of them still left, are as willing and as ready to shed their blood for the honour and dignity, of your crown, and the safety of your person and family, as their fathers were for your grandsires. Then allow not this noble race to be extirpated, nor deteriorated in their soul, mind, chivalry, character, and persons; allow it not, your majesty, to be told in "Gath," nor published in the streets of Askelon, that other nations have to feed and keep alive your Highland Scotch warriors, while you require their service in the battle field; while the nursery where these brave men, who carried many a laurel to the British crown from foreign strands, are now converted to game preserves, hunting parks, and lairs for wild animals. Come them, like a *God* fearing, God loving and Christian queen; like a subject-loving and beloved Sovereign, and demand the restitution of their inalienable rights to your Highland lieges, and the restoration of the Highland straths and glens to their natural and appropriate use. Examine like "*Ahasuerous*," the book of records of the chronicles, and find what service the Highlanders rendered you and your forefathers, and how they are requited. "Who knoweth whether thou art come to the kingdom for such a time as this?" and "how can you endure to see the evil that came upon your people, or how can you endure to see the destruction of your kindred?" people, and then like good Queen Esther, declare boldly and publicly that you shall not have a Hamanite, or a Hamanitess about your person, in your household, or in your council. I know many of them will raise a Rob Roy cry, when the real owner of the cattle he has taken away, came and got possession of them, (I am plundered of my just rights.) Highland proprietors hold the lands and other rights they plundered of the people, on the principle that Rob Roy maintained his right to the cattle he stole from his distant neighbour in Badenoch. But the day is drawing nigh when these rank delusions in high quarters will be dispelled. It is a Satanic imposture, that the stewardship of God's soil is freely convertible into a mischievous power of oppressing the poor. The proper use of property is to make property useful; where this is not done, it were better for land owners to have been born beggars, than to live in luxury while causing the wretched to want and weep. I know that if our Sovereign Lady was to make such a demand as this, that she would incur the ire and displeasure of the turf and sporting classes, (a consuming but not a producing body) the most destructive, vicious, cruel, disorderly, unvirtuous, revelling, and the most useless of all her Majesty's subjects. On the other hand her Majesty would gain for herself the praise and admiration of all the most wise, prudent, liberal, humane, virtuous and most exemplary of the nation; the blessings of the people and of heaven would rest upon her, and remain with her, and Highland proprietors, their children, and children's children would have cause to hold her name and memory in grateful recollection. Their estates would in a few years double their rents, and they and their heirs would be redeemed from insolvency, and secured from beggary. The poor law would become a dead letter. The poaching game law expenditure, along with many other unrighteous laws, which are hanging heavily upon the nation, would fall to disuse ; the people would prosper, and nothing would be lost but hunting grounds for the younger branches of the aristocracy and English snobs, and that same could easily be supplied by Her Majesty directing the attention of this cruel, cowardly class to the Hudson's Bay and Nor' West Territories, where they might have plenty of useful sport, destroying animals much of their own disposition, *though not half so injurious.* In concluding this long letter to you Madam, permit me to tell you my opinion of you on your landing in Britian, after taking notice of the parties who invited you, and with whom you have associated, and the parties you have shunned, as if unclean or unworthy of your society and countenance. I concluded at once your service for the emancipation of the American slaves was for ever lost, and not only lost, but be the means to screw their chains tighter than ever they were before. Is there a class under heaven this day more unlikely to have any influence over the minds of republic Americans than English inhuman, ambitious, slave making aristocracy ? I answer, *no, no!* Hence I was convinced that English gold was your main object. But had you come to Britain, and got up an Uncle Donald, Uncle Jock, and Uncle Geordy's Cabin, where you would not need *colouring,* nor steep your brains to get up sublime falsehood, and impossible achievements of runaway slaves, where the naked unvarnished truths were more than could be believed. Then to return with these British cabins to the United States you would have a good chance to reap as rich a harvest of them in the States, as you have reaped of Uncle Tom in Britain, and establish your name and memory immortal and unsullied. Forming these opinions, I published the following letter in the "*Northern Ensign*" newspaper, Wick, and addressed a copy of it to you :—

SIR.—In my last, of the 18th ult., upon the late member for the Northern Burghs, I stated that I was not half through, but that I would need to forbear. The Stafford House meeting has diverted my attention at present from following up the subject as I intended, so as to make the best use I can of this aristocratic movement in behalf of the African slaves while it was warm before the public. Many thanks to you and your Perth correspondent for your talented comments upon the hollow hypocrisy of this meeting and the injurious effects it will have, if their (so called) Christian affectionate address, headed by the Duchess of Sutherland, her two daughters of Argyle and Blantyre, Duchess of Bedford, Lady Trevellyan, Lady John Russell, and many more, be presented to their sisters, the ladies of America.

I believe your Perth correspondent has given us the true brief version or exact reply of the American ladies to this affectionate address— 'Look at home.' But I must go further and instruct the American ladies in what they should tell their English sisters to look at, at home. Not with a view to justify the American traffic in human beings—God forbid, but merely to tell them that they can meet this feminine, English, Christian, affectionate appeal, with the same argument that the Cannibal Queen met a French philosopher when he was remonstrating with her upon the hateful, horryifying, and forbidden practice of eating human flesh, and recommending her to discontinue and forbid the practice in her dominions. 'Well,' replied the Cannibal Queen, 'Volaire, what is the difference between your people and us? You kill men, and allow them to rot; we kill men, and to crown our victory we eat them, and we find them as good for food as any other flesh; besides, our law demands of us to eat our enemies.' Now, Sir, though two blacks will never make a white, yet the American ladies may justly reply and ask their English sisters, 'What is the difference between you and us? We buy black African slaves; but when we buy them, we feed, clothe and house them. No doubt some of us whip them at times for disobedience or for our own caprice; but we heal their stripes, and take care of them, that they may do our work. But you, English sisters, you make white slaves paupers and beggars; and when you make them this, by depriving them of all means to live by their own industry, then you turn them adrift—you *raze, plough-up,* or *burn down* their habitations, and allow them to die (in hundreds,) the agonizing, lingering death of starvation on the road-sides, ditches, and open fields. Dear sisters, look at the history of Ireland for the last six or seven years, and you will see how many thousands you have allowed to die by hunger; and consider how many thousands more you would have allowed to die a similar death, had we not come to their rescue, and sent them food until we could remove them from your tender mercy and from your territories, to feed, clothe, and house them, and to find employment and fair remuneration for their labour among ourselves. Look for instance at an Irishman arraigned at the bar of justice for sheep-stealing, and his counsel offering to prove that before he stole the sheep, three of his children perished for want of food, and in the case of the last of them who died a sucking infant, the mother peeled the flesh off its legs and arms; she boiled it, and both she and her husband (the prisoner) ate it to save their own lives, and the mother died soon after. At this time you, our English sisters, were riding upon chariots, rolling smoothly over your extensive, uncultivated, depopulated domains, upon the wheels of splendour, and cushions of the finest texture, and your husbands, sons, and daughters sharing of your festivities, luxuries, and unnecessary grandeur; expending more money and human food upon useless dogs and horses than would have saved thousands of the poor useful Irish (with the image of God upon them) from a premature agonizing death. We have read with horror of one of your husbands urging with might and main upon the government (who bestirred themselves at the time for fear the famine might cause disease among the Irish landlords,) to feed the people with *curry powder·*; and you must recollect, when the curry powder scheme of destroying the Irish could not be approved of, that Sir A. Trevellyan was sent over to Ireland with the test starving commission, and conducted the Irish destruction with more humanity, for he allowed one pound of meal as meat and wages for every starving Irishman who would work ten hours per day at making roads, draining, and improving the estates of Irish landlords. Ah! English sisters, though we could bring no more against you, the public will judge and decide that you should be the defenders, and not the pursuers, in this case; but since you began to expose us, we will expose you to the letter, for there is no case or cases brought out against us in 'Uncle Tom's Cabin,' with all Harriet Beecher Stowe's capabilities of colouring, that is equal to this. We tell you emphatically that our law would neither sanction or tolerate such inhuman cruelty—our religion forbids it; and that any man or number of men who would be guilty of such would be branded with infamy and chased from our states and from our societies as inhuman, irrational, irreligious, and immoral monsters, unworthy of christian society, or to have a voice in the civil or religious government of our country. But by taking a retrospective view of the history of your christianized nation, we find that inhumanity, oppression, cruelty, and extortion, are qualifications required to fit a legislator, commander, commissioner, or any other functionary to whom you may safely entrust the law making, the law administration, and the government of your people; but qualifications specially required to entitle them to dignified high sounding titles and distinction, as will be shown afterwards.'

'"Uncle Tom's Cabin" has aroused the sympathy and compassion of the Duchesses of Sutherland, Argyle, Bedford, and Ladies Blantyre and Trevellyan, and many thousands of the women of England, over the fate of Ham's black children. But we would seriously advise the Duchess of Sutherland and her host to pause until Uncle Donald M'Leod's Cabin comes out, and until he himself comes across the Atlantic with it among the thousands of those and their offsprings who have fled from their iron sway and slavery to our shores. He, poor man, has been expostulating with you for the last twenty years against your cruel, unnatural, irrational, unchristian, and inhuman treatment of the brave, athletic, Highland *white sons of Japhet*, but no English or Scottish Duchesses and Ladies took any notice of him, nor convened a meeting to sympathise with him or to remonstrate with Highland despotic slave-making proprietors to discontinue their unrighteous depopulation of the country, and their ungodly draining away of the best blood from the nation. Hence we aver that these ladies would never convene a sympathising meeting for the benighted Africans, should their own African Chiefs, kings, and queens destroy them by the thousand; but because they sell them, and we buy them and take care of them, English feminine hearts sympathise with them. This is a fine opportunity for Donald M'Leod. Let him now speak out, *and make haste*, and we promise him a quick and an extensive sale for his Cabin of unvarnished facts.'

The Duchess of Sutherland got very warm on the subject. After she read the sympathising remonstrating address (which need not be quoted here, being long ago before the public), she with great emphasis said, 'I hope and believe that our efforts, under God's blessing, will not be without some happy result; but whether it will succeed or fail, no one will deny that we shall have made an attempt, which had for its beginning and end, "Glory to God in the highest, on earth, peace and good will to men."' It seems that effrontery is become very lofty and high-voiced under the protection of high-sounding English titles, when the Duchess of Sutherland could presume to mix such notorious hypocritical whinings as these with, 'Glory to God in the highest, on earth peace and good will to men,' for no other cause or design than to whitewash from some public odium already out, or to screen from some that is expected, come from what quarter it may. Surely this cannot be the Duchess of Sutherland who pays a visit every year to Dunrobin Castle, who has seen and heard so many supplicating appeals presented to her husband by the poor fishermen of Golspie, soliciting liberty to take mussels from the Little Ferry Sands to bait their nets—a liberty which they were deprived of by his factors, though paying yearly rent for it; yet returned by his Grace; with the brief deliverance, that he could do nothing for them. Can I believe that this is the same personage who can set out from Dunrobin Castle (her own Highland seat), and after travelling from it, then can ride in one direction over thirty miles, in another direction forty-four miles, in another direction (by taking the necessary circuitous route) sixty miles, and that over fertile glens, valleys, and straths, bursting with fatness, which gave birth to, and where were reared for ages, thousands of the bravest, the most moral, virtuous, and religious men that Europe could boast of; ready to a man, at a moment's warning from their chiefs, to rise in defence of their king, queen, and country; animated with patriotism and love to their chief and irresistable in the battle contest for victory. But these valiant men had then a *country*, a *home*, and a *chief*, worth the fighting for. But I tell her that she can now ride over these extensive tracts in the interior of the country without seeing the image of *God* upon a man travelling these roads, with the exception of a wandering Highland shepherd, wrapped up in a gray plaid to the eyes, with a colly dog behind him as a drill serjeant to train his *ewes* and to marshall his *tups*. There may happen to travel o'er the dreary tract a geologist, a tourist, or a lonely carrier, but these are as rare as a pelican in the wilderness, or a camel's convoy caravan in the deserts of Arabia. Add to this a few English sportsmen, with their stag-hounds, pointer dogs, and their servants, and put themselves and their bravery together, and a company of French soldiers would put ten thousand of them to a disorderly flight to save their own carcasses, leaving their ewes and tups to feed the invaders! The question may arise, where those people, who inhabited this country at one period have gone? In America and Australia the most of them will be found. The Sutherland family and the nation had no need of their services; hence they did not regard their patriotism or loyalty, and disregarded their past services. Sheep, bullock, deer, and game, became more valuable than men. Yet a remnant of them, or in other words a *skeleton* of them is to be found along the sea-shore, huddled together in motley groups upon barren moors, among cliffs and precipices, in the most impoverished, degraded, subjugated, slavish, spiritless condition that human beings could exist in. If this is really the lady who has ' Glory to God in the highest, peace on earth, and good will to men,' in

view, and who is so religiously denouncing the American statute which
'denies the slave the sanctity of marriage, with all its joys, rights, and
obligations—which separates, at the will of the master, the wife from the
husband, the children from the parent,'—I would advise her in *God's
name* to take a tour round the sea-skirts of Sutherland, her own estate,
beginning at Brora, then to Helmsdale, Portskerra, Strathy, Farr, Tongue,
Durness, Eddrachillis, and Assynt, and learn the subjugated, degraded,
impoverished, uneducated, condition of the spiritless people of that sea-
beaten coast, about two hundred miles in length, and let her with similar
zeal remonstrate with her husband, that their condition be bettered; for
the cure for all their misery and want is lying unmolested in the fertile
valleys above, and all under his control; and to advise his Grace, her
husband, to be no longer guided by his Ahithophel, Mr. Loch, but to discontinue his depopulating schemes, which have separated many a wife
from her husband, never to meet—which caused many a premature death,
and that separated many sons and daughters, never to see them; and by
all means to withdraw that mandate of Mr. Loch, which forbids marriage
on the Sutherland estate, under the pains and penalties of being banished
from the county; for it has been already the cause of a great amount of
prostitution, and augmented illegitimate connections and issues fifty per
cent, above what such were a few years ago, before this unnatural, ungodly
law was put in force. When the Duchess will do this, then, and not till
then, will I believe that she is in earnest regarding the American slaves.
Let her and the other ladies who attended the Stafford House meeting be
not like the believers and followers of Jupiter, who were supplied with
two bags each, the one bag representing their own faults, the other their
neighbours' faults—the one representing their neighbours' faults suspended before them, and the one representing their own faults suspended
behind them, so that they could never see their own faults, but their
neighbours' were seen at all times. Ah! ladies, change your Jupiter
bags, that you may discern your inconsistency and connection with those
to whom you owe your position, your grandeur, your greatness, and all
your enjoyments.

I am encroaching too much at this time, and will forbear, but will soon
be at them again.

Yours, &c.,   DONALD M'LEOD.

16 South Richmond Street,
Edinburgh, December 25, 1852.

To the Editor of the Northern Ensign.

Sir,—In dealing with those who convened and attended this meeting, I am not so uncharitable as to include the whole of them under the same denomination; for I am willing to believe that some of them are genuine sympathisers, with generous christian feeling towards their trodden-down, broken-hearted, oppressed fellow-creatures, whether black or white, or whatever nation they belong to, and who have been despoiled of the provision which God in his infinite love and unlimited goodness made, without distinction or respect of titles or personages of the human family, and who became the victims of cruel avarice and boundless ambition. But being unacquainted with them personally, I am not in a position to separate the genuine from the spurious, and must leave them together until they separate themselves, or till some other one higher favored than I am, do it.

No one living would rejoice more earnestly than I would, to see the American slaves, and all slaves liberated; but if they are only to be liberated equally with Highland slaves, and subjected to similar oppression, degradation, and want, I pray to the good Lord to deliver them from such liberation. Being altogether free from personal spleen, and without any other motive in view but pure respect for my country, I request the genuine christian benevolent portion of our ladies, in the name of all that is sacred, if they have a genuine desire for the liberation of the American Slaves, and do not want their chains rivetted tighter, and their slavery prolonged, not to subscribe their names, nor mingle with the Stafford House sophistical mockery of God and men. For the Americans are a proud, discerning people, and when they will see the iniquity of slavery they will abolish it as effectually as they did under the command of immortal Washington abolish English tyranny and slavery among themselves; but they will be neither dogged, dictated to, nor bullied, to abolish it, especially by people who are a hundred-fold more guilty than themselves; whose hands are never but soiled in blood, and who, when they could not maintain or uphold slavery in their own dominions abroad, demanded and obtained for their compliance to abolish it, twenty millions out of the public money in compensation, then turned round upon the industrious producing classes, (who were taxed and peeled, to refund this money, who had fought for them, wrought for them, and paid for all, and told them they had no use for them—laid their land waste, supplanted a portion of the people with bulls, bullocks, cows, sheep, deer, and dogs, others with steel men, or machinery; banished the rest from the coast, with the exception of those they would require to make and attend their machinery, and as many as would allow themselves to be transmitted to animals called soldiers, to keep the rest of the people quiet, or kill them.

But the first question our ladies should ponder well and discuss seriously before they would subscribe this appeal to the American ladies in behalf of the slaves is: How are they prepared to stand the campaign of retaliation under such leaders ?—For I predict they will be put to the blush, and that their affectionate address will soon find its way unceremoniously to a very disrespectful purpose. The Americans are not to be dogged or

cajoled; many of them have sad, sad recollections of the mandates which
used to be "issued" from Stafford House, and from Dunrobin Castle,
dictated and composed by James Loch, Esq., chief commissioner, approved
of by his patron, and executed by their minions: whose names I might
mention; gentlemen, upon the whole, with one or two exceptions, whose
inhumanity and injustice throws the American slave-traders, slave-breeders
and slave-owners, completely into the shade.—Yes, I say mandates, not
announcing for their beginning and end " Glory to God in the highest,
on earth peace, and good will to men;" *no*, woes me! no, but

> Far worse than Egypt's wasting plague,
> Wrought dismal desolation;
> Glens, straths, yea, parishes, at once
> Were swept of population.

Mandates with every line of them announcing schemes for the destruction,
dispersion, and utter ruin of the innocent religious, and patriotic brave
aborigines; laying waste the land provided and appointed by God for their
maintainence, to feed brute beasts (for whose rights to themselves in common with their chieftains, they and their forefathers so often fought and
cemented with their blood), commanding to burn down the habitations
they and their grand-sires occupied for time immemorial per the hundred
year after year, leaving the people houseless and homeless—old and young
weak and strong, sick and hale, without a sanctuary; calumniated in their
moral and religious character, by specially hired emissaries, without an eye
to pity them that could render them any assistance. Mandates pregnant
with confusion, despair, dismay, weeping, wailings, anguish, and bitter
lamentations; separation of the dearest and nearest, never to meet; breaking assunder the most sacred ties of associations, to describe which must
remain incredible to those who have not seen it, beyond description; thank
God with few precedents of parallels in the annuals of ancient or modern
history—yea, in the darkest or most brutal times;—and mandates, indeed
equal in sum and substance to the mandates issued by the Protestant pious
King William, and his secretary Master of Stair, at the instigation of the
Duke of Argyle and Breadalbane, and executed by the infamous Campbell
of Glenlyon, Hamilton, Hill, Duncanson, and Lindsay, purporting the
horrible massacre of the brave loyal McDonalds of Glencoe, which left an
infamous stain upon King William's memory, his Government, and accomplices, that time will not wipe away. And I emphatically tell her Grace
that the evolution of years or of ages will not efface the tragical depopulation of Sutherland, and that the waters of Jordan, and all the fuller's earth
and soap in Europe, will not cleanse from the guilt; and that the time is
bygone when the blood of bullocks, and rams, sheep and deer, would atone
or satisfy Divine justice for guilty deeds, where there was nothing wanting
but the wielding operation of the unsheathed sword (and the same weapon
was threatened and attempted) to make the scene upon a larger scale—a
second Glencoe. Yet, I am perfectly satisfied, if the blood of such animals
would atone, that abundance of it could be procured in Sutherland, and if
money and the influence of priests established by law could procure a

scape-goat, that the second, third or fourth generation would have nothing to fear.

But how can I believe, who was an eye witness to these appalling scenes, without an ample proof, that absolution was diligently sought for from the only source where remission of sins can be obtained, and conversion manifested by visible genuine contrition, demonstrated by a restoration of the undoubted rights of the people of which they were dispoiled—I say, how can I believe that the Duchess of Sutherland, her co-operators, and those who followed the house of Sutherland, or, more properly speaking, Mr. Loch's extirpating example, have a genuine desire to bestow liberties and blessings upon the American slaves, which they so sternly and Malthusian-like deny to their own people, who are more unfortunate, and who have a hundred fold stronger claims upon their sympathy? Monstrous sophistry! The Stafford House meeting is nothing more or less than a revival of Sutherland's deceptive dodges, with which I have been well acquainted for the last forty-five years at least, and of which I will give you a few specimens in my next. At present, for fear of encroaching too much on your liberality, I will conclude by merely telling you that at this moment I am informed that female agents are employed in Edinburgh to procure subscribers to the Stafford House BUBBLE in a clandestine way, not paying so much respect to our Edinburgh ladies as to convene a meeting, and send even one of their female pages to preside, should they consider it below their own station to preside or address our Scottish Ladies. It is evident they could not be favoured by the Duchess of Sutherland, as in all likelihood by this time she is admitted Mistress of the Robes.

Meantime, yours, &c.,

Donald Macleod.

Farewell, Mrs. H. B. Stowe, at present; expecting when your *Delight* upon Dunrobin Castle, or the *Sublimity* of Sutherlandshire (which you visited last year) comes to hand, that I will afford me an extensive scope for animadversion, if I will be spared to see it.

Prince De Ligne, in his amusing memoirs, gives an entertaining account of an imperial visit of Catharine II. to her ultra-Russian dominions in the Crimea. The Tartarian tracts of desolation were as dispeopled as Kildonan and Strathnaver are; but, in timely advance of the august cortege, workmen were employed to construct nice temporary cottages, in which picturesque peasants greeted their sovereign lady as she glided past; and when the monarch was fairly out of sight, the theatrical tenants were ejected, and the make-shift little mansions were tumbled to the ground! Prince Potemkin was the author of this stupendous deception, and Prince De Ligne, who was in the secret, and travelling in the imperial carriage, could hardly refrain from chuckling as they passed through a succession of sham villages. I have been informed by a correspondent who is in the secrets of the Potemkins of Sutherland, that similar preparations were in contemplation, should Her Majesty consent to visit Dunrobin Castle: but the dodge was in reality practised upon you, Madam, with success. A goodly number of cottages for the poor were in the process of building in the neighbourhood of Golspie and not far from the castle, when it was made known that you were to visit Dunrobin. All the carpenters, masons, slaters, painters, and plumbers that could be procured, and that could get room to work, were employed day and night—superintended during the day by her Grace. The furniture of the old castle, and a good deal of furniture borrowed from the sheep farmers and factors, to replenish or furnish these domiciles of the poor in a splendid style, which with the old castle mirrors, carpets, and hair-bottom chairs and sofas, made a very nice and agreeable appearance. These abodes were presented to you as a sample of Sutherlandshire comforts, and I admit it would be the natural conclusion of your mind, if the poor paupers are so well provided for, and so comfortable, surely the condition of the peasantry must be enviable above any condition of people that ever came under my notice. But, says my correspondent, Mrs. Stowe could not be the length of Inverness on her way back, when every stick of this splendid replenishing was returned, and the poor cottages furnished after the order of the other poorhouses: he adds, "however, they are pretty comfortable, if the necessaries of life will correspond with the building, a question to be decided after this." The Potemkins of Sutherland, exultingly chuckling in a suppressed tone —we have dodged the Yankee-ess, have we not? but, poor old lady, she was much easier dodged than we expected. Ah! what glorious praise we may now expect, when her Delight, or Sublimity of Dunrobin Castle, and of our noble family, and of our humane factors and servants, comes out! Good bye, Madam, for the present time.

This leads me again to the operations of the new and disgraceful Poor Law of Scotland, which is without precedent on the Statute book of any Christian civilized nation on earth. Indeed, when pondering over its details, crooks, chicanery and deception, I am tempted to question whether epidemic blindness and hardness of heart have not seized hold of the ruling and influential classes of society ; and it seems as if Providence had de-termined to destroy the baneful system on which the population of the Highlands has so long grown poor and wretched, by destroying the potato crop; in order to arouse the nation from their culpable apathy, regarding the Highland portion of His vineyard, where He was more beloved, more feared, and His statutes more strictly obeyed than any other portion of His creation, by giving this sharp warning of their danger, in tolerating a system pregnant with disastrous results, and cutting deep at the root of national ruin ; you may easily perceive, if all Scotch and English proprie-tors would follow the example of the Highland and Irish Nimrods, what the result would be. Their rights of property conveys the same power to every one of them, to do with their properties what they please, as they do to Highland lairds. In this age of utility we should expect to find the forest ground of Scotland rapidly decreasing, but the reverse is the case. The Highlands is an outer kingdom that moves under different laws of progress from any other portion of Britian. Here the Nimrods of England made a desperate rally. As they have seen their privileges falling

H

off one after another by the blows of public opinion, and their parks and game preserves invaded and ruined by the rise of towns, factories, railways, and other democratic nuisances, the sons of the mighty aristocratic ancestors have cast their eyes to the far North, and by universal reign in that quarter, resolved to make up for all they have lost. Highland proprietors considered that a deer forest was both a necessary and profitable appendage of an estate. If it wanted that it wanted dignity. Hence (according to Mr. Robert Somers, editor of the *North British Mail*, Glasgow, a gentlemen to whom the Highlanders are much indebted) "Deer forests were introduced in much the same spirit as powdered wigs and four-wheeled carriages at the beginning and end of the last century." Now, it is a notorious fact that Highland glens and mountain ranges laid out in forests, is more profitable to a proprietor than when let as a sheep walk, (not speaking of agricultural purposes at all). Not so to the tacksman or to the country, but if it yields more rent to the owner, that one fact is sufficient to decide the disposal of it. The huntsman who wants a deer forest, limits his offers by no other calculation than the extent of his purse. He expects no pecuniary return ; his object is simply to spend his money and to have sport, and if means will allow, and man be capacitated capacious enough, he will out-bid every opponent. But had the Legislature taken care as they should, and have made the rapidly increased rents of the proprietors reponsible for the employment and maintenance of the people, which the system of sheep walks, deer forests and game preserves, deprived of their usual means of livelihood, the Highlanders might not have had occasion to regret the change so much; or if the Legislature did not see fit to retain and secure their clansmen in those rights of tenure which they and their ancestors had possessed for time immemorial, in the same way as the English copyholders were secured in the reign of Charles II, it ought to have vigorously enforced the Poor Law of James VI and supplemented it with a leaf or two from the 43rd of Queen Elizabeth, the true tenor of which was to provide sufficient food, clothing and lodgings, to those among the lieges who are proveably destitute, and who cannot obtain support without public aid. When this law was enforced (in Scotland as I said before) in 1845, the Poor Law Amendment Act was enacted, and the administration of this law entrusted or committed to two sets of men, rather say two Boards, viz., the Board of Supervision and Parochial Board. The Board of Supervision consisted of two able men, (no mistake,) Sir John MacNeil and Mr. Smyth were the responsible parties. The Parochial Boards were composed principally of proprietors, factors, and sheep-farmers, established by-law ministers, doctors, parish schoolmasters, rich merchants, (if favourites of the powers that be) with a very thin mixture from any other denomination, who hold monthly or quarterly meetings, as they think proper, to deliberate and consider who is deserving relief and who is not. (God help the poor for the tender mercies of the wicked are at the best cruel.) When a poor person puts in a claim, the officer of the Board waits upon him to examine his case, and his report is submitted for judgment at the next meeting of the Board ; in most cases the relief is refused, or if granted is so small that it is inadequate to sustain life; in most cases from nine pence to sixpence per week, and often below that sum, especially if there are more than one pauper in the same house. The only course open for the poor supplicant is to demand a schedule to make their cases known to the Board of Supervision, rather say Sir John MacNeil. These schedules are a printed form with a great amount of interrogatories and large blanks left for answers, something like this—

What is your name?

What is your age?

Where were you born?

Have you any children?

About forty questions are asked which must be all answered in writing. The other side of this large sheet is left blank for the Inspector of the Poor to make his answers to the complaint. Yes, (but behold where the secret of iniquity and injustice are concealed which brand the concocters, supporters and enactors of this new Poor Law of Scotland with infamy, and should consign the Law itself to everlasting destruction) when the poor pauper gets his or her side of the schedule made up with answers, then it is handed over to the Inspector, who, in general, is the Factor, Parish Schoolmaster or the Doctor of the District, (who of course must be a creature of the Proprietors and Factors) to make up his side of the schedule, he is at liberty to state the truth or the greatest falsehood imaginable, (one thing evident he must please the Factor or he will not occupy his situation long) he seals up the schedule in a Parochial Poor Board envelope, under the Board's stamp, and hands it to the supplicant to pay it and post it to the Board of Supervision. This is all the liberty and recourse for obtaining justice the British-enacted Poor Law of Scotland left for their paupers, should the supplicant be as poor, moral, upright and honest as Job. The Inspector may represent him or her immoral, intemperate, lazy or thievish, having plenty to eat and drink; for the law enacts that no other evidence can be taken or produced to prove the supplicant's claim; and should the Board of Supervision think proper to reverse the decision of the Parochial Board, what can they do? they can only (by enacted law) recommend the claimant to get relief; they dare not state what amount he is entitled to get; all they can do if the Parochial Board continues obstinate and allow nothing, they can give the claimant a certificate to employ a Solicitor to bring his case before the Supreme Court at Edinburgh, but this is seldom done. I was six years in Edinburgh during the operation of this law, and only one poor case was permitted to pass the Bar of the Board of Supervision all that time. That case was successful in the Court of Session, but carried to the House of Lords, and how it was decided there I have not heard. The fact is that these Boards, the Law, and Highland Proprietors are going hand in hand to demoralize, pauperize and extirpate the race. You have a pointed illustration of this in the following brief account of their co-operation for the consummation of their designs. In the year 1850, Ministers of the Free Church and other dissenting bodies in the Isle of Skye and other districts in the Highlands, forwarded many grievous complaints in behalf of the poor to the Board of Supervision, showing the culpable carelessness and malversation and partiality of the Parochial Board, detailing many extreme cases of poverty and actual death by famine. The public press took up the case, and so urgent were the public requests, that Government ordered Sir John MacNeil and Mr. Smyth to repair to the scene of poverty and fields of famine and death, to make enquiry into the truth of these alarming reports. In a few days they landed among the valleys of famine, death and complaints. These Commissioners of justice and humanity summoned the Parochial Board and the reverend reporters of distress, before them, and enquired where extreme cases of poverty were to be found; being told, they then enjoined upon the parties to accompany them early next morning, at daylight, to examine these cases. So at daylight they started, and they were in the first instance directed to a poor widow's abode. Is this one of the worst cases you have to show? enquired Sir John; being answered in the affirmative, then says he, Mr. Smyth we must see what is within; in they go, the widow with her three fatherless children were in bed. *Holo*, cries Sir John, have you any food in the house? Very little indeed sir, was the reply. Sir John, by this time was searching and opening boxes, where nothing but rags and emptiness was to be found; at last he uncovered a pot where there was about three pounds of cold pottage; Smyth discovered a small bowl or basin of milk. Sir John bawls out with an authoritative tone, holding out the cold pottage in one hand and the basin of milk in the other, "Do you presume, gentlemen, to call this an extreme case of poverty, where so much meat was left after being satisfied at supper?" Some of the party ventured to mutter out, "that is all the poor woman has." "Hush" says Sir John, "she was cunning enough to hide the rest." Sir John's dog made a bolt at the pottage and devoured the most of it; the party left; did not go far when the dog got sick. "That d—n cold pottage has poisoned my valuable dog," says Sir John; the servant was ordered back to the inn to physic the dog. The whole investigation of the day was conducted in a similar manner; only the dog was taken care of, and not allowed among the pots of the perishing people. Next day Sir John summoned the Parochial Board to appear before him, to get instructions for their future proceedings. The Board attended, and Sir John addressed them nearly as follows :—

GENTLEMEN OF THE BOARD—The Government who sent me out, will not compel you to give out more relief than you are giving, until extreme cases of famine are made out. Extreme cases means death by famine; such cases makes you culpable and responsible to the law of the land. Gentlemen, (understand me) who are almost to a man, Ministers of the Gospel, Missionaries, Priests, Sheepfarmers, Factors, Game Keepers, Foresters, Doctors, and Proprietors, to whom the Government look for truth; whose prerogative, by a special Act of Parliament, is to report the cause of death in the Isle of Skye during these clamorous times (understand me), be very careful about making out your reports; how can you prove the death of any one to be caused by want of food without having first a *post mortem* examination of the body by more than one medical man. There are many other distempers and diseases that may linger about people, that may cut away life very quick when a person is in a weak state for want of nourishment, which cannot be attributed to famine. So, be aware of what you are about, for I assure you if you continue to report extreme cases and death by famine, you shall (gentlemen) find yourselves in a sad dilemma when you have to defend yourselves at the bar of a Justiciary Court for culpable homicide.

These instructions and definition of the Scotch new Poor Law Bill enactment were forwarded to every Parochial Board in Scotland, and had the desired effect. We never heard, nor never will hear of an extreme case of death by famine in the Highlands of Scotland. It could not be expected that such *valuable* men as constitutes the Parochial Boards in Scotland, would criminate themselves for the sake of making up a faithful report of the cause of deaths among the unfortunate despised Highlanders. Yet vengeance for all these evils doings, says God, is mine; I am forbearing but not an all-forbearing God.

> "Hence then, and evil go with thee, along
> Thy offspring the place of evil—hell
> Thou and thy wicked crew; there mingle broils
> Ere this avenging sword begin thy doom,
> Or some more sudden vengeance wing'd from God
> Precipitate thee with augmented pains.—*Paradise Lost.*

May we not exclaim in the language of immortal Burns, "Man's inhumanity to man . . ."—and borrow a short paragraph from Shylock, but to change the names, which is quite applicable to the Highland Board, proprietors and their accomplices: "Are we not Highlander: have Highlanders no eyes; have Highlanders no hands, organs, dimensions, senses, affections, passions, and appetites, that should be fed with the same food with you; are Highlanders not hurt with the same weapon, and healed by the same means as you are, warmed and cooled by the same summer and winter as you are? If you prick us, do we not bleed and feel it? If you tickle us, do we not laugh? If you poison and starve us, do we not die? If you persecute us and wrong us, shall we not be revenged? If we are like you in the rest, we will resemble you in that. The villany you have taught us we will execute, and it will go hard with us, or we will better the instructions when our turn of revenge will come." To detail the preconcerted destructive schemes manifested in every chapter of this bill, (which, indeed, we may say, was conceived in sin and brought forth in iniquity;) the malversation of its administration, the fatal effects of its operations, would require more room than I can spare: you will have to be content with the foregoing specimen; and I think it should convince you of the length that the machinations of evil doers in *high places* may go, to rob and punish their fellow creatures, and to make the credulous world believe that all they do is for the good of their victims. Look at a Board of Supervision sitting in secret at Edinburgh, a distance of about 400 miles from some of the most impoverised districts in Scotland, hearing the complaints of the poor only upon schedules, refusing them a right of reply to the allegations of hostile inspectors, and giving no reasons for its decisions, though involving questions of life or death to the poor. The sheriffs of counties were even debarred from giving them justice when deprived of adequate relief. All these precautions were taken lest the poor might have power to impose upon the parochial boards. A grosser misapprehension of the relative position and strength of the two parties could not possibly be acted upon. A Highland pauper is one of the most helpless of mortals: a Highland Poor Board, so far as its jurisdiction extends, is all-powerful, embracing in its ranks the whole wealth and influence of a parish. If the legislature had had any sincere intention of giving the poor a chance of justice against the prejudices of the boards, it would have thought of strengthening instead of weakening their position, but the blunder or the crime. whichever it may be, of 1845, ought now to be atoned for. Let the sheriffs be empowered to review the decisions of the parochial board in respect to the amount of relief; let the old right of appeal, free of let or hindrance, to the Court of Session be restored; let the Board of Supervision itself be made amenable in all its acts to that supreme tribunal to which all classes and bodies of Scotchmen are accustomed to bow in respectful deference; and, in short, let every possible facility be given to the poor of stating their complaints in the courts of justice of having their claims impartially investigated, and of obtaining decisions in accordance with the law, and not with the narrow and illiberal views of bodies which have a palpable interest in depriving the poor of an adequate maintenance. As for the objection that the expense of maintaining the poor would soon consume the entire rental of the Highlands, it has no foundation in fact. The total amount expended on the poor in the four counties of Sutherland, Ross, Inverness, and Argyle, though embracing six months of the severe and universal distress occasioned by the failure of the potato crop, was only £37,618 11s. 7¾d., being scarcely 6½ per cent. of the valued rent. This sum may be considerably increased, without exceeding the rate of assessment in many parts of the country in ordinary years. But even supposing that the expenditure on the poor should rise to a height extremely inconvenient to the proprietors, I do not perceive that this would be disastrous. The proprietors have the means of correcting this evil in their own hands. There is no country on earth where the duty of children to support their aged and disabled parents, and the ties of kindred generally, are more profoundly respected than in the Highlands. As long as a Highlandman has a bite and a sup he shares it with an aged father or mother. It is only when reduced to poverty himself that he allows any of his near kindred to claim the benefit of the poor's roll. The policy of the Highland lairds for many years has been to deprive the able-bodied of their holdings of land, to reduce them to the verge of destitution, and compel them, if possible to emigrate. The direct tendency of these measures has been to increase the number of the aged and infirm dependent upon parochial relief. The proprietors have only to reverse their policy, to keep the able-bodied at home, to lay open the soil to their industry, and to promote their industry, their comfort and independance, in order to reduce the burden of the aged and disabled poor. This is the safety-valve of a liberal and effectual Poor Law. While it would protect the poor from starvation and suffering, it would constrain the owners of property, by the bonds of self-interest, to consult the happiness of the people, to strive for their employment, and to introduce that new division and management of the soil which lie at the foundation of permanent improvement. The same considerations which induced the proprietors would dispose the sheep-farmers to submit to the new order of things. Farewell to the Poor Law at present.

Bad and inadequate as the relief for the poor was, there were still more inconsistent and imbecile schemes tried, and propositions were made to relieve them: such as the Patriotic Society schemes, headed by the Duke of Sutherland, and the most notorious portion of his co-depopulators in the Highlands, which brougut me out in the following letter to the *Northern Ensign*, when the emigration of the Highlanders to the waste bogs of Ireland and Wales, and the Russian war opened a field for me. I am sorry that I cannot refrain from repetitions, as I had to contend with so many deceivers of my countrymen and of the public, almost single-handed, and had often to use the same arguments with them, so you must excuse me for repetitions. This Patriotic Society employed a sneaking scoundrel to bring their scheme of relief of the Highlanders before the public, which, as may be seen at a glance, was a scheme to plunder the credulous public. After his first tour in the Highlands, on his return he had the effrontery to advertise a public meeting in the Waterloo Rooms, Edinburgh, to give an account of success in the Highlands. I had an opportunity to confront him, face to face, at this meeting, and I assure you it was not much in his favour I did meet him: he had good cause to understand that his knavery was dismantled before we parted.

To the Editor of the Northern Ensign.

Sir,—How proud I would be, and what pleasure it would afford me, if I could but give vent to my feelings of gratitude towards you, for your manly, timely and practical interposition in behalf of my ill-used, mis-represented and long-neglected countrymen, at a time when all other philanthropists who have exerted themselves in their behalf as yet seem to content themselves with merely suggesting plans and remedies, which will take years before they can bring relief ; and, alas, after thousands of the Highlanders will after the most agonizing sufferings, drop into a premature grave. Look, for instance, at Mr. Bond, Secretary for the Royal Patriotic Association, (under the patronage of the Duke of Sutherland, his commis-sioner, Mr. Loch, and others,) travelling in the Highlands, with about half a cwt. of cottage models on his back, going from one duke's palace to another, from one marquis to another, from one factor to another, from one grade of proprietors and other underlings to another, including ministers, schoolmasters, sheriffs, and fiscals, collecting information about Highland destitution, and the cause of it, and consulting them upon the best scheme to remedy the evil. Yes, consulting men whose predecessors and them-selves have been steeping and racking their brains for the last half century, contriving how to destroy and extirpate the Highland peasantry from the land of their fathers, and reduce them to their present deplorable condition

—men, I emphatically say, that instead of being consulted, should be arraigned at the bar of public justice, dealt with as traitors, and their property confiscated, for they of verity destroyed and trod under foot the best portion of the national bulwork. But this assuming Mr. Bond comes before the public so ostentatiously, just as if men could believe his information, or be assured that the plans he and the oppressors of the people had devised could save their victims from perishing or bettering their condition in future.

During Mr. Bond's perambulations in the Highlands, he had to travel over extensive tracts of fine lands and fertile glens, bursting with fatness and teeming with everything that is necessary to make the people comfortable and independent of charity, but locked up from them, and lying a solitary waste, or under brute beasts, where no sweeter strains are heard than the screeches of the night owl, or the barking of the collie dogs, and the image of *God* upon man dare not approach the spot. This Mr. Bond did see, though often gliding smoothly over these tracts, shut up snugly (*with his models*) in the laird's coach, or in the Commissioner's dog cart. But then comes Mr. Bond upon the portion of the Highlands allotted to the people, viz., the creeks, precipices, bogs, barren moors and bye-corners, places found both dangerous and unprofitable to rear sheep and bullocks, in most cases dangerous for deer and goats to approach, and never designed by the *God of Nature* for cultivation or the abode of human beings. Here he found them in clusters and motley groups, where they were huddled together after being expelled from their fertile valleys, and without leases or encouragement to improve, should it be possible to do so. If I am not mistaken, (*for I don't hear well,*) Mr Bond admitted at a public meeting in Edinburgh, that he had seen some of the people tearing or cultivating moss which was as tough as India rubber, and as unsusceptible of rearing human food as gutta percha; that the seed they sowed in the evening was wholly eaten up by birds before morning, as nothing could be torn out of the spongy moss to cover the seed, though *he himself were to try on the harrow.* Mr. Bond found the people without food, money or clothing; they were dirty, starving looking creatures; they were living in turf hovels, (houses he could not call them) The lords of the soil complained that the wretches would neither *pay rent* nor go away; that all their means were nearly eaten up with poor rates; and that they were alarmed out of measure, as the case and cries of the poor wretches had already reached the ears of Government, and that an able-bodied poor law was likely to be the result. Besides, Dr. Begg, of Edinburgh, had bestirred the Free Church ministers and other influential bodies in behalf of these miserable-looking wretches, and the public are becoming very indignant at being called upon year after year for subscriptions to keep them alive, even though it is the desire of the Highland landlords that they were all *dead* or *banished.* Oh! exclaimed Mr. Bond, I see what will remedy the whole evil. These dirty, unshapely, and uncomfortable turf hovels must be changed to cleanly stone-built cottages, of which this is a model, and if our Association can procure money from the Government, or from the public, and that you, gentlemen, will grant sites, we

will undertake the building. This suggestion met at once the approbation
of Highland Dukes, Lords and Commons, cunning enough to know as well
as I do, (however utopian the suggestion was) that if the public, through
the high-sounding names connected with this society, could be gulled to
join it and subscribe to its funds, and Government to grant a large sum of
the public money, and the Royal Patriotic Society to build houses with it,
I say they knew it was a scheme which would at least take a hundred
years in its operation, and then vanish like a burst bottle of smoke. But
the houses would be found useful to the proprietors, for the dwellings of
shepherds and dogs, or, as some churches in the Highlands just now, for
sheltering sheep during stormy nights, or for wool stores, and *manses* for
the abodes of gamekeepers, fox-hunters and foresters. Let the public and
Government be guarded against such futile sophistry and preconcerted
machinations, and let me tell them that it is not neat cottages that the
Highlanders now need to redeem them from their miserably pauperised
condition, or to better their condition in future, and elevate their position
in society. It is *the land* the Highlanders would require, yes, the land
now under beasts; and unless they get that, it is in vain to suggest or
devise remedies; they will ultimately perish unless they become State
paupers. But if they get the land which God designed for cultivation,
they will soon cease to be objects of commisseration, and they will pay
rents and become independant of charity. Then let them build such
houses as will suit themselves, whether of mud, turf or stones. Many a
brave Highlander was reared in a turf house, whose intrepidity and valor
gained many victories and immortal fame and praise to the nation which
has callously, cruelly, and carelessly allowed a few despotic minions to
reduce the progeny of the heroes of Bannockburn, Sheriffmuir, Killie-
crankie, Prestonpans, Fontenoy, Egypt, Corunna, Salamanca, Vittoria,
and Waterloo, to their present deplorably destitute condition, a by-word
and an eye-sore to the nation, which often had cause to be proud of them
in many a battlefield, and would be proud of them still more if they had
but half fair play.

Contrast the present race of Highlands with those of forty-five, who,
when only a few clans of them joined together, *shook* this empire to its
very centre, and were within a very little of placing the crown of England
upon the *head* of one who (with all his faults,) would not see nor hear of a
Highlander dying for want of food while there would be a bullock, deer,
ram, sheep, or lamb living in the land, not speaking of allowing thousands
of acres of fertile land in his dominions to lie waste to feed such animals—
and after you compare them, (without any reference to the cause in which
our predecessors were engaged,) ask what is the cause, and who were, and
are to be blamed for such fearful deterioration of everything that was
recommendable or characteristic of our forefathers? Mr. Bond and his
patrons will reply, the Highlanders are exceedingly lazy—yes, lazy, they
will not make bricks without straw. I am encroaching too much on your
liberality ; perhaps I will recur to the subject again. Hoping the Government and the nation will respond to the voice of heaven, that the High-

landers will be saved from dying for want of food, and this nation from a stain on their profession of Christianity that ages will not wipe off.

I am, &c.,

DONALD M'LEOD.

16, S. Richmond St.,
Edinburgh, February 4, 1851.

The emigration of the Highlanders to the wastes of Ireland, and to send them Gælic Bibles and Psalm Books to supply the spiritual famine then discovered among the dying people, brought me out in the following :—

To the Editor of the Northern Ensign.

Sir,—Though I confess my inability to ascertain the exact amount of money expended to meet the spiritual and temporal destitution of the Highland population, by preaching and teaching the Protestant Christian religion, and promoting British civilization in the Highlands and Islands of Scotland, yet I am confident that any one who could ascertain the amount, would be ready to conclude that the Highlanders should be the most religious, the most enlightened, the most civilized, and the most comfortable people under the canopy of heaven. In my opinion, the amount cannot be less, or not more, than three millions sterling. To prevent such conclusions, I am resolved in my old simple style to prove to you and your readers, that it had been well for the Highlanders if they had never seen a farthing of the immense sum, and that the progress of civilization and religion were left to Heaven and their own exertions. This will be easier credited, when we candidly and impartially compare the present state of religion, comfort and civilization in the Highlands, with that which existed about fifty years ago, or before one farthing of these enormous sums was expended to improve either. Besides, I am at no loss to prove to your satisfaction, that the principal contributors to those societies who squandered the money, were the chief plunderers of the people; hence, that it was neither for the glory of God nor the elevation of the Highlanders that the money was contributed and expended. Bestowing charity in all ages has had the most effectual tendency to make beggars. Only think of men in power depriving their subjects of their corn fields and of every means of their subsistence, then to cloak their unrighteous doings would subscribe liberally that the poor would receive Gælic Bibles and Psalm Books in lieu of their plunder.

I am now advanced in years, and have a pretty correct recollection of passing events and of the movements of society for the last fifty years. At that period, and down to the period at which the calamities accompanying the clearing system overtook us, and before we came under the Loch iron rod of oppression, and drank of that bitter cup of many withering ingredients which accompanied that ever cursed and condemned by God system, I say that we lived what might be termed a happy life, when

compared with the present. Some years our corn crops would fail, but
we had cattle which we could sell, and purchase food with the price of
them ; we had sheep and goats which we could take and eat ; we had
salmon and trout for the taking ; we had abundance of milk, butter and
cheese ; and none of us ever died by famine. To the stranger every door
was open ; to the lame, needy, and poor every hand was stretched with
relief ; to the sick and afflicted every breast was full of sympathy. Sabbath desecration, profane swearing, drunkenness, disobedience to parents,
immorality of every description, in short, every violation of the laws of
God and rules of society, was considered as a heinous crime, and not
allowed to pass with impunity. I may add, without fear of refutation,
that there was not exceeding four families in the county of Sutherland
but who worshipped God morning and evening in their respective families.
Weekly, monthly, and yearly prayer meetings were held in every district.
The pulpits of our respective parish churches were occupied by ministers
worthy of their vocation, who were making themselves well acquainted
with their flocks by visiting them often, besides having *Men* known for
their piety and exemplary virtues, (chosen by the people), appointed to
examine, instruct, admonish, and reprove, when required. There was no
need for fiscal, constables, thief-catchers, or policemen to keep us quiet
and protect property; till of late years these hateful names were not known
in the Gælic language. Now, this is a brief sketch of the state of religion
and civilization in the beginning of this century. Query, what is it now ?
Yet, though these are stubborn facts which challenge refutation, I am
aware, while I confine my observations to Highland character and Highlanders among these secluded glens, romantic mountains, and cascades,
for many years their religion and moral virtues have become an easy prey
to every vile calumniator, theologian and historian, down from M'Culloch
and Loch of Sutherland, to the *Scotsman* and your own contemporary at
the Bridgend ; so that I am unprotected from the literary scourges of
Highland happiness, civilization, and religion. Hence I must extend my
remarks to a period when the Sutherland Highlanders were embodied, and
came before the world in such a position that their character could neither
be concealed nor villified with impunity, and we will hear what competent
impartial judges said of them, among other Highland regiments. General
Stewart of Garth, in his 'Sketches of the Highlands,' says : In the words
of a general officer by whom the 93d Sutherlanders were once reviewed,
" They exhibit a perfect pattern of military discipline and moral rectitude.
In the case of such men disgraceful punishment would be as unnecessary
as it would be pernicious." ' Indeed,' says the general ' so remote was the
idea of such a measure in regard to them, that when punishments were to
be inflicted on others, and the troop in garrison assembled to witness their
execution, the presence of the Sutherland Highlanders was dispensed with,
the effects of terror as a check to crime being in their case uncalled for,
as examples of that nature were not necesssary for such honourable soldiers.
When the Sutherland Highlanders were stationed at the Cape of Good
Hope, anxious to enjoy the advantage of religious instruction agreeably to
the tenets of their national church, and there being no religious service in

the garrison except the customary one of reading prayers to the soldiers on parade, the Sutherland men,' says the general, 'formed themselves into a congregation, appointed elders of their own number, engaged and paid a stipend (collected among themselves) to a clergyman of the Church of Scotland, and had divine service performed agreeable to the ritual of the Established Church every Sabbath, and prayer meetings through the week.' This reverend gentleman, Mr. Thom, in a letter which appeared in the *Christian Herald* of October 1814, writes thus: 'When the 93rd Highlanders left Cape Town last month, there were among them 156 members of the church, including three elders and three deacons, all of whom, so far as men can know the heart from the life, were pious men. The regiment was certainly a pattern of morality, and good behaviour to all other corps. They read their Bibles and observed the Sabbath. They saved their money to do good. 7,000 rix dollars, a sum equal to £1,200 sterling, the non-commissioned officers and privates saved for books, societies, and for the spread of the Gospel, a sum unparalleled in any other corps in the world, given in the short space of eighteen months. Their example had a general good effect on both the colonists and the heathen. If ever apostolic days were revived in modern times on earth, I certainly believe some of those to have been granted to us in Africa.' Another letter of a similar kind, addressed to the Committee of the Edinburgh Gaelic School Society (fourth annual report), says: 'The 93d Highlanders arrived in England, when they immediately received orders to proceed to North America; but, before they re-embarked, the sum collected for your society was made up and remitted to your treasurer, amounting to seventy-eight pounds sterling.' 'In addition to this,' says the noble minded immortal General, 'such of them as had parents and friends in Sutherland did not forget their destitute condition, occasioned by the operation of the (*fire and faggot*) "*mis*-improved state of the country." During the short period the regiment was quartered at Plymouth, upwards of £500 was lodged in one banking-house, to be remitted to Sutherland, exclusive of many sums sent through the Post-office and by officers; some of the sums exceeding £20 from an individual soldier. Men like these do credit to the peasantry of a country. 'It must appear strange, and somewhat inconsistent,' continues the general, 'when, the same men who are so loud in their profession of an eager desire to promote and preserve the religious and moral virtues of the people, should so frequently take the lead in removing them from where they imbibed principles which have attracted the notice of Europe, and of measures which lead to a deterioration, placing families on patches of potato ground as in Ireland, a system pregnant with degradation, poverty, and disaffection.' It is only when parents and heads of families in the Highlands are moral, happy, and contented, that they can instil sound principles into their children, who in their intercourse with the world may become what the men of Sutherland have already been, "an honourable example worthy the imitation of all."

I cannot help being grieved at my unavoidable abbreviation of these heart-stirring and heart-warming extracts, which should ornament every mantle-piece and library in the Highlands of Scotland; but I could refer to other authors of similar weight; among the last, (though not the least), Mr. Hugh Miller of the *Witness*, in his 'Sutherland as it was, and is: or, How a country can be ruined;' a work which should silence and put to shame every vile, malignant, calumniator of Highland religion and moral virtue in bygone years, who in their sophistical profession of a desire to promote the temporal and spiritual welfare of the people, had their own sordid cupidity and aggrandisement in view in all their unworthy lucubrations, (as I will endeavour to show at a future period.) Come then, ye perfidious declaimers and denouncers; you literary scourges of Highland happiness, under whatever garb, whether political economist or *theology mongers*, answer for yourselves—What good have you achieved, after expending such enormous sums of money? Is it possible that the world will believe you, or put confidence in you any longer? Before I am done with you, come, you professing preachers of the everlasting gospel of peace and of good will to men, stand alongside and on the same platform with the Highland Destitution Relief Board, exhibited before *God* and the world, and accused of misapplying and squandering away an enormous amount of money, and of having in your league, and combination with political economists—treacherous professing civilizers and improvers of the Highlands and Highland population,—produced the most truly deplorable results that ever were recorded in the history of any nation, the utter ruin and destruction of as brave, moral, religious, loyal, and patriotic a race of men as ever existed. Spiritual and temporal destitution in the Highlands has been a profitable field for you these many years back. Many a scheme have you tried (hitherto successful) to extract money from the pockets of the credulous benevolent public, who unfortunately believed your fabulous accusation and misrepresentation of the Highlanders, and who confided in your honesty; and although you, yourselves, may see; the public, yea, and he that runneth may see, that the *Lord* (not without a cause) has discountenanced you, still you continue your appeals to the public, that your traffic may continue likewise; appeals from respectable quarters have lately been made for Gaelic teachers, Gaelic bibles, and psalm books, and tracts, for the poor Highlanders, who are dying for want of food; depend upon it that there is a squad of students out of employment, and a great deal of these books unsold somewhere, that must be turned to money. We have now an association forming in Edinburgh, got up by men from whom better things should be expected, who have for their object to export these dying, penniless Highlanders to Ireland, to mix location with the poor Irish—who have gone through many a fiery ordeal for the last sixty years—that the wastes of Ireland may be reclaimed from nature, and cultivated by Highlanders; just as if there was no waste land in the Highlands and Islands of Scotland to reclaim and cultivate; or, as if there was something *devilish* or unnatural in the Highland soil, and detrimental to the progress of its inhabitants. Perhaps they have in view to have the Highlanders trained in the school and discipline of that *great* and useful lady (to the fiscal department) *Molly M'Guire*, to partake of her uncouth freaks. Very likely the next speculative experiment will be the exportation of Highlanders to Wales, to learn the humoursome freaks of *Rebekah*, since all the ingenuity of evildoers, evil teachers, the effects of famine, oppression, and false accusation, have been baffled to make them *murder*, *rob*, *steal*, or destroy property, while on the (stubborn and unproductive of crime) Highland soil.

You, benevolent public, *pause*, for a little while, till I have time to explain myself better, and draw the curtain of the stage of devices, chicanery, and deception, and be no longer the abettors and accomplices of Highland depopulators—the legitimate parents of Highland calamities.

Britain will some day bewail the loss of her Highland sons, Highland bravery, loyalty, patriotism and Highland virtue. May God hasten the day, that I may live to see it.

Meantime, yours, &c.,
DONALD M‘LEOD.

[NOTE,—Molly McGuire was Chief Judge of what was termed the Lynch Law of Ireland. When a evictor or a man used intrigues to supplant any of Molly's society, he was at once summoned to her bar, to be judged by Molly, yet the man did not know where to attend, being a secret court; yet the case would go on and Molly would employ a counsel to defend the accused, where I am told every facility was afforded him and rewarded provided he could exonerate the accused; otherwise there was nothing for him. If the accused was found innocent he got notice to that effect, that he had nothing to fear; but if found guilty he was next day warned to leave the country or prepare for eternity, that upon a certain day and hour he was to be dispatched by order of Molly M‘Guire, which orders were in general punctually executed. Again, when farmers raised the price of butcher's meat so high that her disciples could not buy it, Molly (in order to keep the meat market down at a reasonable price) would order so many of her subjects to proceed to the town or district where such high prices were wrung from the poor people to (what they termed) houghing all the fat cattle and sheep in the district, so as to compel them to sell cheap. Yet we have writers of no small reputation maintaining that "however diabolical Molly M‘Guire's laws, rules, and operations were, still there was more humanity and justice discerned than in the new Poor Law of Scotland." Rebekah was the leader of the Toll breakers in Wales, South of England, some few years ago, but solely on account of being English, Rebekah and her children claimed redress for their grievances, and the offensive Tolls were removed.]

To the Editor of the Northern Ensign.

SIR,—If in my last I have suceeded in making out a claim upon the sympathy and interposition of the nation, in behalf of my unfortunate countrymen, where is the Christian heart so void of sympathy as not to *throb heavily*, or the eye so void of pity as not to shed a bitter tear over the lamentable fate of this peaceable, inoffensive, and once brave people? Or where is the Christian heart that is not full of indignation, or the eye that will not look with abhorrence, upon the criminal men who are the legitimate parents and sole cause of all the sufferings and premature agonizing death to which the Highland population are doomed? Napoleon Bonaparte, at one period of his horrible career in Turkey, ordered four hundred Musselmen whom he had taken prisoners, to be shot, because he could not provide them with food, and to let them go free he would not, and he saw that they would die by famine—hence mercy dictated that they would be formed into a solid square, and 2,000 French muskets loaded with ball cartridges levelled at them, which was done, and this disarmed mournful square mass of human beings were quickly put out of pain. All the Christian nations of Europe were horrified, and every breast was full of indignation at the perpetrator of this horrible tragedy, and France wept bitterly for the manner in which the tender mercies of their wicked Emperor were exhibited. Ah! but guilty Christian, your Protestant law-making Britain, *tremble* when you look towards the great day of retribution. Under the protection of your law, Colonel Gordon has consigned 1,500 m n, women, and innocent children, to a death a hundred fold more agonising and horrifying. With the sanction of your law he (Colonel Gordon) and his predecessors, in imitation of His Grace the Duke of Sutherland and his predecessors, removed the people from the land created by *God*, suitable for cultivation, and for the use of man, and put it under brute animals; and threw the people upon bye-corners, precipices, and barren moors, there exacting exorbitant rack-rents, until the people were made penniless, so that they could neither leave the place nor better their condition in it. The potato-blight blasted their last hopes of retaining life upon the unproductive patches—hence they became clamourous for food. Their distress was made known through the public press; public meetings were held, and it was managed by some *known knaves* to saddle the *God* of providence with the whole misery—a job in which many of God's professing and well-paid servants took a very active part. The generous public responded; immense sums of money were placed in the hands of Government agents and other individuals, to save the people from death by famine on the British soil. Colonel Gordon and his worthy allies were silent contributors, though terrified. The gallant gentleman solicited Government through the Home Secretary to purchase the Island of Barra for a penal colony, but it would not suit; yet our humane Government sympathised with the Colonel and his coadjutors, and consulted the honourable and brave M'Neil, the chief pauper gauger of Scotland, upon the most effective and speediest scheme to relieve the *gallant* Colonel and colleagues from this clamour and eyesore, as well as to save their pockets from able-bodied poor rates. The result was, that a liberal grant from the public money, which had been granted a twelvemonth before for the purpose of improving and cultivating the Highlands, was made to Highland proprietors to assist them to drain the nation of its best blood, and to banish the Highlanders across the Atlantic, there to die by famine among strangers in the frozen regions of Canada, far from British sympathy, and far from the resting-place of their brave ancestors; though the idea of mingling with kindred dust to the Highlanders is a consolation at death, more than any other race of people I have known or read of under heaven. Oh! Christian people, Christian people, Christian fathers and mothers, who are living at ease, and never experienced such treatment and concomitant sufferings; you Christian rulers, Christian electors, and representatives, permit not Christianity to blush and hide her face with shame before heathenism and idol-

atry any longer. I speak with reverence when I say, permit not Mahomet
Ali to deride *our Saviour* with the conduct of his followers—allow not
demons to exclaim in the face of Heaven, What can you expect of us when
Christians, thy chosen people, are guilty of such deeds of inhumanity to
their own species? I appeal to your feelings, to your respect for Christianity and the cause of Christ in the world, that christianity may be redeemed from the derision of infidels, Mahommedans, idolaters, and demons
—that our beloved Queen and constitutional laws may not be any longer a
laughing stock and derision to the despots of the Continent, who can justly
say: You interefere with us in our dealings with our people; but look at
your cruel conduct toward your own. Ye hypocrites, first cast out the
beam out of your own eye, before you meddle with the mote in ours. Come,
then, for the sake of neglected humanity and *prostrated Christianity,* and
look at this helpless unfortunate people—place yourselves for a moment in
their hopeless position at their embarkation, decoyed, in the name of the
British Government, by false promises of assistance, to procure homes and
comforts in Canada, which were denied to them at home—decoyed, I say,
to an unwilling and partial consent, and those who resisted or recoiled
from this conditional consent, and who fled to the *caves* and *mountains* to
hide themselves from the brigands, look at them, chased and caught by
policemen, constables, and other underlings of Colonel Gordon, handcuffed,
it is said, and huddled together with the rest on an emigrant vessel. Hear
the sobbing, sighing, and throbbings of their guileless, warm *Highland
hearts,* taking their last look, and bidding a final adieu to their romantic
mountains and valleys, the fertile straths, dales, and glens, which their
forefathers for time immemorial inhabited, and where they are now lying
in undisturbed and everlasting repose, in spots endeared and sacred to the
memory of their unfortunate offspring, who must now bid a mournful farewell to their early associations, which were as dear and as sacred to them
as their very existence, and which had hitherto made them patient in sufferings. But follow them on their six weeks' dreary passage, rolling upon
the mountainous billows of the Atlantic, ill fed, ill clad, among sickness,
disease and excrements. Then come ashore with them, where death is in
store for them—hear the captain giving orders to discharge the cargo of
live-stock—see the confusion, hear the noise, the bitter weeping and bustle—hear mothers and children asking fathers and husbands, where are we
going? hear the reply, *cha 'n 'eil fhios againn*—we know not—see them in
groups in search of the Government agent, who they were told was to give
them money—look at their despairing countenances when they came to
learn that no agent in Canada was authorised to give them a penny—hear
them praying the Captain to bring them back that they might die among
their native hills, that their ashes might mingle with those of their forefathers—hear this request refused, and the poor helpless wanderers bidding
adieu to the captain and crew, who showed them all the kindness they
could, and to the vessel to which they formed something like an attachment during the voyage—look at them scantly clothed, destitute of food,
without implements of husbandry, consigned to their fate, carrying their
children on their backs, begging as they crawl along in a strange land, un-

qualified to beg or buy their food for want of English, until the slow-moving and mournful company reach Toronto and Hamilton in Upper Canada, where, according to all accounts, they spread themselves over their respective burying-places, where *famine* and *frost-bitten* death was waiting them. Mothers in Christian Britain, look, I say, at these Highland mothers who conceived and gave birth, and who are equally as fond of their offspring as you can be ; look at them by this time, wrapping their frozen remains in rags and committing them to a frozen hole—fathers, mothers, sons, and daughters, participants of similar sufferings and death, and the living who are seeking for death (yet death fleeing from them for a time) performing a similar painful duty. This is a painful picture ; the English language fails to supply me with words to describe it : I wish the spectrum would depart from me to those who could describe it and tell the result. But how can Colonel Gordon, the Duke of Sutherland, James Loch, Lord Macdonald, and others of the unhallowed league and abettors, after looking at this sight, remain in Christian communion, ruling elders in Christian churches, and partake of the *emblems* of Christ's broken body and shed blood ? But the great question is, can we as a nation be guiltless, and allow so many of our fellow creatures to be treated in such a manner, and not exert ourselves to put a stop to it and punish the perpetrators? Is ambition which attempted to *dethrone God*, become omnipotent, or so powerful when *incarnated* in the shape of Highland dukes, lords, esquires, colonels, and knights, that we must needs submit to its revolting deeds? Are parchment rights of property so sacred that thousands of human beings must be sacrificed year after year, till there is no end of them, to preserve them inviolated? Are sheep walks, deer forests, hunting parks, and game preserves, so beneficial to the nation that the Highlands must be converted into a hunting desert, and the aborigines banished and murdered ? I know that thousands will answer in the negative ; yet they will fold their arms in criminal apathy until the extirpation and destruction of my race will be completed. Fearful is the catalogue of those who have already become the victims of the cursed clearing system in the Highlands, by famine, fire, drowning, banishment, vice, and crime. What is to be done, and how to proceed, will be the subject of my next—expecting the co-operation of the advocates and sympathisers of suffering humanity.

I am, meantime, yours, &c.,

DONALD M'LEOD.

16, South Richmond St., Edinburgh.

To the Editor of the Northern Ensign.

SIR,—There is assuredly no lawful day to which I look forward with such intense interest as Friday, being the day (if favourable) on which the *Ensign* crosses the tempestuous Pentland Firth. It is generally the bearer of something new, and very often brings tidings of importance to me from the once happy home of my youth, a home which nothing but death can ever sever from my remembrance.

I

The *Ensign* is not only the bearer of something new, something cheering, something teeming with acts of Christian charity and benevolence, but, I am sorry to say, it also brings intelligence mournful, deplorable. and inhuman. Who has perused its columns for the last year, and does not feel within his breast the deepest sympathy for the sick and the dying, the helpless and the destitute, the hoary locks and the furrowed cheek, yea, the aged, the friendless, and the infirm, with one foot in the grave and another upon its brink, driven by cold-hearted lordlings to seek for shelter and beg a morsel of bread in foreign wilds? Certainly few, indeed! How awful is the idea to the cherisher of his native plains, which are still as dear to him as life, to be driven far, far away from the land of his forefathers, the sepulchres, of those whose dust, although now covered with the green sward, and it may be trodden upon by some coveteous man's favourite quadrupeds, is deposited there as a momento of a glorious resurrection to the departed in Christ, and a coming judgment to the oppressors of the widow and the fatherless! The pages of the *Ensign* inform us in rending language, piercing to the inmost core, that—

'Man's inhumanity to man,
Makes countless thousands mourn.'

Is it possible that man, a being of a few years existence, and perhaps only days, every moment a dependant upon God for the air he breathes, the food he eats, and the raiment he puts on, can, with the impartial sword of death unsheathed to strike him down as a tyrant and a cumberer of the ground, spend so many sleepless nights devising schemes, the result of which sinks him as low as were he the companion of the lion, the tiger, or the hyena? Can he, as a being possessed of an immortal soul, primitively formed in the moral image of God, and destined for eternity, look around him upon the cottages of his less temporally favoured and humbler fellow mortals, from whence, at morning, night, and noon-day, have arisen to the throne of God on high the sacred song and pious prayer, and yet deliberately scatter before the four winds of heaven from off his bit of idolised soil those beings whose actions in the sight of heaven are more acceptable than his? Yes; such hearts as are deceitful above all things and desperately wicked can do these and more:

'Unmindful, though a weeping wife
And helpless offspring mourn!'

Strange as it is, that such a being as man, exposed to numberless calamities, coming naked into the world, and who at last must return to the ground from whence he was taken, to become the companion and food of worms, can, during a few and uncertain years, be guilty of glaring harassings and inhuman treatment to his fellow men, as if his present little brief authority, his few perishing pence, and the gay clothing which so pompously adorns his polluted clay, were to be his companions through eternity. Strange, indeed, thus to act, with a coming judgment and an endless eternity before him, either to spend a glorious immortality in the beatific mansions of the eternal, or wretchedness and woe with the devil and his angels. Are pride and oppression the highways to the latter?

So says the Word of God. Then, ostentatious and puny tyrants, grieve no more the Holy Spirit of your Judge. Death, that matchless marksman, is hovering over you, from whose icy grasp, the potency of your wealth, with all its self-destroying allurements, will not be able to rescue you. The bar of God is before you, and there assuredly you must stand and receive a sentence conformable to your actions done here below ; and then eternity will receive you into its everlasting embrace, and as the tree falleth so shall it lie. Why, then my fellow worm, with theses awful realities before you, do you oppress and grind the face of the poor? Remember Lazarus and the rich man. With you, as well as the beggar who begs at your door a morsel of bread, from which you too often spurn him as abject, mean, and vile, a few square yards of your depopulated domains will *only* be your share in the 'narrow house', over which, in a few years hence, sheep and cattle may graze.

I am, Sir, yours &c.,   D. M'LEOD.

The following is from the pen of a man of affluence, and an independent, patriotic, Scotch Lowlander, who has travelled in the Highlands for to obtain personal knowledge of what was going on there, and whose sympathy for the oppressed Highlanders often *graced* the pages of the Scotch public press :—

To the Editor of the Scottish Herald.

Sir,—An unaccountable apathy has come over the press this some time past regarding Highland affairs. Twelve months ago the nation was made to ring with indignant exclamations at the oppressions and privations under which our Celtic countrymen have been long groaning ; but *now* there is as little said on the subject, as if the people on whose behalf so much had been written were living in perfect tranquility, and had nothing to complain of. This, however, is not the case. The grievances of the Gael still remain unredressed. They still continue to live, steeped in the same poverty and degradation which have been their lot since they were burned out of their ancient habitations in the valleys, and planted like sea fowls on the outskirts of their country. While a Highlander is left to shiver out a miserable existence on that dismal, sea-begirt locality which he has been compelled to exchange for his once comfortable inland farm—while one glen remains unoccupied, capable of affording adequate shelter and nourishment to him, the public ought not to be satisfied, and the press betrays its trust by remaining silent.

I have been led into these remarks in consequence of accidentally perusing an admirable work on the state of the Highlands, published in 1785 by Mr. John Knox, a man celebrated for his patriotism and enlightened philanthropy. About the period Mr. Knox wrote his book, the depopulating projects of the Highland lairds were in full operation, and this warmhearted individual resolved, if possible, to avert the ruin he saw impending over his country. He accordingly travelled alone through the glens and mountains of the north on horseback, with the view of convincing the chieftains of the cruelty and error of their conduct towards their unoffending clansmen, and devising schemes for the immediate relief and perma-

nent elevation of those unhappy sons of toil; and since Mr. Knox's day
no author that I am aware of has written so powerfully on the distress of
the Highlanders, or displayed so minute and accurate a knowledge of the
remedies best adapted for their condition. True, Mr. Knox was no flat-
terer of the great, no visionary dreamer. He did not, as is the modern
custom, go to the Highlands to calumniate the natives, to represent them
as drones and cumberers of the ground, in order to minister to the designs
of a few rapacious capitalists and hard-hearted landowners; no, he went
there to console the inhabitants under the hardships they were suffering—
to proclaim to the world their patient industry, and the many noble virtues
by which they were distinguished. But he was sensible his work was only
half done when he accomplished these things. A *practical benefactor*, he
examined into the fishing and agricultural capabilities of the country, and
having, after incredible labour, satisfied himself that the Highlands teem-
ed with resources, sufficient to sustain ten times the number of human
beings that were starving in those regions, he points out how the resources
he had discovered might be called forth, and the aboriginal tribes thereby
kept at home, and made useful citizens, instead of being banished like
felons into far distant climes. O that Scotchmen of the present day would
imbibe a little of Mr. Knox's wisdom and fervour in this cause, and look
with the same compassionate eye that he did towards the neglected hills of
Caledonia: but, alas! I fear everything like a disinterested, manly, public
spirit is dead among us, and the age is vanished when the Highlanders
would have disdained to ask any other aid save that of their own good
swords to right their own wrongs. But did Mr. Knox content himself
with using soft words while witnessing those terrible exhibitions of havoc,
oppression, and expulsion which were then prevalent in the Highlands?
Very far from it; being convinced that the chieftains were for their own
mean and selfish ends madly bent on destroying a community that might
be the glory and stay of their country in the hour of peril, his indignation
rose in proportion to the magnitude of crime those infatuated men were
committing, and he speaks of their doings in the following emphatic
terms:—

"I shall not waste paper on arguments which with some minds pass as
tinkling sounds. Since neither the precepts of Christianity nor philosophy
can make any impression—since humanity and avarice never can assimi-
late—we must change our ground, and trace the subject to its origin. The
earth which we inhabit was given for the general support and benefit of
all mankind, by a Being who is incapable of partiality or destinction; and
though in the arrangements of society the earth is divided into very unequal proportions, and these confined to a few individuals, whilst the great
body of the people are totally cut off, this distribution *doth not give the
possessors a shadow of right to deprive mankind of the fruits of their labour.* The earth is the property of Him by whom it was called into existence; and, strictly speaking, no person hath an exclusive right to any
part of it who cannot show a charter or deed handed down from the original and only Proprietor of all nature; if otherwise, *they hold their possessions upon usage only.* Grants of land were made by princes to their

champions, friends and favourites; and these have been handed down from father to son, or by them transferred to new possessors ; *but where are the original charters from the Author of nature to those monarchs ?* In vain may we search the archives of nations from one extreme of the globe to the other. If so, and who can controvert it? the man who toils at the plough from five o'clock in the morning to sunset, and who sows the seed, hath undoubtedly a right to the produce thereof, preferably to the lounger who lies in bed till ten, and spends the remainder of the day in idleness, extravagance, and frivolous or vicious pursuits. The tenure of the former is held from God, founded on the eternal law of justice ; the claim of the latter *is from man, held in virtue of the revolutions and casual events of nations.*

" He therefore who denies his fellow-creatures the just earnings of their labour counteracts the benovelent intentions of the Deity—deprives his king and country of an industrious and useful body of the community, whom he drives from starvation at home to slavery abroad—*ought to be considered as an avowed enemy of society*, particularly the man who can take the cow from the aged widow, and afterwards the bed, the kettle, and the chair—thus turning out the decrepid at fourscore to wander from door to door, till infirmities and grief close the scene of tribulation.

" Since human laws do not reach such persons, while petty rogues are cut off in dozens, *their names ought to be published in every newspaper within these kingdoms, and themselves excluded from any place of honour or profit, civil or military.*"

Now, Sir, let it be observed, these are not the sentiments of a person who had revolutionary or party purposes to serve, but the deliberate opinions of a philosophic, humane, generous, and independent spirit ; who could take an enlarged view of the matter he had in hand, and sincerely feel for the distresses, and show that he had a thorough perception of the inalienable rights of his fellow-creatures. But I fatigue you, and I would just add in conclusion, let your readers ponder well the quotation I have just given them from Mr. Knox's publication, and ask themselves the question, whether it is not as capable of being applied to landowners, both in the Highlands and Lowlands, in the 19th, as it was in the 18th century. I could instance facts to prove this ; but, as I understand Mr. Donald M'Leod is to give you a few sketches of some pictures of wretchedness he saw in Sutherland lately, I forbear in the meanwhile, and shall simply refer you to him for practical illustrations of the truth of the general statements contained in this epistle. I am, Sir, your obedient servant,
Edinburgh, 24th July, 1844. JOHN STEILL.

I know many will consider that I am unwarrantably attacking the character of Ministers of the Gospel ; and may say what could they do as they had no control over the proprietors. Thank God that the Gospel or religion is not to be measured by the conduct of its preachers, and that they are not all alike. Read the following from the pen of a reverend gentleman, whom I believe to be a faithful Minister of Christ, upon the subject I have handled a little ago, and I think when you will read the

evidence of so many witnesses upon oath, you will admit at once that I
have not exaggerated Colonel Gordon's strictures, and none, I hope, who
will read the conduct and co-operation of this infamous hireling, Henry
Beatson, Minister of Barra, with Colonel Gordon in the evictions in that
island, cannot but admit that such vicious dogs should be exposed, and
classed in this world, among their companions through *eternity*, viz., oppressors of the poor, with the Devil and his angels : read 10th chapter,
Gospel of St. John.

THE EXILED BARRAMEN AND THEIR CALUMNIATORS.

" What I have written, I well know, will give offence to many petty tyrants : but
I am actuated by motives of humanity, and of duty to the common Parent and Lord
of all mankind. And I thank God, who has given me grace to speak the truth
with boldness, notwithstanding the menaces of certain unprincipled oppressors."—
REV. J. L. BUCHANAN.

" Since the dawn of the creation, when wicked Cain imbrued his hands
in the blood of his brother Abel, there has been two opposite classes in
the world, viz,—oppressors and oppressed. There are generally other
two classes who step in as seconds in this unequal contest between right
and wrong; and that is the fawning party who put their Amen to the
most cruel deeds of the arch-oppressors, and also those who are, like Moses
grieved at the sufferings of their brethren, and who, like Job, do what
they can to " break the arm of the oppressor."
Since the overthrow of West Indian Slavery the friends of human freedom in Britain have been resting on their oars, with the exception of an
occasional fling at American despots, and no doubt congratulating themselves, as well they might, for their achievements in the cause of liberty.
But let them not conclude that a complete victory is obtained even at
home. The following disclosures will at once convince every philantro-
phist that he should be up and doing; and that there is much need that
a share of that noble and disinterested sympathy which was shown to the
sable sons of Africa should now be imparted to our brethren in the
Western Hebrides.
It was a most unlucky day to the Highlands that Sir John-M'Neil was
commissioned to investigate their condition; and the one-sided Report
which he has laid before the Legislature of our country shows how incom-
petent he was for the undertaking. Our analysis of the annexed document, which he obtained from the Parochial Board of Barra, and which,
by the way, was considered by the pro-clearings and expatriating Press the
cream of his trashy Report, will show every unprejudiced reader how little
confidence may be placed in Sir John's evidence. Our readers probably
recollect the excitement which was caused in Glasgow and Edinburgh
about 18 months ago, by the appearance of some expatriated and starving
Barramen. The unfeeling conduct of the proprietor, Colonel Gordon, and
his underlings on that occasion was the subject of many well-merited

animadversions , both from the platform and the press.   But in order to shield Colonel Gordon from these castigations, the Barra authorities, headed by Henry Beatson their minister, have thrown their mantle around him. and besides have made a malicious, but a most silly attack upon the expatriated Barramen.   This attack is now fully six months before the public ; but till within a few days these caluminated creatures have not heard a word of it.   The following is a verbatim copy of the infamous document :—

" We are acquainted with Barr Macdougall, Donald M'Lean, commonly called Donald Hecterson, Roderick M'Neil, senior, and Roderick M'Neil junior, who have been referred to in the newspapers as persons who had left Barra and gone to Edinburgh because of their inability to obtain the means of subsistence here.   They were all provided with houses at the time of their departure.   They were all, either employed by the Relief Committee or might have been so at the date when they left Barra.   With the exception of Roderick M'Neil, senior, who left this in the first week of September, all the others left Barra in July.   Barr Macdougall was notoriously lazy, and before Colonel Gordon had acquired this property, had voluntarily surrendered his croft at Greine, and subsisted thereafter by begging, for which purpose he perambulated the country.   On the failure of the potatoes he became altogether destitute, and was received upon the lists of the Relief Committee.   Roderick M'Neill, junior, was employed by Mr. M'Alister at 1s a day, which he voluntarily relinquished, declaring that the wages was too low.   He then applied to the inspector of poor for assistance, and was refused, on the ground that he had left Mr. M'Alister's service, where he could have obtained the means of subsistence   He was an able-bodied man.

Donald M'Lean was an indolent man who never did much work even when wages could be earned ; whose wife perambulated the country begging from house to house.

Roderick M'Neill, senior, was several times accused of theft, and once apprehended on a charge of sheep stealing, but was not convicted.

Of Ann M'Pherson or M'Kinnon, nothing is known in Barra, unless she be a sister-in-law to Roderick M'Neil, senior, who had an illegitimate child to a person of the name of M'Pherson, and whose own name is M'Kinnon.

We are of opinion that the eleemosynary relief afforded to the people has had a prejudicial effect upon their character and habits ; that it has induced many to misrepresent their circumstances with a view to participate in it ; that it has taught the people generally to rely more upon others, and less upon themselves; and that we have reason to believe that, relying upon this source of subsistence, some persons even neglected to sow their lands."

(Signed) Henry Beatson, Minister.
D. W. M'Gillvray, J.P., Tacksman.
Wm. Birnie, Manager for Colonel Gordon,
Donald M. Nicolson, M.D. Tacksman.
Archibald M'Donald, Elder, Tenant.

The following declaration which we have obtained from three of the individuals mentioned in the preceding document is a true statement of the case; being corroborated by other parties who are well acquainted with the state of affairs in that island :—

Declaration of Barr M'Dougall, Roderick M'Neill, senior, and Ann M'Kinnon, being three individuals of the expatriated people of Barra.

"It is not true that we were all provided with houses before we left Barra ; neither were we employed, nor might have been employed by the Relief Committee at the date when we left Barra. Barr M'Dougall, and Donald M'Lean occupied houses on the farm rented by Dr. M'Gillvray, and got notice to quit them a week before the term of Whitsunday, 1850. They did not remove till their houses had been partly stripped and their fires put out. Donald M'Lean did not remove till his house was totally unroofed and remained for ten days within the bare walls without any covering but the sail of a boat : though he was at the time lingering under the disease of which he has since died. Barr M'Dougall did not give up his croft at Greine voluntarily ; but when his rent was augmented without any corresponding advantages he fell into arrears, like all his neighbours.* His stock was seized by the factor and sold for the arrears—consequently had to surrender his croft, and finally his native country along with it. Does not deny that he sought assistance when pressed by famine ; but always laboured when he could find employment.

Donald M'Lean was not indolent, as is falsely reported ; but, the poor man was quite incapable of standing fatigue or hard labour, as he was for a long while labouring under the consumptive disease which relieved him from the fangs of his pampered calumniators, six weeks after he went to Edinburgh.

Roderick M'Neil senior, was not several times accused of theft, and never apprehended. There was an attempt made once to implicate him, by another man who broke into a grocer's shop and who afterwards (in order to lighten his own punishment) accused Roderick M'Neil, senior, as being art and part ; but the said Roderick appeared before the Fiscal, Mr. Duncan M'Nee, at Lochmaddy, North Uist, where he was honourably acquitted, and was paid the sum of twelve shillings for his trouble.

Roderick M'Neil, junior, laboured for a long time for the Relief Committee, at roads and other works for 10½ lbs of meal per week, which was all the means of subsistence allowed for himself, his wife and two children. Finding death staring them in the face, Roderick's wife went to the su-

---

* For the information of our readers we may here notice the manner in which the Barra crofters have been reduced to their present condition. When kelp was in great demand the former proprietor, started a kelp manufactory, at which the services of all the spare hands in the island were required. He always preferred labour to money ; and when he found that the crofters could pay their rent in three months he increased his claims gradually, until each crofter required to keep a labourer there all the year round. After the manufacturing of kelp stopped the rents continued at the same figure. This is the whole secret of the Barra destitution.

perintendent of the Relief Board and begged of him to allow her to work in her husband's place that he might go to the fishing, which the superintendent granted ; and for this favour Roderick shared the fish with him. There were many females labouring for 10 hours a day in the island of Barra at that time. They were compelled from the system of labour to work with wheelbarrows and carry burdens. The method taken to load them was as follows :—The female being ordered to turn her back to the turf-cutter and to place her hands behind in a position almost on her knees, the turfs were laid on her back in succession till she had a sufficient burded—enough to rise under and carry for some distance—there lay them down to come back for more. They had often to gather their petticoats about the sod in order to keep it on their back, while, in wet weather, the water, sometimes the melted snow, streamed down their back and sides. At this work Roderick M'Neil's wife continued till within two days of her confinement ! ! !

Ann M'Kinnon acknowledges having had a child ten years ago ; but neither herself nor her child ever became a burden on the Parochial Board of Barra ; though (in consequence of the father's death) the maintenence of the child fell entirely on herself. She also laboured at both the turf-carrying and the wheelbarrow so long as she could get work, at the rate of 4½ lbs of meal per week.

We further declare that we went to Henry Beatson, minister, requesting certificates of character, which he refused, alleging that he was not in the habit of giving such to any one. However we see that he has sent one after us ; though to his eternal shame he has given it in direct violation of the Holy Scriptures which he pretends to expound to the people, and which says, ' Thou shalt not raise a false report ; put not thine hand with the wicked to be an unrighteous witness '.—Exod. xxiii. 1. That the said Henry Beatson is a most unfeeling person. He once told James M'Donald, an indigent man, when he solicited aid, ' Go to the mountains and eat grass and heather !' He has been most energetic in assisting Colonel Gordon's underlings in forcing away from their fatherland the 2000 which were transported to America from Barra and South Uist, and who are now begging and starving in Upper Canada. That there are at the present time men and women working about his manse, raising fences, trenching, &c., for one pound of meal per day, and although they would perish of cold, they dare not approach the minister's kitchen fire. That the meal which is doled out on these hard conditions, under the superintendence of Mrs. Beatson, is believed to be the remains of the old Relief Committee meal.

We also know D. W. M'Gillvray, J.P., Tacksman, and think he should be the last to speak of ' illegitimate children,' as a poor idiotic female who perambulated the country fathered a child on him, and declared that various stratagems were tried to prevent disclosures which cannot be mentioned here.

We have nothing particular to say of Wm. Birnie, Manager for Colonel Gordon, as he is but seldom in the island.

Of Donald N. Nicolson, M.D.,Tacksman, we will only wait to say that after continuing for years, 'adding house to house and field to field,' the woes which are pronounced against such have at last overtaken him; his whole effects having been sold by his creditors a few weeks ago.

Archibald M'Donald, Elder, Tenant, is a bastard son; and the *gallant* Colonel himself had no fewer than three bastard children to grace the name of Gordon."

The above declaration was taken at Glasgow, on the 26th of January, 1852, in the presence of the undersigned witnesses, and was read in Gaelic to the Declarants, who affirm that it is correct.

ARCHIBALD SINCLAIR, Witness.
DUNCAN M'DOUGALL,   do.
NEIL CAMPBELL,   do.
WILLIAM LIVINGSTONE, do.

As the Declarants have not said anything in reference to the last paragraph in the accusations, we would simply ask, What person in his senses will believe that "eleemosynary relief," as administered by the Barra Authorities, would have the tendency to make the recipients "neglect to sow their land" so long as they are allowed to gather the crumbs that fall from the Parochial Board!

To follow these investigations a little farther, we cannot do it better than by giving the following well authenticated communication received from a gentleman who had resided for some time in Barra, and was an eyewitness of the enormities perpetrated there during the summer of 1851:—

"The unfeeling and deceitful conduct of those acting for Colonel Gordon, in Barra and South Uist last summer, cannot be too strongly censured. The duplicity and art which was used by them in order to entrap the unwary natives is worthy of the craft and cunning of an old slave-trader. Many of the poor people were told in my hearing, that Sir John M'Neill would be in Canada before them, where he would have every thing necessary for their comfort prepared for them. Some of the officials signed a document binding themselves to emigrate in order to induce the poor people to give their names; but in spite of all these stratagems many of the people saw through them and refused out and out to go. When the transports anchored in Loch Boisdale the tyrants threw off their mask, and the work of devastation and cruelty commenced. The poor people were commanded to attend a public meeting at Loch Boisdale where the transports lay, and according to the intimation, any one absenting himself from the meeting was to be fined in Two Pounds. At this meeting some of the natives were seized and in spite of their entreaties were sent on board the transports. One stout Highlander, named Angus Johnstone, resisted with such pith that they had to hand-cuff him before he could be mastered; but in consequence of the priest's interference his manacles were taken off and marched between four officers on board the emigrant vessel. One morning, during the transporting season, we were suddenly awakened by the screams of a young female who had been recaptured in an adjoining house; having escaped after her first apprehension. We all rushed to the door and saw the broken-hearted creature with dishevelled hair and swollen face, dragged away by two constables and a ground officer. Were you to see the racing and chasing of policemen, constables, and ground officers, pursuing the outlawed natives you would think, only for their colour, that you had been by some miracle transported to the banks of the Gambia on the slave coast of Africa.

"The conduct of the Rev. H. Beatson on that occasion is deserving of the censure of every feeling heart. This "Wolf in sheep's clothing" made himself very officious, as he always does when he has an opportunity of oppressing the poor Barramen and of gaining the favour of Colonel Gordon. In fact, he is the most vigilant and assiduous officer Colonel Gordon has. He may been seen in Castle Bay, the principal anchorage in Barra, whenever a sail is hoisted, directing his men, like a game-keeper with his hounds, in case any of the doomed Barramen should escape, so that he might get his land cultivated and improved for nothing. They offered one day to board an Arran boat who had a poor man concealed, but the master, John Crawford, lifted a hand-spike and threatened to split the skull of the first man who would attempt to board his boat, and thus the poor Barramen escaped their clutches.

"I may state in conclusion that two girls, daughters of John M'Dougall, brother of Barr M'Dougall whose name is mentioned in Sir John M'Neill's Report, have fled to the mountains to elude the grasp of the expatriators, where they still are, if in life. Their father, a frail old man, along with the rest of the family, have been sent to Canada. The respective ages of these girls is 12 and 14 years. Others have fled in the same manner, but I cannot give their names just now."

Let us now follow the exiled Barramen to the "new world" and witness their deplorable condition and privations in a foreign land. The *Quebec Times* says:—

"Many of our readers may not be aware that their lives such a personage as Colonel Gordon, proprietor of large estates, South Uist and Barra, in the Highlands of Scotland; we are sorry to be obliged to introduce him to their notice, under circumstances which will not give them a very favourable opinion of his character and heart.

"It appears that tenants on the above mentioned estates were on the verge of starvation, and had probably become an eye-sore to the gallant Colonel! He decided on shipping them to America. What they were to do there, was a question he never put to his conscience. Once landed in Canada, he had no further concern about them. Up to last week, 1,100 souls from his estates had landed in Quebec, and begged their way to Upper Canada; when in the summer season, having only a morsel of food to procure, they probably escaped the extreme misery which seems to be the lot of those who followed them.

On their arrival here, they voluntarily made and signed the following statement:—"We the undersigned passengers per Admiral from Stornoway, in the Highlands of Scotland, do solemnly depose to the following facts,—That Colonel Gordon is the proprietor of the estates of South Uist and Barra; that among many hundreds of tenants and cotters whom he has sent this season from his estates to Canada, he gave directions to his

factor, Mr. Fleming of Cluny Castle, Aberdeenshire, to ship on board of
the above named vessel a number of nearly 450 of said tenants and cottars
from the estate in Barra—that accordingly, a great majority of these people, among whom were the undersigned, proceeded voluntarily to embark
on board the Admiral, at Loch Boisdale, on or about the 11th August,
1851 ; but that several of the people who were intended to be shipped for
this port, Quebec, refused to proceed on board, and in fact, absconded
from their homes to avoid the embarkation. Whereupon Mr. Fleming
gave orders to a policeman, who was accompanied by the ground officer of
the estate of Barra, and some constables, to pursue the people who had
ran away among the mountains ; which they did, and succeeded in cap-
turing about twenty from the mountains and islands in the neighbourhood ;
but only came with the officers on an attempt being made to handcuff them ;
and that some who ran away were not brought back, in consequence of
which four families at least, have been divided, some having come in the
ships to Quebec, while other members of the same families were left in the
Highlands.

" 'The undersigned further declare, that those who voluntarily em-
barked did so under promise to the effect, that Colonel Gordon would
defray their passage to Quebec ; that the Government Emigration Agent
there would send the whole party free to Upper Canada, where, on arrival
the Government Agents would give them work, and furthermore, grant
them land on certain conditions.

" 'The undersigned finally declare, that they are now landed in Quebec
so destitute, that if immediate relief be not afforded them and continued
until they are settled in employment, the whole will be liable to perish
with want.'

(Signed) HECTOR LAMONT,
and 70 others.

" This is a beautiful picture. Had the scene been laid in Russia or
Turkey the barbarity of the proceeding would have shocked the nerves of
the readers ! but when it happens in Britain, emphatically the land of
liberty where every man's house, even the hut of the poorest, is said to
be his castle, the expulsion of these unfortunate creatures from their
homes—the man-hunt with policeman and Bailiffs—the violent separation
of families—the parents torn from the child, the mother from her daughter
—the infamous trickery practised on these who did embark—the aban-
donment of the aged, the infirm women, and tender children in a foreign
land—form a tableau which cannot be dwelt on for an instant without
horror. Words cannot depict the atrocity of the deed. For cruelty less
savage, the dealers of the South have been held up to the execration of
the world.

And if, as men, the sufferings of these our fellow-creatures find sympathy
in our hearts, as Canadians their wrongs concern us more dearly. The
fifteen hundred souls whom Colonel Gordon has sent to Quebec this season,
have all been supported for the past week at least, and conveyed to Upper
Canada at the expense of the Colony ; and on their arrival in Toronto and
Hamilton, the greater number have been dependent on the charity of the

benevolent for their morsel of bread. Four hundred are in the river at present and will arrive in a day or two, making a total of nearly 2,000 of Colonel Gordon's tenants and cotters whom the province has to support. The winter is at hand, work is becoming scarce in Upper Canada. Where are these people to find food?"

Having laid a great mass of conclusive evidence before the public, we must now " sum up." We are certain that every man who has any sense of honour and justice cannot but condemn Colonel Gordon and his officials for these hitherto unheard of cruelties, and will loudly protest against the woes which are being heaped upon the head of the poor Hebridean. Is such conduct as we have now recorded to be winked at and tolerated by a nation who have laboured more in the sacred cause of human liberty than any other nation from the beginning of the world? Are those very men who have ungrudgingly paid £20,000,000 for the freedom of the negroes on a few of the West Indian islands : and who have effected the emancipation of every captive within the British dominions, to stand by with folded arms and not offer a helping hand to their own flesh and blood in the Western Isles—to those who have victoriously fought their battles and kept foreign invaders from their shores? Are they to remain calm and unmoved, while British laws are being violated, and the poor inoffensive, unprotected, and down-trodden Celt is hand-cuffed and dragged from his country and his kinsman with less regard to his comfort than if he were a beast of burden? Certainly not. And we are confident that all an enlightened and a benevolent public require to stir them up to cause a proper and impartial investigation being made is to lay the case explicitly before them. Instead of trusting to a " broken reed," as Sir John M'Neil has proved himself to be, let a disinterested public act in this case as they have done in that already mentioned. In 1838, when conflicting accounts of the cruelties endured by the Africans were wafted across the Western Ocean, instead of confiding in the report brought by Government Officials, the friends of the Negro sent a deputation of enlightened and fearless men who brought back a trustworthy report, and they went to work accordingly. Let them do the same now and send men who will not pass by the cottage of the poor but will listen to what he has to say—neither will accept of the gifts of the rich, and we have no doubt that the result will be the same—the emancipation of the poor Hebridean and his restoration to his rights and his responsibilities as a British subject. Then petty tyrants will see that however well concocted their plans—however far removed from the public eye " that their sins will find them out."

I ask Mrs. Stowe, what is your *Uncle Tom's Cabin* or your *Dred* in comparison to such treatment as this? and dare you say in the face of such (living) evidence that my narrative is a ridiculous unfounded calumny, and ridiculous and absurd accusation. I am told when writing this that you were lately in ROME paying homage to his Holiness and his Jesuit Ministers and kissing his toe; but whatever indulgence he may grant you for perverting truth and falsifying philosophy, and whatever promises he has made to you for absolutions for such sins, I tell you in plain

Heeland Scotch terms that you will find all his promises insufficient to screen or protect you from me, in your future praise of Highland Proprietors. And may I not ask, why is not all the Christian nations of the world up with a united universal cry of disapprobation of the system, law, and reprobation of the foul deeds committed under the protection of such law and system, and demand of the British Legislature their abolition and erasement from the Statute book, and retribution of their rights to their victims—a cry and demand in which the slave owners of America would have a tenfold better right to join than the English aristocracy had to remonstrate with them on American Slavery.

The following is my appeal published before I left Scotland :

To the Editor of the Northern Ensign.

SIR,—Highland destitution and famine in the Highlands have become proverbial and so familiar that people think and speak of them as a calamity hereditary to the Highlanders ; and, indeed, since they have become so burdensome to the public for the last half century (keeping them alive upon charity), the more fortunate portion of the Christian world are beginning to think, and say, that they should not exist any longer, and that the sooner they are exterminated the better. The appellation Gael, Celt, or Gaul, has now become a reproach ; yet those to whom the titles originally belong were at one time the terror and admiration of all Europe. They at one period inhabited Upper Asia, and took possession of Italy, and marched upon Rome 390 years before the advent of Christ —defeated the Roman army, laid the city in a heap of ruins, and levied one thousand pounds weight of gold of the then invincible Romans to purchase their departure. They were the people of whom *Cæsar* said— after a fearful struggle of ten years fighting, in which his army cut off one million of them—that he never observed one Gael turning his back, but that they all died fighting in their ranks without yielding one foot. But to come nearer home. They were a race of men who, when they had to encounter the Romans at the foot of the Grampian Hills (under the command of Galgacus), defied the Roman legion (under the command of Agricola, the most renowned of the Roman generals), whose discipline, science, and civilization, on that bloody occasion, drew forth the admiration of Tacitus, the Roman annalist, who declared that the Caledonian Celts were the most formidable enemy and the bravest people that ever Rome encountered—that, indeed, they were unconquerable. That learning and civilization followed this race of people is evident, and could be proved from a chain of Scottish historians whose works are still extant. ' I am tired,' said a distinguished writer many centuries ago, ' of having Roman authors quoted when the commencement of our civilization is spoken of, while nothing is said of the Celts, or of our obligations to them.' It was not the *Latins*, it was the Celts, who were our first instructors. Aristotle declared that philosophy was derived by the Greeks from the Gauls, and not imparted to them.—(*See introduction to Logan's " Scottish Gael."*)

You will pardon me, should I ask, through you, the most avowed and inveterate enemies of the Highlander, where, or when, has the *Highland Celt* stained the character given them by the Roman annalist at the early period of our history? If we turn up the annals of European bloody battle fields, from the Grampians to Waterloo, where will we find bravery to excel Highland bravery? If we look for discipline, morality and religion, among the British army, we must find such in the Highland regiments.

We have now a small remnant of the progeny of this mighty *race* of men who conquered civilized and enlightened Europe, yea more, who converted Europe from heathenism and paganism to Christianity ; I say we have them in obscure corners of the West and North Highlands of Christianized, vain, vaunting, civilized Scotland, DYING by FAMINE, to the everlasting disgrace, confusion, and abhorrence *here* and *hereafter*, of those, and their abettors, to whose cupidity, ambition, and steel hearted inhumanity, thousands of deaths in the Highlands could be attributed, Let this be told and proclaimed throughout the length and breadth of the land, on every market-cross, and in every place of resort, all over Europe—that Roman Catholic and Mahommedan nations may record it against them, when endeavours are making to proselytise them. But thank *God* that Christianity is not to be measured by the conduct of Christians ; if it were the heathens would do well to reject it.

Let the Legislature of this nation (to their shame) know it, that the only portion of Her Majesty's subjects who, by language and appearance, legitimately can lay claim to be the progeny of those who chastised and forced many a formidable invader from Britain's shore—who fought the battles of this nation at home and abroad, from the day of the Grampians to Waterloo, and who brought immortal praise and laurels of victory home to Britain—let the representatives of Scotland (the dumb dogs, with one honourable exception, MR. COWAN) know it—that in return for their ancestor's services to the nation, they, the progeny are doomed to die by famine, or be exterminated from the land, so dear to them by many sacred ties, by compulsory emigration, that they were made subject to, and left the victims of the most wanton cruelty, ingratitude, and injustice that the most avaricious barbarians could devise. That the most fertile valleys, straths, and glens of Caledonia, which they have been for ages defending, and purchased so often with their dearest blood, are depopulated, and converted by a few selfish minions, who have neither ancestry nor bravery to boast of, if they were properly searched, into deer-forests and hunting-parks, for the amusement of English snobs and sporting gents, where the image of God upon a Gael dare not approach ; while the Celts, who can boast of both bravery and ancestry, are turned adrift as beings of no value, upon barren, unproductive moors and precipices, and on skirts exposed to all the casualties of the season, deprived of every means to better their condition. Here they are dying, or living, what we may term a lingering, agonizing death, fed by the cold, sparing, stinted hand of charity, when twenty-four lines (upon an octavo) of an Act of Parliament would cure all.

In the days of one of the Cæsars (during what are called the dark ages) there was a law in Rome, that none would be allowed to sit in the State Council, ride in a chariot, hold any public office, or sit at a public feast, while it was known that any of his dependents were in want; and during the prosperous and victorious days of Greece, they had two temples built, one for virtue and one for honour, and so constructed that it was impossible to enter the temple of honour without going through the temple of virtue,—intended for a noble purpose, and it had the desired effect in those days. Would to God we had such qualifications, and we would not have so many direful revolting deeds perpetrated, and so many ignobles raised to honour and titles till there is no room to ascend. Let the ministers of the everlasting Gospel, the ambassadors of Christ, hear it, that in proportion as the people are diminished and extirpated, their services will be less required—sheep, bullocks, deer, blackcocks, and pheasants, will require no ministry. It is a part of their commission to plead the widow, the fatherless,. and the orphan's cause—to resist and denounce the oppressors,—to follow the example of their Master and the prophets in reproving evil doers. How can they prostrate themselves at the throne of mercy, pleading with God for the spiritual wants of their flocks, and not utter a word against these wolves who are trampling under foot, scattering their flocks by banishment (under the name of emigration) depriving them of the land created for their subsistence, and bestowing it upon brute-beasts—thus ushering thousands to a premature grave? How can they see this, and not interpose, plead with God, and call upon the nation to their assistance, that the ungodly, unnational, and unjust law which tolerates and protects such evil-doers, may be expunged from the Statute book? This is their duty—they may seek a subterfuge to disregard it, but if they will, *The day is coming when they shall repent, if they can find a place for repentance.* Thank God we have a Rev. Charles Thomson in Wick, a Dr. Begg in Edinburgh, and others—*For woe's me, my people are robbed and sold, and those who rob them say, Blessed be the Lord, for I am rich, and their own shepherds pity them not.*

I would ask the mercantile and manufacturing portion of this nation,. will you stand by carelessly and callously, seeing the home market destroyed, millions of those that should and would be the consumers of your goods banished from our shores, dying by famine, or living in a state of misery and wretchedness, that they can be of no service to you, but the reverse—a burden to you? I leave you to reflect upon this for a time. Sheep and bullocks may supply you, but they will take very little in exchange; but supply and demand, when corresponding, are the very life of the *home market.* I ask you, literary men or knowledge manufacturers,—How are the people ignorant? The people are in misery, dying by famine, and cannot buy knowledge. There is abundance of wealth in the land, and abundance of work before you; but if the people are banished from the land or die by famine, you may shut your shops, for sheep, bullocks, deer, black cocks, and pheasants will not employ you, and you need not attempt to teach them. Rise, then, from.

your lethargy, and stand no longer in your criminally callous indifference regarding the producing classes. You are the fourth estate, and to whom much is given, much shall be required. To the Government of this nation I would say, and put them in mind, that this kingdom was often invaded before, and often threatened, and it may happen yet. You have allowed the best part of the national ramparts to be trodden down and razed to the foundation, you have allowed the patriotism or love of country which was characteristic of Highlanders and which was so powerful to animate them at all times when encountering an enemy, to be destroyed ; you have allowed, and helped to banish them from your shores, to foreign strands, where, at no distant period, they or their off-spring may become as formidable enemies as their sires were formidable friends. Then you will find that cruel Highland proprietors, English snobs, and sporting gents, sheep, bullocks, rams, deer, blackcocks, and pheasants, will make but a poor stand for your nation's defence. I say, reflect. This is the time, this is the day to retract, to retrieve, and to re-claim lost confidence, and make reparation to the unfortunate Highland victims of mal-administration and of cruel short-sighted policy.

The accounts received daily by the Secretary of the Highland Destitu-tion Relief Committee (of which I am a member) are heart-rending and revolting to humanity. A reverend gentleman writes thus :—' You have sent me two pounds ; I bought meal with the money but there were so many applicants for relief that I had to divide it in ounces.' Another writes ;—' I acknowledge the receipt of £5, but I must keep it a secret or the people will storm my house ; yet I am travelling among them, and enquiring, and where I find that death by famine is approaching, I administer relief. I need not trouble you with any more. This is a sample of them all.' People of high standing in society were finding fault with me for advising the poor Highlanders to take sheep or any other animal they could get their hands on and eat them, before they would allow themselves or their children to die ; but I'll warrant you, if these gentlemen were only getting an ounce each of oatmeal to make water gruel for their supper, in Edinburgh, and had no other prospect for food until a few more ounces came from the Isle of Skye, there would not be a hen-roost nor pig-stye in or about Edinburgh but they would pay a visit to before morning, and where they would help themselves. This is a fearful state of matters in a country professing Christianity. Yet, however dreadful and threatening it is, I have often said, and will say it yet, that until the land in the Highlands is under a different system of management, matters will be getting worse and worse. I hope that the Rev. Charles Thomson's exhortation in your last will be followed up by every one whose breast contains a spark of humanity, and who is favoured with an opportunity.—I am, &c.,

DONALD M'LEOD.

16, South Richmond Street,
Edinburgh, July 14, 1851.

K

I have, in the preceding pages, particularized the Duke of Sutherland as chief depopulator of the Highlands ; I must now notice those next to him, Athol, Breadalbane, Lord Macdonald, and Gordon, as you will see from the following :—A gentleman of the name of R. Alister,* in 1853, wrote a work which was inscribed to another patriotic philanthropist of the name of Patrick Edward Dove, Edinburgh, titled "Barriers to National Prosperity," in which he demonstrates the short-sighted policy of Highland proprietors in a style worthy of the author and editor, Mr. Dove. The Marquis of Breadalbane was offended at seeing the work advertised, and wrote the following letter through the public press. As I was not personally acquainted with the extent of the clearance system in that quarter, I consider the most prudent step I can adopt is to give *verbatim* Breadalbane's letter and Mr. Alister's reply :—

COPY LETTER.

To the Editor of the Perthshire Advertiser.

21 PARK LANE, LONDON, }
June 18, 1853. }

" SIR,—My attention has been directed to an article in the *Perthshire Advertiser*, of the 13th ultimo., in which a work, entitled *Barriers to the National Prosperity of Scotland*, is reviewed, and from which are quoted passages tending to give an impression of the management of my estates in the Highlands, which is inconsistent with the facts.

The extract from Mr. Alister's work to which I more particularly allude is the following :—" At the present rate of depopulation, the Highlands must soon be one vast wilderness ; and although their numbers were never great in the British Army, yet we aver that one-tenth of the men who fought in the last war could not be got in the Highlands. Many of the smaller glens are totally cleared, and any of the peasantry remaining do not calculate that they can obtain a home for many years longer. Glencoe, the Black Mount, and Lochtayside, where the Campbells flourished, are swept ; and although no difficulty was experienced by the late Marquis of Breadalbane in raising three battalions of fencibles at the last war, we are sure that 150 men could not now be obtained."

Glencoe does not, and never did, belong to me.

Mr. Alister appears to labour under a mistake as to the history of the Black Mount, inasmuch as he would seem to assert that it was formerly densely inhabited ; whereas the fact is, that, as far back as the records of my family reach (for some centuries) till towards the close of last century, when it was put into very large sheep farms, that country was always a deer forest, and consequently uninhabited, except by the foresters. As I began to convert it again into a forest upwards of thirty years since, it is obvious that it could only have been in the hands of tenants for a (comparatively speaking) short period. The present population of that district is, I believe, as great as it was in the times to which Mr. Alister alludes, and, in point of fact, the number of families employed by me there now, as shepherds and foresters, is much the same as the number who lived there when the ground was tenanted by farmers.

* Mr. Alex. Robertson of Dundonachie.

On my Nether Lorne property, I believe the population to be greater than it was fifty or sixty years ago.

The population on the banks of Loch Tay is certainly not as large as it was twenty years since, and it is fortunate for all parties concerned that it is not, as a continuance of the old system would, before this, have produced disastrous results.

When I succeeded to the property, I found the land cut up into possessions too small for the proper conduct of agricultural operations, or the full employment of the occupiers. The consequence was, that habits of idleness were engendered, great poverty existed, and the cultivation of the land was in a most unsatisfactory state—the social, the moral, and physical condition of the people being thus unfavourably affected.

A continuance of this state of matters was clearly inconsistent with the improvement of the country and the welfare of the inhabitants, subjects to which I at once, on my succession, directed my attention, and to which I have ever since constantly directed my best thoughts.

To carry these views into effect, it was absolutely necessary that the holdings should be so increased in size as to give sufficient employment to the resources of the occupiers, and this could only be done by consolidating some of the smallest possessions, retaining the tenants who appeared most likely to profit by the change.

In no case was this done in the way implied by Mr. Alister, as the changes were always made gradually, and so as to produce as little inconvenience as possible to those whom it was necessary to remove. Indeed, whenever, from the circumstances of the case, it was practicable, those who were removed were offered other houses.

In reality, there has been no depopulation of the district, in the sense in which the word is usually accepted. There is still a large population on both sides of Loch Tay, and almost all the land is still held in, comparatively speaking, small possessions.

The results of the system I have pursued speak for themselves. If any person who saw Lochtayside twenty years since were to see it now, he could not fail to be struck with the change for the better in the face of the country, in the state of the dwellings, and in the appearance and habits of the people.

A very satisfactory proof of the flourishing condition of the people may be found in the fact, that, while the inhabitants of many parts of the Highlands were suffering from famine in the years 1846-47, and were to a great extent indebted for mere existence to the charity of the public, none of the money so collected was expended on, or required by, the inhabitants of my estates, even on the west coast. All were supported by internal, not by external aid, although the failure of the potato crop was quite as complete there as in other parts of the Highlands. Indeed, money was raised in these districts in aid of the general funds collected for the alleviation of the famine.

In no part of the Highlands are the religious and educational wants of the inhabitants better provided for, nor are there fewer public-houses.

In looking over my factorial accounts, I find that, on my Perthshire property, I have expended, in employing the people in useful works, £188,750; on Glenurchay, a part of my Argyleshire property, £19,402; and on the other part a similar sum in proportion—in each case from the period of my succession down to 1852 (eighteen years).

Having stated these facts regarding the management of my property, and my conduct towards those residing upon it, I fearlessly ask, am I justly obnoxious to the imputation of being regardless of the prosperity and happiness of the people upon it? Have I recklessly driven out from its mountains and its glens the interesting and gallant race that formerly resided there?—I remain, sir, your obedient servant,

(Signed)   BREADALBANE.

LETTER I.

To the most noble the Marquis of Breadalbane.

"MY LORD,—For the last fifteen years I have been brought into immediate contact with the middle and lower orders in various parts of Scotland, and during that period I have observed that the section of our population deriving their support from land have been subjected to some grievances, so much so that their means of living have become pinched, and multitudes, who would have submitted to great privations at home, have nevertheless been compelled to expatriate themselves from the country so dearly loved, or, what is worse, take shelter in the dungeons of a large town. For a long time it puzzled me to understand how a country growing in commercial prosperity must be declining in its agricultural population; and while the towns were doubling their residenters, and consequently demanding greater supples of food, yet all the while vast tracts of producing land should be thrown waste! Any enquiries that I could make were generally answered, that the peasantry must make way before the improvements of modern agriculture; but *that* explanation I never was satisfied with, and I never was at peace until I found out what appeared to me to be the real cause of such great evils; for I could not shut my eyes to the fact that rural depopulation and the overpeopling of towns stood linked together as cause and effect. As your Lordship must know, I traced out these evils to the *Laws of Entail*, which have concentrated vast territories into the hand of a single individual, while they prevented peasant proprietorship,—a system that has produced magical benefits wherever it has been allowed to come into operation. The *Game Law rules* I also found to be a wicked instrument, seized by lairds for banishing the peasantry, and for desolating great tracts of land. The *Laws of Hypothec* I also found operated most injuriously against society, by unduly enlarging the size of farms, by giving illegitimate security to lairds for rents, and for increasing the price of rent to a fictitious amount. The abolition of these unjust laws is all the cure that I suggest, and I hesitate not to affirm that if their abolition were secured, a most healthful improvement, both moral and physical, would be apparent in Scotland, and that at no postponed date.

Your Lordship is aware that I brought these views under public notice in a volume entitled, " Barriers to the Prosperity of Scotland ; " at
the same time labouring to prove that a country cannot long survive the
loss of its peasantry, or, if it did exist, it would be—like Samson, deprived of his hair—shorn of all that was morally fair or physically good.
I have laboured to show how the peasant at home loves his country and
his God, but when huddled into the pestiferous alleys of a large town,
he loses his physical strength and his religious principle ; and his family,
which, in the cottaroon, would be brought up in thrift and in virtue,
would, like the rest, be swept into the vortex of vice and dissipation.

This theory of human life your Lordship has not attempted to overturn,
neither have you denied its applicability to the present condition of
Scotland.   But you have attempted to place my statements before the
public as being untrue, and therefore my case against the laws of Game,
Entail, and Hypothec would fall to the ground.   I must confess that I
should have much rather been attacked in my arguments than in any
isolated illustration thereof, because the general argument may be perfectly good, albeit the particular illustration thereof may have been incorrect.   In a former publication I had to complain of this ; for many
busied themselves with the *illustration*, while they overlooked entirely
the principle it was intended to support.

When illustrating the evil effects of our feudalistic legislation, it was
barely possible for me to avoid pointing to certain estates where the evils
were most apparent.   But I certainly did so as seldom as possible, and I
think in only one instance have I condescended on a personal reflection.
Your Lordship's name *is not mentioned at all*, for although I state that
Lochtayside had been cleared, I did not say *by whom* ; and had you not
published the letter of 18th June, your lordship's name and character
might have been forgotten altogether in connection with such a deplorable
state of matters.   Personally, I entertain no grudge towards your Lordship or any other laird, but on the contrary it might have been beneficial
to me to retain the good favour of lairds rather than to excite their ill-will.
But the letter referred to leaves me only two courses,—either to support
the statements of my book, or stand arraigned before the public as guilty
of circulating untruths.   Your Lordship has dragged our dispute promi-
nently before the public ; let the public, therefore, be judge between us.

I have good right to complain that your Lordship's contradiction of my
statements are not brought out in a straightforward manner, but that by
numerous shifts and fallacies you evade the facts altogether.   Considering
the high position of your Lordship, I think you might have condescended
to have met such a humble antagonist as I am openly and frankly ; excuse me, therefore, if I now ask you to answer my statements *seriatim*.

1*st*. Do you deny in general that the Highlands are being depopulated,
and that one soldier could not now be raised for ten who fought in the last
war ?   Your Lordship, I think, would hardly risk the denial of a statement which every person in this country knows to be correct.   I have
given the public an opportunity of denying my statements ; but so far as
I can judge, my figures are under rather than over the mark.   I can point

to a place where thirty recruits that manned the 92d in Egypt came from —men before whom Napoleon's Invincibles had to bite the dust,—and now only two families reside there altogether. I was lately informed by a grazier that on his farm a hundred swordsmen could be gathered at the country's call; and now there is only himself and one or two shepherds. On his neighbour's farm fifty swordsmen formerly lived, and it is now much in the same condition. The Sutherland and Gordon clearings are known to the world, and yet the fact of Highland depopulation is stated as being inconsistent with truth? Under this head your Lordship had ample opportunity of contradicting my statements, but no man with any regard to his standing could do so. But if I am labouring under a delusion here, I am not alone, as will be seen from the following quotation:—

"But in other and in too many instances the Highlands have been drained, not of their superfluity of population, but of the whole mass of the inhabitants, dispossessed by an unrelenting avarice, *which will be one day found to have been as short-sighted as it is unjust and selfish.* Meantime the Highlands may become the fairy ground for romance and poetry, or the subject of experiment for the professors of speculation, political and economical. But if the hour of need should come,—and it may not perhaps be far distant,—the pibroch may sound through the deserted region, but the summons will remain unanswered."—*Sir Walter Scott.*

Let us hear what the great continental historian, Michelet, says :—

"The Scotch Highlanders will ere long disappear from the face of the earth ; *the mountains are daily depopulating*; the great estates have ruined the land of the Gaul, as they did ancient Italy. The Highlander will ere long exist only in the romances of Walter Scott. The tartan and the claymore excite surprise in the streets of Edinburgh : they disappear—they emigrate—their national airs will ere long be lost, as the music of the Eolian harp when the winds are hushed."

It is not necessary for me to say anything about the *result* of this depopulation—whether it is desirable or not—for I am not at present discussing an abstract question in political science, but *the fact* of that depopulation going on is notorious over all. In one week *one hundred* most industrious emigrants left the district of Athole for Canada, while sixty additional were preparing to remove. As the press stated, there is a general "move" of Highland population to Australia and Canada, of their own accord in many instances. The ousted farmers from Athole have thriven so well in Canada, that the remaining friends are desirous of sharing their prosperity. Those who left Badenoch for Australia sixteen years ago have made fortunes rapidly, and now the people *en masse* are flitting. But it is not only in the Highlands this system is at work ; from where I write I see a farm in the occupation of a tenant who has ground that formerly sustained *one hundred lowland Scotch families,* and all in peace and plenty, in contentment and happiness. On hundreds of places might Nicoll sing,—

"Ae auld aik tree, or may be twa,
Amang the wavin' corn,
Is a' the mark that time has left
O' the toon where I was born."

I have never said that the Highlanders *should be kept up* as a nursery for soldiers; my only position is this, do not keep up nor *put them down*. If they cannot work, let them shift for themselves; but if *they* are beaten, it is time for others to look out. Although it is not necessary to keep up the Scottish peasantry by eleemosynary aid, yet does that argue that they should be oppressed as much as possible? that they should be rendered uncomfortable at home, and their crops devoured through the influence of game laws? Surely not.

I say, that "any of the peasantry remaining do not calculate that they can obtain a home for many years longer." Now, on Lochtayside, and especially at Acharn, I certainly understood that some thirty or forty tenants looked at Whitsunday next as the time when their doom would be fixed. Certain ominous examinations have been seen, and whispers were rife that the same dose which their neighbours had been favoured with was in preparation for them. The besom of extermination had left no barrier betwixt them and being thrown upon the wide world for a home and the means of life. To say what your Lordship's plans are for the future is what I cannot do; but I am perfectly correct in saying what is "calculated." On another Highland property, I was aware at the time my book was in the press that extensive warnings had been given for the small tenants to leave. I am glad, however, to say, that such doings have been seen in their true colours, and that if any have to leave that property it will be their own fault, as I learn that every reasonable encouragement will now be afforded them to stay at home. The question was started in high quarters,—"If the people leave, who will be got to work the land?" Well would it be for Breadalbane, and for our country, if your Lordship would set yourself seriously to examine the same question.

In reference to Glnecoe, your Lordship abruptly answers, that it does not, and never did belong to you. I never said that it did. I asserted that it is "swept" of its inhabitants, and perhaps my information is incorrect, but your Lordship has not condescended to state whether it is so or not. If, however, my language can bear any such construction as that your Lordship is proprietor thereof, I willingly withdraw any such ambiguity, and confess that my language should not be equivocal, although at the same time, I believe that the less some Campbells say about Glencoe the better. I have also put the Black Mount among the number of cleared grounds That there were numerous tenants living there was according to my information. In a region of territory covering some 200 or 300 square miles of Scottish ground, the fact is, as I have stated, viz. that it is "swept"—not one tenant on the whole!!! Your Lordship evades the question by saying, that my statement amounts to this, "that it was formerly *densely* populated." I certainly was unable to tell the *number* of families put away, but your Lordship might have done so, and there is nothing to prevent that being done yet. You tell us about the records of your family; your Lordship might have spared such an allusion. It is a painful one to a Scotchman, and particularly to a Highlander. Tradition must be far wide of the truth if the early history of your family be fit for seeing light in the nineteenth century. You tell us that the present population of that district is now as great as the time to which I allude. What time, my Lord?—please explain yourself. You tell us that it is obvious that this land could only have been in the hands of tenants for a short time. I certainly understood that it never was a deer forest until made so by your Lordship, *but I never said so.* The arguments used to excuse the clearing system are not a little unique. Thus, the Black Mount is cleared, having been "but thinly peopled"; and Lochtayside is all but swept, because it was "too densely populated." Some of your Glenquiech tenants' families were in possession 400 years—was that the reason they were "swept?" If not contradictory, these arguments are, at least, somewhat strange; thus the Fens of Lincoln have only been improved lately,—*ergo* there would be no harm in converting them again into marshes. The whole cultivation of America is of comparitively recent origin,—*ergo*, it would be no harm for a tyrant to lay it all waste! Then, you very cooly tell us that your shepherds and foresters make up as great a population as formerly resided there. But you have forgotten to tell how many shepherds you have there, and it would be naturally inferred that the Black Mount is as well grazed as before. Now, allow me to remind your Lordship that such an impression is very far from being borne out by the facts of the case, there being only a *very small* part of the Black Mount under sheep pasture. Then, about the foresters, you would think it no harm in having the whole Highlands under the dominion of that excellent and useful class, would you? Your Lordship must hold very strange doctrines of political science, if you estimate that game-keepers and foresters, who keep the country lying waste, who dissipate the national resources, are for a moment to be compared to the industrious peasant, by the sweat of whose

land, not to lay it waste! The country would be vastly improved if idle keepers, who are a notorious pest to any district, were transformed into respectable and industrious tillers of the ground. Am I not correct, then, in saying that the Black Mount has been swept of its industrious tenants, and that only a few shepherds, (not, I believe, one-tenth of what ought to be) occupy their place? But about the Black Mount more anon.

We have now come to Lochtayside; and if the peasantry be not *virtually* "swept" from there, I shall make all apology that may be deemed meet. By a mere play upon words, your Lordship makes out that it is not "swept," because some tenants remain there still; and yet in another place we are told it was for good to the people themselves that they were cleared off, and, in the same letter, it was for the prevention of pauperism; again, at the conclusion, you triumphantly ask, "Have I recklessly driven out from its mountains and glens the interesting and gallant race that FORMERLY dwelt there?"

In volunteering to correct the impression which every one has, of Lochtayside being virtually cleared of its peasantry, I think if your Lordship *could* have proved that it was *not cleared*, this would have been easily done by a statement of the number of families there were in 1834 and those now in 1843. If my statement was not worth answering, why meddle with it ? If it was worth noticing why not answer it in the only manner it could be answered, viz., by an appeal to facts and figures ? In a passing allusion I think I shall be borne out if, in denouncing the clearing system, four out of five families are thrust out. If I had meant that it was cleared of *every* inhabitant, I should certainly have said " totally cleared ;" but I adopted the everyday expression used whenever Lochtayside is spoken of, both by strangers who see the remains of former houses, &c., AND OF BREADALBANE MEN THEMSELVES. But lest your Lordship's memory should have got rusty on this point, allow me to remind you of Mornish, with its twenty-two families now occupied by one ; of the Cloichran with eight or nine families, without a tenant at all. In Acharn, near Killin, there were nineteen families ; how many now? if there be one tenant, mention his name. How many " toons" have been cleared of four, ten, or fourteen families besides those quoted ? Out with it my Lord ! If you have not been actuated by a desire to banish the people of Breadalbane out of the country, prove it by facts and figures, not by roundabout statements entirely beside the point. It is quite true that many people still live there ; and if your Lordship thinks it anything to your credit that *bothy-men* now usurp the place of honest cottagers, I am willing to allow you all the benefit of the plea, although, at the same time, I think the bothy system is one of the worst that your Lordship could possibly patronise. You can take credit in the population account for the inhabitants of your Lordship's bothies at Newhall, Comrie-farm, Balmacnaughton, Auchmore; and Acharn, near Killin.

And, lastly, as to the fencible men. You must be aware that your late father raised 2,300 men the last war, and that 1,600 of that number were from the Breadalbane estates. My statement is, that 150 could not *now* be raised. Your Lordship has most carefully evaded all allusion to this,—perhaps the worst charge of the whole. From your Lordship's silence I am surely justified in concluding that you may endeavour to evade the question, but you dare not attempt an open contradiction. I have often made enquiries of Highlanders on this point, and the number above stated was the *highest estimate.* Many who should know, state to me that your Lordship would not get *fifty* followers from the whole estates ; and another says,—" Why, he would not get half-a-dozen, and not one of them unless he could not possibly do otherwise." This, then, is the position of the question : in 1793-4, there was such a numerous, hardy, and industrious population on the Breadalbane estates, that there could be spared of valorous defenders of their country in her hour of danger............... 1600
Highest estimate now.. 150

Banished.. 1450

Per Contra.

Game of all sorts increased a hundred fold.

In conclusion, under this head, can you produce any thing farther in confutation of the statements made in my book ? if so, let us have them.

Knowing a good many facts, I am quite prepared to substantiate all I have advanced.

I am, my Lord,
your very obedient humble servant,

July, 1853. R. ALISTER.

LETTER II.

To the most noble the Marquis of Breadalbane.

" MY LORD,—Having attempted to support the original statements made by me in the volume before alluded to, I am now at liberty to examine some of those adduced by you ; and from the manner they are stated, and the semi-official tone in which they are couched, some might believe that I had wantonly undertaken to misrepresent your Lordship. In my book there was not a single imputation thrown upon your Lordship's character, but the manner in which you have endeavoured to clear yourself of blame (not then imputed), convinced many that you had made a personal application of the general charges made in my book.

In the examination which I intend to make of the facts brought forward by your Lordship, I shall confine my observations to two parts, viz.,—1*st*, Destroying the resources of the country for game. 2*nd*, Extermination of the peasantry.

In the factorial accounts to which your Lordship refers, is there any estimate of the territory laid virtually waste for game sports ? The next time your Lordship openly makes reference thereto, perhaps you could without much trouble, favour the public by replies to the following queries :—

How many square miles of valuable pasture are kept waste for deer?

How many sheep could annually be drawn from them, but for the deer ?

How many thousand black cattle could be reared, but for the same cause?

With moderate and judicious outlays in planting, open draining, &c., &c., how much extra produce could be brought into market? Would the increase be 5, 100, 200, or 300 per cent? Opinion differs very much about these figures.

Referring again to the Black Mount, perhaps your Lordship would favour the public with its *geographical* boundaries. I have had great difficulty in arriving at anything like a correct estimate of the extent of territory laid waste. The lowest estimate of its circumference I have heard is *fifty miles*, others say sixty, and some as high as ninety miles. Let us assume that in its present state there are 100,000 acres of the most valuable pasture all but useless to the nation at present, but with the abolition of the Game Law Rules we might guess that it could graze 70,000 sheep. One-third to one-fourth of these could be annually drawn, and thus *twenty thousand sheep* would be yearly brought down for sale, *minus* some 3,000 at present. The *Clashgoure* wedders were said to be the best ever seen in Glasgow market. How many does the hill produce now? Besides 20,000 sheep, there might be 50,000 fleeces sold, in which almost nothing is done at present.

If these statistics approximate the truth, would not such an addition to the supplies of food to our town population be very valuable? Considering the high price of meat at present, the great demand, the limited supply, I am sure that no more wholesome or beneficial change could take place in this country than would the opening up of the Highlands to trade. The supply of black-faced sheep and of black cattle would be increased beyond all conception. Instead of sending to the four quarters of the earth for food, why not let Scotland produce all that it can? why banish the industrious population when such a field of real, not representative, wealth (as gold is) lies inviting them only to reap it?

Your Lordship states, that to the *improvement of the country* and to the welfare of the inhabitants you have directed your attention and your best thoughts. Without disputing your good intentions, allow me to ask you before Scotland what more could you have done, by yourself or your agents, to lay the country waste,—the Black Mount in particular? Was it for the improvement of the country that you have kept some of the finest soil of Perthshire waste,—that is, the forest facing Kenmore? Is it for the improvement of the country that you keep all the land round Drummond Hill merely for sport at deer-stalking? Is it for the encouragement of agriculture that the tenants are bound *by lease* to leave the fields nearest the hill under grass, apparently that the game may have a morsel in winter? Is it for the public good that your deer come to the gardens and destroy the cabbage (some of it having had to be three times planted this year in consequence)? and yet the tenants dare not scare them away; if dogs are set after them they are forthwith shot; if they are frightened by firearms, the tenant is forthwith put off the property! And yet this is all done for " the improvement of the country," or else " for the welfare of the inhabitants!!"

Whatever good has accrued from the unexampled increase of game, must be entirely placed to the credit of your Lordship, for your predecessor (whose memory and good deeds are warmly extolled by thousands) did not favour the increase of game. No doubt he had numbers of deer, but they were principally in parks, few or none being wild; and no tenant was restricted from using his gun (except in the parks) until the efforts of your Lordship introduced a different regime. The late Marquis had a greater respect for his splendid and devoted peasantry than to harass them with gamekeepers, or destroy their crops with hares and pheasants. He wished them to live in the country, and therefore he adopted no measures directly or indirectly, to force them away. There are, however, certain doings about game of which your Lordship must be ignorant, because no nobleman, professing such liberality as you do, could be a party to such transactions. I refer to the case of a tenant at Acharn, who was tempted to shoot a fallow deer, which had perhaps fattened on his own crops or cabbage. His servant, instead of going to church on Sabbath, went to inform your Lordship's keeper of the occurrence; and, if I am correctly informed, that excellent man went shortly after and made a search in the house. He was like to be foiled in the pursuit, when he took off the kail-pot, and carrying it to the door, found therein a piece of venison! What a horrible disclosure! The venison was forthwith carried to Bolfracks, and such a hullabaloo was there! And what was the sentence?—banishment! Although strongly attached to Scotland, yet no remedy could be found for the unpardonable crime—off he had to go. Now it turns out this happened for the man's welfare, for he would hardly return to Breadalbane, although made proprietor of his former occupancy.

How these 200 square miles, laid all but desolate, besides crops in fields and in gardens destroyed, tallies with your Lordship's loud professions for agricultural improvement, is what others must explain for I really confess for once that I am shamefully beaten in the attempt to do so.

I shall now trouble your Lordship with a few inquiries relative to the EXTERMINATION OF THE PEASANTRY. On your Nether Lorne property, you state your belief that the population is as large as ever it was. Previous to the overturn of the Roman empire, the towns multiplied exceedingly, but at the same time the rural population was totally swamped. Would your Lordship be good enough to state whether or not the Nether Lorne *is cleared of the peasantry*, and the land is now tenanted by *south country farmers*, and if the population to which your Lordship refers is not that employed at Easdale slate quarries?

In reference to the removals from Lochtayside, your Lordship claims great credit on that account, alleging that pauperism would have produced "disastrous results before this." Again, you claim great credit, because there was no destitution in 1846-7.* Now, I most flatly deny the insinuations here thrown out upon the peasant population; and not only so, but I aver that *it is to clearing landlords like yourself that we are indebted for the great abundance of pauperism in large towns!* The deplorable destitution on the west coast was in a great measure occasioned by lairds thrusting out the population (which they had previously done so much to develop), and huddling them together in fishing villages along the coast.† I do not remember of any peasantry in Scotland being afflicted with the evils you name. On those parts of the Breadalbane property not yet cleared, did any destitution prevail? Was there any of it felt at the densely populated neighbourhood of Acharn? I can point out to numerous estates, as densely populated as ever Lochtayside was, and in as unfavourable circumstances, and yet destitution was never dreamt of. In Athole, in Strathtay, Moulin, and many other places that suggest themselves to me, where the holdings are almost all small, the people never were more prosperous than they have been since 1846.

---

* Pray, how could there be pauperism when the people were banished?
† See "Theory of Human Progression," page 322, and also Parliamentary Report of 24th May 1841.

Your Lordship takes it for granted that any visitor must see a vast improvement in Lochtayside, dating from 1734,—a statement which demands proof ; for I am informed on the most unquestionable authority, that there is now *less* produced to clothe and feed the human race on Lochtayside than there was twenty years ago ; and I fully believe it. Instead of the improvements on the Breadalbane estates keeping up with the times, I am strongly convinced that they have retrograded rather than advanced since your Lordship's succession.

The former condition of the peasantry seems to have drawn forth an unmerited sneer. In reply to numerous inquiries, the answers all concur in representing the peaceful dwellers by the lake-side as peculiarly social. They lived without guile ; they assisted each other in every respect, and nothing but harmony and good feeling prevailed ; and certainly, if such were the case, it would form a pleasing contrast to the bitterness, rancour, and ill-feeling that is elsewhere displayed. We are also told that "the physical condition was unfavourably affected." Now, of all places in Europe, I certainly understood that physical strength was nowhere better developed than in the Highlands of Scotland. In Lochtayside I have seen some very powerful, hardy, well-knit men. In particular, the most herculean figure that I ever remember to have seen was one of the individuals from a croft on the lake-side ! Although your Lordship has chosen to blacken the Highland peasantry to justify your own doings, yet I shall easily get many who are of a different opinion. The following is the testimony of a Breadalbane man :—" In my young days the people lived happy* and sociably, as well as being healthy and comfortable. There was plenty of animal food, and abundance of milk. There were few or no paupers ; for when a man was worn out he got a cow's haddin, which the neighbours ploughed, sowed, and reaped. Thus he was kept off the poor's box,—a calamity they were dreadfully afraid of."

Your Lordship congratulates yourself for the great efforts made for the religious and educational wants being supplied better than in any other part of the Highlands. Now, it is unfortunate that these laudible efforts are so little known, and the example of such excellent endeavours thereby

---

* I am quite alive to the fact, that nothing is more common among certain would-be-wise theorist than to sneer at the phase of human life here alluded to. Nicoll, on the other hand, is perhaps too *severe* in its favour :—

"We saw the corn and haud the plough,—
We a' work for our living ;
We gather nought but what we've sawn,
A' else we reckon thieving.
And for the loon wha fears to say
He comes o' lowly sma' folk,
A wizened saul the creature has,—
Disown him will the puir folk ! "

Those who scoff at peasant life are often those who hold the ludicrous idea that a man's life consist in the things of which he is possessed ! To such we say, in the words of the poet, "Let not ambition mock their humble toil ;" for beyond all controversy the peasantry were possessed of a rare gem,—contentment ; that which Holy Writ hath pronounced to be better than riches !

lost. As for the educational superiority, I may safely state that the average amount of education, on the best part of the Breadalbane estates, does not nearly approximate to that of Logierait in your own neighbourhood.

In my work I have endeavoured to show that religion takes a much firmer hold in the cotter toons than in the Gallowgates and Cannongates of our large towns, and I adduced Burn's description of a "Cotter's Saturday Night" in proof of my position. I fear that the transforming of honest cottagers into bothy blackguards has not a salutary effect; and if your Lordship desires the religious and social amelioration of the Scottish peasantry, I would strongly advise you to abandon the bothy system in the farms wrought by yourself, and lend a helping hand to put down the system in Scotland generally. Nicoll's description of an evening in a Scottish cottage would not answer for bothies generally :—

> " And when the supper-time was o'er,
> The BEUK was taen as it should be,
> And heaven had its trysted hour
> Aneath that sooty auld roof-tree."

It is quite possible that the population on both sides of the lake might have been too great, but then there was ample room for expanding. In Breadalbane there was no trade, although I believe there is abundant room for a considerable local business. Look at Athole for instance, which has not greater facilities, and yet many branches of commerce are developed there. I could point out from personal experience how this could be accomplished, but it is not wanted,—it would keep too many people in the country, the very rock which is of all others to be avoided. It consists, with my knowledge, that when the Breadalbane farms were small, the rents were paid up to the last farthing, and testimony to this effect will not be wanting if called for. Since the farms have been made large, have the rents been equally well paid? But who caused the population to expand on Lochtayside? Was it not your noble father? Did he not *cram in* the men who returned from the fencible regiments? This method of cutting and carving up human families,—the father increasing, and the son sweeping away,—is what, in my humble opinion, demands investigation. Human beings have acute feelings, and they should not be removed hither and thither to accomodate the caprice of an ill-disposed laird. I shall not inquire about the original rights of the property of the Campbell clan,—I shall not ask whether or not the men whose swords acquired the property had no right to any part of the acquired territory,—I shall not ask whether or not, at a recent date, the clansmen did exercise their rights, and caused their castle to be built where it now stands, yes, after the foundations of another had been raised ground high. All that I beseech and pray for, on behalf of the peasantry is, that they may be allowed to live in Scotland, and that they may be allowed to cultivate the land, paying full rent for their possessions, and that they shall not be harassed by a wicked law, such as the one that protects game. Do I ask, or rather demand, anything but what all would openly admit was bare justice and no favour?

Your Lordship states that in reality there has been no depopulation of the district. This, and other parts of your Lordship's letter would certainly lead any who know nothing of the facts to suppose that there had been no clearings on the Breadalbane estates ; whereas it is generally believed that your Lordship removed, since 1834, no less than 500 families ! ! Some may think this a small matter ; but I do not. I think it is a great calamity for a family to be thrown destitute of the means of life, without a roof over their heads, and cast upon the wide sea of an unfeeling world. In Glenqueich, near Amulree, some sixty families formerly lived, where there are now only four or five ; and in America there is a glen inhabited by its ousted tenants, and called Glenqueich still. Yet forsooth, it is maintained there has been no depopulation here !* The desolations here look like the ruins of Irish cabins, although the population of Glenqueich were always characterized as being remarkably thrifty, economical and wealthy. On the braes of Taymouth, at the back of Drummond Hill, and at Tullochyoule, some forty or fifty families formerly resided where there is not one now ! Glenorchy, by the returns of 1831, showed a population of 1806 ; in 1841, 831 ;—is there no depopulation there ? Is it true that in Glenetive there were sixteen tenants a year or two ago, where there is not a single one now ? Is it true, my Lord, that you purchased an island on the west coast, called Luing, where some twenty-five families lived at the *beginning of this year*, but who are now cleared off to make room for one tenant, for whom an extensive steading is now being erected ? If my information be correct, I shall allow the public to draw their own conclusions ; but, from every thing that I have heard, I believe that your Lordship has done more to exterminate the Scottish peasantry than any man now living ; and perhaps you ought to be ranked next to the Marquis of Stafford in the unenviable clearing celebrities. If I have over-estimated the clearances at 500 families, please to correct me.

Now, my Lord, I did not say how these clearances were affected. I have been told they have been gone about in a covert and most insidious manner, and that a mock ceremony has been gone through of offering the people houses; but where are there houses in Breadalbane to give them ? I never heard of any unoccupied cottages—pray, where are they ? I am credibly informed that many have been offered places unfit for pigs ; and some have got the share of a house, but from which they were shortly driven out, on the shadow of a pretext. But granting that they got houses, what could the people do ? could they live on the wind ? I am aware that your Lordship does give considerable employment to workpeople ; but what kind of wages do the regular workers get ? They travel some three, four, or five miles to and from work daily, and the scanty pittance they obtain is 1s. 2d. per diem in winter, and 1s. 4d. in summer. By the time an able-bodied man pays house-rent out of that sum, and keeps a family, he cannot hoard much money in the banks. That the condition of such people is greatly ameliorated by depriving them of their

---

* A stranger, passing through the glen, inquired what had become of the people whose houses lay in ruins, and a man, apparently weak in intellect, replied, " They are out of my sight, and I know not where they have gone ! "

small holdings is what might be disputed. If they were not comfortable then, it is at least evident they are not in the Garden of Eden now.

Your Lordship states that upwards of £208,000 have been expended on "useful works." Of course, a large amount thereof has been recorded against the future heirs of entail. But how much of this large sum has been expended in a manner that will *yield any benefit to the country?* (for money expended for the gratification of caprice might be as well thrown into Loch Tay.) I am informed that the proportion is miserably small; *but how much is it?* Let it be known to a penny, so that your Lordship may have full justice rendered you. I may safely say that the peasantry have had very little of it appropriated for the improvement of their holdings. But after such a display of figures, you say, "I fearlessly ask, am I obnoxious to the imputation of being regardless of the prosperity of the people upon the property?" That you have been blamed for being *utterly* regardless of the people, is what I have often heard, and that you cared not a farthing what became of them, if they are got quickly out of sight; and all my informants agree to the same assertion (some of them using stronger language.)* But I am bound to admit that one of your factors is blamed for much of the mischief that has been done. If, as it is alleged, he boasted that he could get a south country farmer to rent the whole ground between Drummond Hill and Killin, it did certainly reveal no kindly feeling toward numerous families residing there.

You conclude your famous letter by asking, "Have I recklessly driven out from its mountains and glens the interesting and gallant race that *formerly resided there?* I can prove that the "interesting and gallant race" rather increased than diminished under your father's management. Who, then has driven them out? I know of no one who could but your Lordship or your agents.

But I cannot finish this long letter, without paying a tribute to the memory of the late Marquis of Breadalbane. He was beloved by a numerous and attached tenantry, and it may be some consolation to his descendants to know that his memory is yet respected in Breadalbane. Instead of being feared by his servants, he was greatly esteemed by all of them. Instead of making loud professions abroad and acting the tyrant at home, his practice always stood higher than his professions of liberality. The poor blessed him in the gate, and well might they deplore his departure; and yet he had always plenty himself; he was no niggard, but dispensed a bounteous Highland hospitality; yet he left his estates free of debt, besides leaving nearly half a million sterling to his heirs!

I have shortly alluded to the past and present on the Breadalbane estates, but what shall be said of the future? Hope, that always expects the best, whispers that present evils may come to an end; and, if report speaks correctly, promises to that effect may yet be realised. The tenure of entailed estates makes the possessor only a life-renter on them; and in

---

* Thus, a party, well-known on the Lakeside, is reported to have addressed a certain Marquis, "Ay, my Lord, and you're to put me out! are ye? But if I was a pheasant cock or a pointer dog, *I would get a house,* and meat too."

the course of nature, the Breadalbane estates must some time pass into the possession of others, who, it is hoped, will act more kindly to the people remaining than your Lordship has done. But it is hoped that they will remain as long in the hands of the present possessor as will enable him to make some reparation for the unexampled blunders he has committed.

I could have brought forward many more facts to prove that the systematic extermination of the peasantry, that is being carried on all over Scotland, is particularly felt on the Breadalbane estates; but whether pauperism and other claimant evils are occasioned thereby is what the public can determine; but they will widely differ from me if they do not believe that the Gothic or feudalistic legislation that fosters such enormities is a great obstruction to our prosperity and happiness as a nation.

I am, my Lord, your Lordship's very humble servant,
R. ALISTER.
July, 1853.

P.S.—On same future occasion I may trouble your Lordship with some inquiries about the benefits conferred upon the Highlands by ABSENTEEISM, and ask some questions about the legality of deer forests. which, I believe, cause an annual loss to Scotland of 100,000 sheep, and 10,000 black cattle. I believe they occupy 800 square miles of Scottish territory. Why we should spend so much money and spill so much blood in Africa for the protection of grazings *there*, while such tracts of country in Scotland are locked up from industry, and all but laid desolate?

To trace the scenes of desolation, and the extreme poverty occasioned by the clearing system, in the West Highlands, is more than can be expected in this work. This was done by abler men than me, viz., MR. ROBERT SUMMERS, Editor of the Glasgow *Daily Mail*, and MR. DONALD ROSS, Writer, Glasgow, gentlemen to whom the Highlanders are much indebted for their disinterested advocacy in behalf of the poor, and their disclosure of the cruelty and ungodly conduct of proprietors. But before leaving Perthshire, permit me to make some few remarks upon his Grace of Atholl. The Duke of Atholl, can, with propriety, claim the origin of Highland clearances. Whatever merit the family of Sutherland and Stafford may take to themselves, for the fire and faggot expulsion of the people from the Glens of Sutherland, they cannot claim the merit of originality. The present Duke of Atholl's Grandfather cleared Glen Tilt, (so far as I can learn) in 1784. This beautiful valley was occupied in the same way as other Highland valleys; each family possessing a piece of arable land, while the hill-pasture was held in common. The people held a right and full liberty to fish in the Tilt, an excellent salmon river, and the pleasure and profits of the chase, in common with their chief; but the then Duke acquired a great taste for deer. The people were for time immemorial accustomed to take their cattle in the summer seasons to

L

a higher glen, which is watered by the River Tarfe ; but the Duke appointed this Glen Tarfe for a deer forest, and built a high dyke at the head of Glen Tilt. The people submitted to this encroachment on their rights. The deer increased, and did not pay much regard to the march, they would jump over the dyke, and destroy the people's crops ; the people complained, and His Grace rejoiced : and to gratify the roving propensities of these light-footed animals, he added another splice of some thousand acres of the people's land to the grazing grounds of his favorite deer. Gradually the deer forest extended, and the marks of cultivation were effaced, till the last of the brave Glen Tilt men, who fought and often confronted and defeated the enemies of Scotland and her Kings upon many a bloody battle field, were routed off and bade a final farewell to the beautiful Glen Tilt, which they and their forefathers for ages considered their own healthy sweet home. An event occurred at this period, according to history, which afforded a pretext to the (*villain*) Duke for this heartless extirpation of the aborigines of Glen Tilt. Highland Chieftains were exhibiting their patriotism by raising regiments to serve in the American war ; and the Duke of Atholl could not be indifferent in such a cause. Great efforts were made to enlist the Glen Tilt people, who are still remembered in the district as a strong athletic race. Perpetual possession of their lands, at the then existing rents, was promised them, if they would only raise a contingent force equal to a man from each family. Some consented, but the majority, with a praiseworthy resolution not to be dragged at the tail of a Chief into a war of which they knew neither the beginning nor the end, refused. The Duke flew into a rage ; and press-gangs were sent up the Glen to carry off the young men by force. One of these companies seized a cripple tailor, who lived at the foot of Beney-gloe, and afraid lest he might carry intelligence of their approach up the Glen, they bound him hand and foot, and left him lying on the cold hill-side, where he contracted disease, from which he never recovered. By impressment and violence the regiment was at length raised ; and when peace was proclaimed, instead of restoring the soldiers to their friends and their homes, the Duke, as if he had been a trafficker in slaves, was only prevented from selling them to the East India Company by the rising mutiny of the regiment ! He afterwards pretended great offence at the Glen Tilt people, for their obstinacy in refusing to enlist, and—it may now be added—*to be sold*; and their conduct in this affair, was given out as the reason why he cleared them from the glen—an excuse which, in the present day, may increase our admiration of the people, but can never palliate the heartlessness of his conduct. His ireful policy, however has taken full effect. The romantic Glen Tilt, with its fertile holmes and verdant steeps, is little better than a desert. The very deer rarely visit it, and the wasted grass is burned like heather at the beginning of the year, to make room for the new verdure. On the spot where I found the grass most luxuriant, I traced the seats of thirty cottages, and have no hesitation in saying, that under the skill, the industrious habits, and the agricultural facilities of the present day, the land once occupied by the tenants of Glen Tilt, is capable of maintaining a thousand people,

and leave a large proportion of sheep and cattle for exportation besides.
In the meantime, it serves no better purpose than the occasional play-
ground of a Duke.

> " Proud Nimrod first the bloody chase began,
> A mighty hunter—and his prey was man.
> Our haughty Norman boasts the barbarous name,
> And makes his trembling slaves the royal game.
> The fields are ravished from industrious swains,
> From men their cities, and from gods their fanes.
> In vain kind seasons swell the teeming grain,
> Soft showers distill'd, and suns grow warm in vain;
> The swain, with tears, his frustrate labours yields,
> And, famish'd dies amidst the ripening fields.
> What wonder then a beast or subject slain,
> Were equal crimes in a despotic reign?
> Both, doomed alike, for sportive tyrants bled;
> But, while the subject starved, the beast was fed."—*Pope.*

The Parish of Atholl was at one period a gigantic parish; it is traversed
from end to end by the Great Northern Road, from Perth through the
Grampian Hills to Inverness, formerly a favorite resort for tourists
annually—the natural attraction of the place being so widely known for
its romantic scenery.   The famous Pass of Killicrankie, ushers you from
the south to the Plains of Atholl, a beautiful level strip of land stretching
along the north bank of the River Garry, about three and a half miles
long, and about two miles broad.   Here stands Blair Castle, the Duke's
seat, whose parks and pleasure grounds takes up three-fourths of the whole
plain.   The whole industry of this once populous parish, is compressed
into the remainder one-fourth.   This busy little plain is the terminus of
half a dozen of other great glens, which shoot amongst the Grampians.
The renowned Glen Tilt stretches easterly, Glen Bruan northward, and
Glen Garry westward.   These Glens are intersected by smaller valleys,
presenting varieties of aspects, from the most fertile carses to the bleak
moorland.   But man durst not be seen there.   The image of God is
forbidden to travel there, unless it is stamped upon the Duke, his foresters,
and game-keepers, that His Grace's deer may not be annoyed.   In 1800,
the population of this parish was given in at 2,998; in 1841, the population was given in at 2,304, shewing a decrease of 694.   But those better
acquainted in the parish, say that the population does not exceed 1,800.
For all these highland depopulators manage to keep up a false population to
screen them from the infamy they so well merited.

"Wealth increases, and men decay."

Long since these valliant men of Atholl have been expelled from the
Grampian Nursery.   Still new forests for deer are springing up from east
to west; from the neighbourhood of Aberdeen to the crags of Oban, you
have one continuous line of forests.   In other parts of the highlands they
can scarcely be numbered.   Such as the Forest of Loch Archaig, Glen
Morison, Glen Strathfarar, Dirubh Moor, (Sutherlandshire); and many
more unpronounceable names, which would only weary the reader.   In
short, whether the old Forests of King Fergus and Ceanmore were revived,

or new regions are brought within the mystic circle for the first time, the same devastation precedes the completion of the enterprise ; houses, roads, enclosures, cattle, men, every work of time and progress, the valuable creation of labour, and changes of centuries, are all extirpated by the word of a mortal insignificant worm of the earth, in order that deer, blackcock, and other sporting animals, more valuable than men, may enjoy the pleasing solitude ; and that aristocratic sportmen may monopolise the pleasure and benefits of the chase. Yes my highland Scotch readers, but Britain is now in need of men to fight her battles, to subdue her rebellious subjects or slaves in India, to invade and conquer China, to keep at bay Russia, Persia, and many other formidable enemies. Cringing and making alliance with perjured Napoleon and France, who cannot but remember, and will remember, Waterloo, and who would rejoice to see her glory departed, and her humbled in the dust. Look at her squandering her money away, hiring German paltroons to fight her battles. Pawning her revenues with Jews, to raise money to pay them, while her own nursery of the brave, irresistable in the battle field, who always fought for glory and honour, not for her shilling per day ; who at all times, and especially in need, increased her army and navy with men by the thousands worthy of the name—not with hired foreign cowards, who in most cases, do more harm than good—but with men who were never known to turn their back to an enemy, but when prudence and good discipline required it. Yes I say this nursery is converted into a howling desert, to afford amusement and sporting ground for a number of these aristocratic locusts, who were, and will continue to be, the desolating curse of every land and nation they are allowed to breed in. This Royal Caledonian Forest they destroyed by fire ; the oaks and cedars of this Lebanon have been hewn down and up-rooted. They are (to my joy) taking firm root and spreading fast in foreign climes. But the question is, has Britain or their mother, any claim upon their sympathy or assistance wherever they (her children) are to be found. Let me not say no, though she deserved it—I say yes. However cruel she dealt with us, she is still our mother ; and bad and short-sighted as she acted, she is still, I hope, open to conviction ; and this is the time to convince her of her folly, when she is under the unerring chastising *Rod of God*, when her sins have found her out. And every true Scotchmen should exert himself, wherever he is, to persuade her of her past folly, and help on her conviction and conversion. She has hearkened to sound reasoning in many instances this some years back ; and it is to be hoped her Rulers will do so yet ; and that the Highlands of Scotland will be re-peopled, and flourish as in the days of yore. The people have only to demand it in earnest, and it will be done ; whereas in other nations the people's demands are answered by the cannon. Let no Scotchman, Highland or Lowlander, wish to see their mother trampled down by Mahomedans, Pagans, Idolators, and Despots, who erased liberty and freedom from their vocabularies, and even the very word is not found in their nations.

But I am sorry that through evil agency and mal-administration of Highland proprietors, sympathy for Britain in her late and present trouble disappeared in the Highlands of Scotland ; a proof of it is to be seen in the following letter which I received shortly after leaving Scotland :

My correspondent says: "MacLeod, your predictions are making their appearance at last, great demand are here for men to go to Russia, but they are not to be found. It seems that the Secretary of War has corresponded with all our Highland Proprietors, to raise as many men as they could for .the Crimean War, and ordered so many officers of rank to the Highlands to assist the proprietors in doing so—but it has been a complete failure as yet. The nobles advertised by placards, meetings of the people; these proclamations were attended to, but when they came to understand what they were about, in most cases the recruiting proprietors and staff were saluted with the ominous cry of Maa! maa! boo! boo! imitating sheep and bullocks, and, send your deer, your roes, your rams, dogs, shepherds, and gamekeepers, to fight the Russians, they never done us any harm. The success of his Grace the Duke of Sutherland was deplorable,. I believe you would have pitied the poor old man had you seen him.

In my last letter I told you that his head commissioner, Mr. Loch, and military officer, was in Sutherland for the last six weeks, and failed in getting one man to enlist; on getting this doleful tidings the Duke himself left London for Sutherland, he arrived at Dunrobin about ten days ago, and after presenting himself upon the streets of Golspie and Brora, he called a meeting of the male inhabitants of the parishes of Clyne, Rogart, and Golspie; the meeting was well attended, upwards of 400 were punctual at the hour, his Grace in his carriage with his military staff and factors appeared shortly after, the people gave them a hearty cheer; his Grace took the chair. Three or four clerks took their seats at the table, and loosened down bulky packages of bank notes, and spread out platefulls of glittering gold. The Duke addressed the people very serious, and entered upon the necessity of going to war with Russia, and the danger of allowing the Czar to have more power than what he holds already, of his cruel despotic reign in Russia, &c., likewise praising the Queen and her government, rulers and nobles of Great Britain, who stood so much in need of men to put and keep down the Tyrant Russia, and foil him in his wicked schemes to take possession of Turkey. In concluding his address, which was often cheered, he told the young able-bodied men that his clerks were ready to take down the names of all those willing to enlist, and every one who would enlist in the 93rd Highlanders that the clerk would give him, there and then, £6 sterling, those who would rather enter any other corps would get £3, all from his own private purse, independent of the government bounty; after advancing many silly flattering decoyments, he sat down to see the result, but there was no movement among the people; after sitting for a long time looking at the clerks, and them at him, at last his anxious looks at the people assumed a somewhat indignant appearance, when he suddenly rose up and asked what was the cause of their non-attention to the proposals he made, but no reply; it was the silence of the grave—still standing, his Grace suddenly asked the cause; but no reply; at last an old man leaning upon his staff, was observed moving towards the Duke, and when he approached near enough, he addressed his Grace something like as follows: 'I am sorry for the response your Grace's proposals are meeting here to-day, so near the spot where your maternal mother, by giving forty-eight hours notice, marshalled fifteen hundred men, to pick out of them the nine hundred she required, but there is a cause for it, and a grievous cause, and as your Grace demands to know it I must tell you, as I see none else are inclined in this assembly to do it. Your Grace's mother and predecessors applied to our fathers for men upon former occasions, and our fathers responded to their call, they have made liberal promises which neither them nor you performed; we are, we think, a little wiser than our fathers, and we estimate your promises of to-day at the value of theirs, besides you should bear in mind that your predecessors and yourself expelled us in a most cruel and unjust manner from the land which our fathers held in *lien* from your family for their sons, brothers, cousins, and relations, which was handed over to your parents to keep up their dignity, and to kill the Americans, Turks, French, and the Irish; and these lands are devoted now to rear dumb brute animals, which you and your parents consider of far more value than men. I do assure your Grace that it is the prevailing opinion in this country, that should the Czar of Russia take possession of Dunrobin Castle and of Stafford House next term, that we could not expect worse treatment at his hands than we have experienced at the hands of your family for the last fifty years. Your parents, yourself, and your commissioners, have desolated the glens and straths of Sutherland, where you should find hundreds, yea, thousands of men to meet you and respond cheerfully to your call, had your parents and yourself kept faith with them. How could your Grace expect to find men where they are not, and the few of them which are to be found among the rubbish or ruins of the country, have more sense than to be decoyed by chaff to the field of slaughter; but one comfort you have, though you cannot find men to fight, you can supply those who will fight with plenty of mutton, beef, and venison.' The Duke rose up, put on his hat and left the field."

Whether my correspondent added to the old man's reply to his Grace or not, I cannot say, one thing evident, it was the very reply his Grace deserved.

I know for a certainty this to be the prevailing opinion throughout the whole Highlands of Scotland, and who should wonder at it? How many thousands of them who served out their 21, 22, 25, and 26 years, fighting for the British aristocracy, and on their return, wounded, maimed, or worn out, to their own country, promising themselves to spend the remainder of their days in peace, and enjoying the blessings and comfort their fathers enjoyed among their healthy Highland delightful hills, but found to their grief their parents were expelled from the country to make room for sheep, deer, and game, the glens where they were born desolate, and the abodes which sheltered them at birth and where they were reared to manhood, burnt to the ground; and instead of meeting the cheer, shaking-hands, hospitality and affections of fathers, mothers, brothers, sisters, and relations, met with with a desolated glen, bleating of sheep, barking of dogs, and if they should happen to rest their worn-out frame upon the green sod which has grown upon their father's hearth, and a game-keeper, a factor, or water bailiff to come round, he would very unceremoniously tell them to absent themselves as smart as they could, and not annoy the deer. No race we have on record has suffered so much at the hands of those who should be their patrons, and proved to be so tenacious of patriotism as the Celtic race, but I assure you it has found its level now, and will disappear altogether soon, and as soon as patriotism will disappear in any nation, so sure that nation's glory is tarnished, victories uncertain, and her greatness diminished, and decaying consumptive death will be the result. If ever the old adage, which says, " Those whom the Gods determine to destroy, they first deprive them of reason," was verified, it was, and is, in the case of British aristocracy, and Highland proprietors in particular. I am not so void of feeling as to blame the Duke of Sutherland, his parents or any other Highland absentee proprietor for all the evil done in the land, but the evil was done in their name and under the authority they have invested in wicked cruel servants. For instance, the only silly man who enlisted from among the great assembly his Grace addressed, was a married man with three of a family and his wife; it was generally believed *that his bread was baked for life*, but no sooner was he away to Fort George to join his regiment than his place of abode was pulled down, and his wife and family turned out, and only permitted to live in a hut, from which an old female pauper was carried a few days before to the church-yard; there the young family were sheltered, and their names registered upon the poor roll for support; his Grace could not be guilty of such low rascality as this, yet he was told of it, but took no cognizance of those who did it in his name. It is likewise said that this man got a furlough of two weeks, to see his wife and family before going abroad, and that the factor heard he was coming and ordered the ground officer of the parish of Rogart, of the name of M'Leod, to watch the soldier, and not allow him to see nor speak to his wife, but in his, the officer's presence. This was cruelty to prevent the poor fellow who was three months absent from his wife, and could not be allowed to kiss, or have one night's pleasure with her before he would embark for the Crimea, but in presence of an officer. None could think his Grace to be so devoid of natural feelings, yet it was done in his name. The factor alleged as an excuse for it, that he did not want the parish of Rogart to be burdened with any more children to keep up. *Economy! Economy!!* We have then in the same parish an old bachelor of the name of John Macdonald, who had three idiot sisters, whom he upheld independent of any source of relief, but a favorite of George, the notorious factor, envied this poor bachelor's farm, and he was summoned to remove at next term. The poor fellow petitioned his Grace, and Loch, but to no purpose, he was doomed to walk away, on the term day as the factor told him, "to America, Glasgow, or to the devil if he choosed." Seeing he had no other alternative, two days before the day of his removal he yoked his cart, and got neighbours to help him to haul the three idiots into it, and drove away with them to Dunrobin Castle; when he came up to factor Gunn's door he capsized them out upon the green, and wheeled about and went away home, the three idiots finding themselves upon the top of one another so sudden, they raised an inhuman-like yell, and fixed into one another to fight, and scratched, yelled, and screeched so terrific that

Mr. Gunn, his lady, his daughters, and all the clerks and servants, were soon about them, but they hearkened to no reason, for they had none themselves, but continued their fighting and inharmonious music; messenger after messenger was sent after John, but of no use; at last the great Gunn himself followed and overtook him, asked him how did he come to leave his sisters in such a state? He replied. "I kept them while I had a piece of land to support them, you have taken that land from me, then take them along with the land, and make of them what you can, I must look out for myself, but I cannot carry them to the labour market." Gunn was in a fix, and had to give John assurance that he would not be removed if he would take his sisters, so John took them home, and has not been molested as yet.

I have here beside me a respectable girl of the name of Ann Murray, whose father was removed during the time of the wholesale *faggot* removal but got a lot of a barren moor to cultivate; however barren-like it was, he was raising a family of industrious young sons, and by dint of hard labour and perseverence, they made it a comfortable home, but the young sons one by one left the country, (and four of them are within two miles of where I sit), the result was, that Ann was the only one who remained with the parents. The mother who had an attack of palsy, was left entirely under Ann's care after the family left; and she took it so much to heart that her daughter's attention was required day and night, until death put an end to her afflictions, after twelve years' suffering. Shortly after the mother's death, the father took ill, and was confined to bed for nine months; and Ann's labour re-commenced until his decease. Though Ann Murray could be numbered among the most dutiful of daughters yet her incessant labour for a period of more than thirteen years, made visible inroads upon her tender constitution; yet by the liberal assistance of her brothers, who did not lose sight of her and their parent, (though upon a foreign strand) Ann Murray kept the farm in the best of order, no doubt expecting that she would be allowed to keep it after her parent's decease; but this was not in store for her, the very day after her father's funeral, the officer came to her, and told her that she was to be removed in a few weeks, that the farm was let to another, and that Factor Gunn wished to see her. She was at that time afflicted with jaundice, and told the officer that she could not undertake the journey, which was only ten miles. Next day the officer was at her again, more urgent than before, and made use of extraordinary threats; so she had to go. When she appeared before this Bashaw, he swore like a trooper, and damned her soul, why she disobeyed his first summons; she excused herself trembling, that she was unwell; another volley of oaths and threats met her response, and told her to remove herself from the estate next week, for her conduct; and with a threat, which well becomes a Highland tyrant, not to take away nor sell a single article of furniture, implements of husbandry, cattle, or crop; nothing was allowed but her own body clothes: that every thing was to be handed over to her brother, who was to have the farm. Seeing there was neither mercy nor justice for her, she told him the crop, house, and every other thing belonging to the farm, belonged to her and brothers in

America, and that the brother to whom he (the factor) intended to hand over the farm and effects, never helped her father or mother while in trouble ; and that she was determined that he should not enjoy what she laboured for, and what her other brother's money paid for. She went and got the advice of a man of business, advertised a sale, and sold off in the face of threats of interdict, and came to Canada, where she was warmly received by brothers, sisters, and friends, now in Woodstock, and can tell her tale better than I can. No one could think nor believe that his Grace would even countenance such doings as these ; but it was done in his name.

I have here within ten miles of me, Mr. William Ross, once Taxman of Achtomeleeny, Sutherlandshire, who occupied the most convenient farm to the principal deer-stalking hills in the county. Often have the English and Irish lords, connected in marriage with the Sutherlands, dined and took their lunch at William Ross' table, and at his expense ; and more than once passed the night under his roof. Mr. Ross being so well acquainted among the mountains and haunts of the deer, was often engaged as a guide and instructor to these noblemen, on their deer-stalking and fishing excursions, and became a real favorite with the Sutherland family, which enabled him, to erect superior buildings to the common rule, and improve his farm in a superior style ; so that his mountain-side farm was nothing short of a Highland paradise. But unfortunately for William, his nearest neighbour, one Major Gilchrist, a sheep farmer, *(Ahab)* coveted Mr. Ross's vineyard, and tried many underhand schemes to secure the place for himself, but in vain. Ross would hearken to none of his proposals. But *Ahab* was a chief friend of Factor Gunn ; and William Ross got notice of removal. Ross prepared a Memorial to the first and late Duchess of Sutherland, and placed it in her own hand. Her Grace read it, and instantly went in to the Factor's office, and told him that William Ross was not to be removed from Achtomeleeny while he lived ; and wrote the same on the petition, and handed it back to Ross, with a graceful smile, saying, "you are now out of the reach of Factors; now, William, go home in peace." William bowed, and departed cheerfully; but the Factor and Ground Officer followed close behind him, and while Ross was reading Her Grace's deliverance the officer, David Ross, came and snapped the paper out of his hand and ran to Factor Gunn with it ; Ross followed, but Gunn put it in his pocket saying, "William, you would need to give it to me afterwards at any rate, and I will keep it till I read it, and then return it to you," and with a tiger-like smile on his face said, "I believe you came speed to-day, and I am glad of it ;" but William never got it in his hand again. However, he was not molested during Her Grace's life. Next year she paid a visit to Dunrobin, when factor Wm. Gunn advised Ross to apply to her for a reduction of rent, (under the mask of favouring him.) He did so, and it was granted cheerfully. Her Grace left Dunrobin this year never to return ; in the beginning of the next Spring she was carried back to Dunrobin a corpse, and a few days after she was interred in Dornoch, William Ross was served with a Summons of Removal from Achtomeleeny, and he had nothing to shew. He petitioned the present Duke and his

Commissioner, Mr. Loch, and related the whole circumstance to them, but to no avail, only he was told that factor Gunn was ordered to give him some other lot of land, which he did; and having no other resource William accepted of it to his loss; for between loss of cattle, building and repairing houses, he was minus of one hundred and fifty pounds sterling of his means and substance, from the time he was removed from Achtomeleeny till he removed himself to Canada. Besides he had a written agreement or promise for melioration or valuation for all the farm improvements and house building at Achtomeleeny, which was valued by the family surveyor at £250. William was always promised to get it, until they came to learn that he was leaving for America, then they would not give a cent of it. William Ross left them with it to join his family in Canada ; but he can in his old age sit at as comfortable a table, and sleep on as comfortable a bed, with greater ease of mind and a clearer conscience, among his own dutiful and affectionate children, than the tyrant Factor ever did or ever will among his. I know as well as any one can tell me that this is but one or two cases out of the thousand I could enumerate, where the liberality and benevolence of His Grace, and of his parents, were abused, and that to their patron's loss. You see in the above case, that William was advised to plead for a reduction of rent, so that the Factor's favourite, Ahab Gilchrist, would have the benefit of Naboth Ross' improvement, and the reduction he got on his rent, which would not be obtained otherwise. The long and the short of it is, that the unhallowed crew of factors and officials, from the highest to the lowest grade of them employed by the family of Sutherland for the last 54 years, were so well qualified in rascality that they in their combination, could rob both proprietor and people. They got the corrupt portion of the public press on their side, to applaud their wicked doings and robbing schemes, as the only mode of improvement and civilization in the Highlands of Scotland. They have got what is still more to be lamented, all the established ministers, with few exceptions, on their side; and in them they found faithful auxiliaries in crushing the people. Any of them could hold a whole congregation by the hair of their heads over hell-fire, if they offered to resist the powers that be, until they submitted. If a single individual resisted, he was denounced from the pulpit, and considered afterwards a dangerous man in the community; and he might depart as quick as he could. Any man, or men, may violate the laws of God, and violate the laws of heaven as often as he chooses; he is never heeded, and has nothing to fear, but if he offends the Duke's Factor, the lowest of his minions, or violates the least of their laws and regulations it is an unpardonable sin. The present Duke's mother, was no doubt a liberal lady of many good parts, and seemed to be much attached to the natives, but unfortunately for them, she employed for her factors a vile, unprincipled crew, who were their avowed enemies; she would hearken to the complaints of the people, and would write to the ministers of the Gospel to ascertain the correctness of complaints, and the factor was justified, however gross the outrage was that he committed—the minister dined with the factor and could not refuse to favour him. The present Duke is a simple, if not a silly, narrow minded gentleman, who concerns himself very little, about even his own pecuniary affairs ; he entrusts his whole affairs to this set of vile, cunning knaves, called factors, and the people are enslaved so much that it is now considered the most foolish thing a man can do to petition his Grace, whatever is done to him, for it will go hard with the factor, or he will punish and make an example of him to deter others.

To detail what I knew myself personally, and what I have learnt from others of their petty roguery and robbery, it would, as I said before, fill a volume. For another instance :—When a marriage in the family of Sutherland takes place, or the birth of an heir, a feast is ordered for the Sutherland people, consisting of whiskey, porter, ale, and plenty of eatables. The day of feasting and rejoicing is appointed, and heralded throughout the country, and the people are enjoined in marshal terms to assemble —barrels of raw adulterated whiskey are forwarded to each parish, and some raw adulterated sugar, and that is all. Bonfires are to be prepared upon the tops of the highest mountains. The poorest of the poor are warned by family officers to carry the materials consisting of peats and tar barrels, upon their backs ; the scene is lamentable to see groups of these wretched, half-clad and ill-shod, climbing up these mountains with their loads ; however, the work must be done, there is no denial, and the evening of rejoicing arrived, and the people are assembled at their different Clachans ; the barrels of whiskey are taken out to the field, and are poured into large tubs, and a good amount of abominiable-looking sugar is mixed with it, and a sturdy favourite is employed to stir it about with a flail handle, or some long cudgel—all sorts of drinking implements are produced, such as tumblers, bowls, ladles, and tin jugs. Bagpipers are set up with great glee. In the absence of the factor, the animal called the ground officer, and in some instances the Parish Minister will open the jolification, and show an example to the people how to deal with this coarse beverage ; after the first round the respectable portion of the people will depart, or retire to an inn, where they could enjoy themselves ; but the *drouthies*, and ignorant youthful, will keep the field of revelling until tearing of clothes and faces come to be the rule ; fists and cudgels supplant jugs and ladles, and this will continue until king Bacchus enters the field and hushes the most heroic brawlers, and the most ferocious combatants to sound snoring on the field of rejoicing, where many of them enters into contracts with death, from which they never could extricate themselves. With the co-operation and assistance of factors, ministers, and editors, a most flourishing account is sent to the world, and to the absentee family in London, who knows nothing about how the affair was conducted. The world will say how happy must the people be who live under such good and noble liberal minded patrons, and the patrons themselves are so highly pleased with the report, that however extraordinary the bill that comes to them on the rent day, in place of money, for roast beef and mutton, bread and cheese, London porter, and Edinburgh ale, which was never bought nor tasted by the people, I say they consider their commissioners used great economy ; no cognizance are taken, the bill is accepted and discharged, the people are deceived and the proprietors robbed, and the factors divide the spoil, which is not a trifle; no wonder that the Duke of Sutherland receives so little rent from his Sutherland Estates. Were it not for the many channels of wealth pouring in upon him he would be bankrupt long ago; but all these robberies of his Grace will no doubt be among the items which makes up the £60,000 sent down to save the people from dying by famine, as Loch says; but I will leave the Duke and his factors to settle their own accounts; one thing is evident, his factors and commissioners have disgraced him, and left a stain of immortal dye upon him and the family of Sutherland, that time and revolution of years will not wipe away.

Let me now conclude by taking a few extracts from other authors who wrote faithfully and without any hostile feeling towards his Grace, or his family, nor any other Highland proprietor who followed the Atholl and Sutherland clearing example. The first of these extracts is from the pen of that noble minded Scotchman, General Stuart, of Garth, who wrote largely upon the clearing system :—

"It is painful to dwell on this subject" [the present state of Sutherland]; "but as information communicated by men of honour, judgment, and perfect veracity, descriptive of what they daily witness, affords the best means of forming a correct judgement, and as these gentlemen, from their situations in life, have no immediate interest in the determination of the question, beyond what is dictated by humanity and a love of truth, their authority may be considered as undoubted."—*General Stewart of Garth.*

"It is by a cruel abuse of legal forms,—it is by an unjust usurpation,—that the *tacksman* and the tenant of Sutherland are considered as having no right to the land which they have occupied for so many ages. * * A Count or Earl has no more right to expel from their homes the inhabitants of his county, than a King to expel from his country the inhabitants of his kingdom."—*Sismondi.*

THE BELOVED AND GREAT HUGH MILLER ON SUTHERLAND AS IT WAS AND IS.

"There appeared at Paris, about five years ago, a singularly ingenious work on political economy, from the pen of the late M. de Sismondi, a writer of European reputation. The greater part of the first volume is taken up with discussions on territorial wealth, and the condition of the cultivators of the soil; and in this portion of the work there is a prominent place assigned to a subject which perhaps few Scotch readers would expect to see introduced through the medium of a foreign tongue to the people of a great Continental State. We find this philosophic writer, whose works are known far beyond the limits of his language, devoting an entire essay to the case of the late Duchess of Sutherland and her tenants, and forming a judgement on it very unlike the decision of political economists in our own country, who have not hesitated to characterize her great and singularly harsh experiment, whose worst effects we are but beginning to see, as at once justifiable in itself and happy in its results. It is curious to observe how deeds done as if in darkness, or in a corner, are beginning. after the lapse of nearly thirty years, to be proclaimed on the house-tops. The experiment of the late Duchess was not intended to be made in the eye of Europe. Its details would ill bear the exposure. When Cobbett simply referred to it only ten years ago, the noble proprie-trix was startled, as if a rather delicate family secret was on the eve of being divulged ; and yet nothing seems more evident now than that civi-lized man all over the world is to be made aware of how the experiment was accomplished, and what it is ultimately to produce. It must be obvi-ous, further, that the infatuation of the present proprietor, in virtually setting aside the Toleration Act on his property, must have the effect of spreading the knowledge of it all the more widely, and of rendering its results much more disastrous than they could have possibly been of them-selves.

In a time of quiet and good order, when law, whether in the right or the wrong, is all-potent in enforcing its findings, the argument which the philosophic Frenchmen employs in behalf of the ejected tenantry of Sutherland, is an argument at which proprietors may afford to smile. In a time of revolution, however, when lands change their owners, and old families give place to new ones, it might be found somewhat formidable, —sufficiently so, at least, to lead a wise proprietor in an unsettled age rather to conciliate than oppress and irritate the class who would be able in such circumstances to urge it with most effect. It is not easy doing justice in a few sentences to the facts and reasonings of an elaborate essay : but the line of the argument runs somewhat thus :—

Under the old Celtic tenures,—the only tenures, be it remembered, through which the Lords of Sutherland derive their rights to their lands, —the *Clann*, or children of the soil, were the proprietors of the soil ;— "the whole of Sutherland," says Sismondi, belonged to "the men of Sutherland." Their chief was their monarch, and a very absolute mon-arch he was. " He gave the different *tacks* of land to his officers or took them away from them, according as they showed themselves more or less useful in war. But though he could thus, in a military sense, reward or punish the clan, he could not diminish in the least the property of the clan itself ;"—he was a chief, not a proprietor, and had " no more right to expel from their homes the inhabitants of his county, than a king to expel from his country the inhabitants of his kingdom." " Now, the Gaelic tenant," continues the Frenchman, " has never been conquered ; nor did he forfeit, on any after occasion, the rights which he originally possessed ;"—in point of right, he is still a co-proprietor with his captain. To a Scotchman acquainted with the law of property as it has existed among us, in even the Highlands, for the last century, and everywhere else for at least two centuries more, the view may seem extreme ; not so, however, to a native of the Continent, in many parts of which, prescrip-tion and custom are found ranged, not on the side of the chief, but on that of the vassal. " Switzerland," says Sismondi, " which in so many respects resembles Scotland,—in its lakes, its mountains,—its climate,—

and the character, manners, and habits of its children,—was likewise at the same period parcelled out among a small number of Lords. If the Counts of Kyburgh, of Lentzburg, of Hapsburg, and of Gruyeres, had been protected by the English laws they would find themselves at the present day precisely in the condition in which the Earls of Sutherland were twenty years ago. Some of them would perhaps have had the same taste for *improvements*, and several republics would have been expelled from the Alps, to make room for flocks of sheep." "But while the law has given to the Swiss peasant a guarantee of perpetuity, it is to the Scottish laird that it has extended this guarantee in the British empire, leaving the peasant in a precarious situation." "The clan,—recognised at first by the captain, whom they followed in war, and obeyed for their common advantage, as his friends and relations, then as his soldiers, then as his vassals, then as his farmers,—he has come finally to regard as hired labourers, whom he may perchance allow to remain on the soil of their common country for his own advantage, but whom he has the power to expel so soon as he no longer finds it for his interest to keep them."

Arguments like those of Sismondi, however much their force may be felt on the Continent could be formidable at home, as we have said, in only a time of revolution, when the very foundations of society would be unfixed, and opinion set loose, to pull down or reconstruct at pleasure. But it is surely not uninteresting to mark how, in the course of events, that very law of England which, in the view of the Frenchman, has done the Highland peasant so much less, and the Highland chief so much more than justice, is bidding fair, in the case of Sutherland at least, to carry its rude equalizing remedy along with it. Between the years 1811 and 1820, fifteen thousand inhabitants of this northern district were ejected from their snug inland farms, by means for which we would in vain seek a precedent except perchance in the history of the Irish masssacre.

Mr Miller goes on. He visited Sutherland at the the time of the disruption, in the Church of Scotland, and found the people in a deplorable state; their complaints and sorrow were heard by him thus—" We were ruined and reduced to beggary before," they say, "and now the gospel is taken from us."

Nine-tenths of the poor people of Sutherland are adherents to the Free Church,—all of them in whose families the worship of God has been set up,—all who entertain a serious belief in the reality of religion,—all who are not the creatures of the proprietor, and have not stifled their convictions for a piece of bread,—are devotedly attached to the dis-established ministers, and will endure none other. The Residuary clergy they do not recognise as clergy at all. The Established Churches have become as useless in the district, as if, like its Druidical circles, they represented some idolatrous belief, long exploded,—the people will not enter them ; and they respectfully petition his Grace to be permitted to build other churches for themselves. And fain would his Grace indulge them, he says. In accordance with the suggestion of an innate desire, willingly would he permit them to build their own churches and support their own ministers. But then, has he not loyally engaged to support the Establishment? To permit a religious and inoffensive people to build their own places of worship, and support their own clergy, would be sanctioning a sort of persecution against the Establishment; and as his Grace dislikes religious persecution, and has determined always to oppose whatever tends to it, he has resolved to make use of his influence, as the most extensive of Scottish proprietors, in forcing them back to their parish churches. If they persist in worshipping God agreeably to the dictates of their conscience, it must be on the unsheltered hill-side,—in winter, amid the frosts and snows of a severe northern climate,—in the milder seasons, exposed to the scorching sun and the drenching shower. They must not be permitted the shelter of a roof.

We have exhibited to our readers, in the *clearing* of Sutherland a process of ruin so thoroughly disastrous, that it might be deemed scarcely possible to render it more complete. And yet with all its apparent completeness, it admitted of a supplementary process. To employ one of the striking figures of Scripture, it was possible to grind into powder what had been previously broken into fragments,—to degrade the poor inhabitants to a still lower level than that on which they had been so cruelly precipitated,—though persons of a not very original cast of mind might have found it difficult to say how, the Duke of Sutherland has been ingenious enough to fall on exactly the one proper expedient for supplementing their ruin. All in mere circumstance and situation that could lower and deteriorate, had been present as ingredients in the first process; but there still remained for the people, however reduced to poverty or broken in spirit, all in religion that consoles and ennobles. Sabbath-days came round with their humanizing influences; and, under the teachings of the gospel, the poor and the oppressed looked longingly forward to a future scene of being, in which there is no poverty or oppression. They still possessed, amid their misery, something positively good, of which it was impossible to deprive them, and hence the ability derived to the present lord of Sutherland of deepening and rendering more signal the ruin accomplished by his predecessor.

These harmonize but too well with the mode in which the interior of Sutherland was cleared, and the improved cottages of its sea-coasts erected. The plan has its two items. No sites are to be granted in the district for Free Churches, and no dwelling-house for Free Church ministers. The climate is severe,—the winters prolonged and stormy,—the roads which connect the chief seats of population with the neighbouring counties, dreary and long. May not ministers and people be eventually worn out in this way? Such is the portion of the plan which his Grace and his Grace's creatures can afford to present to the light. But there are supplementary items of a somewhat darker kind. The poor cotters are, in the great majority of cases, tenants-at-will; and there has been much pains taken to inform them, that to the crime of entertaining and sheltering a Protesting minister, the penalty of ejection from their holdings must inevitably attach. The laws of Charles have again returned in this unhappy district, and free and tolerating Scotland has got, in the nineteenth century, as in the seventeenth, its intercommuned ministers. We shall not say that the intimation has emanated from the Duke. It is the misfortune of such men, that there creep around them creatures whose business it is to anticipate their wishes; but who, at times, doubtless, instead of anticipating, misinterpret them; and who, even when not very much mistaken, impart to whatever they do the impress of their own low and menial natures, and thus exaggerate in the act, the intention of their masters. We do not say, therefore, that the intimation has emanated from the Duke; but this we say, that an exemplary Sutherlandshire minister of the Protesting Church, who resigned his worldly all for the sake of his principles, had lately to travel, that he might preach to his attached people, a long journey of forty-four miles outwards, and as much in return, and all this without taking shelter under cover of a roof, or without partaking of any other refreshment than that furnished by the slender store of provisions which he had carried with him from his new home. Willingly would the poor Highlanders have received him at any risk; but knowing from experience what a Sutherlandshire removal means, he preferred enduring any amount of hardship rather than that the hospitality of his people should be made the occasion of their ruin. We have already adverted to the case of a lady of Sutherland threatened with ejection from her home because she had extended the shelter of her roof to one of the Protesting clergy,—an aged and venerable man, who had quitted the neighbouring manse, his home for many years, because he could no longer enjoy it in consistency with his principles; and we have shown that that aged and venerable man was the lady's own father. What amount of oppression of a smaller and more petty character may not be expected in the circumstances, when cases such as these are found to stand but a very little over the ordinary level?

The meanness to which ducal hostility can stoop in this hapless district, impress with a feeling of surprise. In the parish of Dornoch, for instance, where his Grace is fortunately not the sole landowner, there has been a site procured on the most generous terms from Sir George Gunn Monro of Poyntzfield; and this gentleman, believing himself possessed of a hereditary right to a quarry, which, though on the Duke's ground, had been long resorted to by the proprietors of the district generally, instructed the builder to take from it the stones which he needed. Here, however, his Grace interfered. Never had the quarry been prohibited before, but on this occasion, a stringent interdict arrested its use. If his Grace could not prevent a hated Free Church from arising in the district, he could at least add to the *expense* of its erection. We have even heard that the portion of the building previously erected had to be pulled down and the stones returned.

How are we to account for a hostility so determined, and that can stoop so low? In two different ways, we are of opinion, and in both have the people of Scotland a direct interest. Did his Grace entertain a very intense regard for Established Presbytery, it is probable that he himself would be a Presbyterian of the Establishment. But such is not the case. The church into which he would so fain force the people has been long since deserted by himself. The secret of the course which he pursues can have no connection therefore with religious motive or belief. It can be no prosleytising spirit that misleads his Grace. Let us remark, in the first place, rather however, in the way of embodying a fact, than imputing a motive, that with his present views, and in his present circumstances, it may not seem particularly his Grace's interest to make the county of Sutherland a happy or desirable home to the people of Scotland. It may not to be his Grace's interest that the population of the district should increase. The *clearing* of the sea-coast may seem as little prejudicial to his Grace's welfare now, as the *clearing* of the interior seemed adverse to the interests of his predecessor thirty years ago; nay, it is quite possible that his Grace may be led to regard the *clearing* of the coast as the better and more important *clearing* of the two. Let it not be forgotten that a poor-law hangs over Scotland—that the shores of Sutherland are covered with what seems one vast straggling village, inhabited by an impoverished and ruined people—and that the coming assessment may yet fall so weighty that the extra profits accruing to his Grace from his large sheep farms, may go but a small way in supporting his extra paupers. It is not in the least improbable, that he may live to find the revolution effected by his predecessor taking to itself the form not of a crime, for that would be nothing,— but of a disastrous and very terrible blunder.

There is another remark which may prove not unworthy the consideration of the reader. Ever since the completion of the fatal experiment which ruined Sutherland, the noble family through which it was originated and carried on have betrayed the utmost jealousy of having its real results made public. Volumes of special pleading have been written on the subject,—pamphlets have been published, laboured articles have been inserted in widely spread reviews,—statistical accounts have been watched over with the most careful surveillance. If the misrepresentations of the press could have altered the matter of fact, famine would not be gnawing the vitals of Sutherland in a year a little less abundant than its predecessors nor would the dejected and oppressed people be feeding their discontent, amid present misery, with the recollections of a happier past. If a singularly well-conditioned and wholesome district of country has been converted into one wide ulcer of wretchedness and woe, it must be confessed that the sore has been carefully bandaged up from the public eye,—that if there has been little done for its cure, there has at least been much done for its concealment. Now, be it remembered, that a Free Church threatens to insert a *tent* into this wound, and so keep it open. It has been said that the Gaelic language removes a district more effectually from the influence of English opinion than an ocean of three thousand miles, and that the British public know better what is doing in New York than what is doing in Lewis or Skye. And hence one cause, at least, of the thick obscurity that has so long enveloped the miseries which the poor Highlander has had to endure, and the oppressions to which he has been subjected. The Free Church threatens to *translate* her wrongs into English, and to give them currency in the general mart of opinion. She might possibly enough be no silent spectator of conflagrations such as those which characterized the first general improvement of Sutherland,—

M

nor yet of such Egyptian schemes of house-building as that which formed part of the improvements of a later plan. She might be somewhat apt to betray the real state of the district, and thus render laborious misrepresentation of little avail. She might effect a diversion in the cause of the people, and shake the foundations of the hitherto despotic power which has so long weighed them down. She might do for Sutherland what Cobbett promised to do for it, but what Cobbett had not character enough to accomplish, and what he did not live even to attempt. A combination of circumstances have conspired to vest in a Scottish proprietor, in this northern district, a more despotic power than even the most absolute monarchs of the Continent possess; and it is, perhaps, no great wonder that that proprietor should be jealous of the introduction of an element which threatens, it may seem, materially to lessen it. And so he struggles hard to exclude the Free Church, and, though no member of the Establishment himself, declares warmly in its behalf. Certain it is, that from the Establishment, as now constituted, he can have nothing to fear, and the people nothing to hope.

After what manner may his Grace, the Duke of Sutherland, be most effectually met in this matter, so that the cause of toleration and freedom of conscience may be maintained in the extensive district which God, in his providence, has consigned to his stewardship? We shall in our next chapter attempt giving the question an answer. Meanwhile, we trust the people of Sutherland will continue, as hitherto, to stand firm. The strong repugnance which they feel against being driven into churches which all their ministers have left, is not ill founded. No church of God ever employs such means of conversion as those employed by his Grace; they are means which have been often resorted to for the purpose of making men worse,—never yet for the purpose of making them better. We know that with their long formed church-going habits, the people must feel their now silent Sabbaths pass heavily ; but they would perhaps do well to remember amid the tedium and gloom, that there were good men who not only anticipated such a time of trial for this country, but who also made provision for it. Thomas Scott, when engaged in writing his Commentary, used to solace himself with the belief that it might be of use at a period when the public worship of God would be no longer tolerated in the land. To the great bulk of the people of Sutherland that time seems to have already come. They know, however, the value of the old divines, and have not a few of their more practical treatise translated into their expressive tongue,—*Alleine's Alarm,*—*Boston's Fourfold State,*—*Doddridge's Rise and Progress,*—*Baxter's Call,*—*Guthrie's Saving Interest.* Let these and such as these be their preachers, when they can procure no other. The more they learn to relish them, the less will they relish the bald and miserable services of the Residuary Church. Let them hold their fellowship and prayer meetings,—let them keep up the worship of God in their families : the cause of religious freedom in the district is involved in the stand which they make. Above all, let them possess their souls in patience. We are not unacquainted with the Celtic character, as developed in the Highlands of Scotland. Highlanders, up to a certain point, are the most docile, patient, enduring of men ; but that point once passed, endurance ceases, and the all too gentle lamb starts up an angry lion. The spirit is stirred that maddens at the sight of the naked weapon, and that in its headlong rush upon the enemy, discipline can neither check nor control. Let our oppressed Highlanders of Sutherland beware. They have suffered much; but, so far as man is the agent, their battles can be fought on only the arena of public opinion, and on that ground which the political field may be soon found to furnish. Any explosion of violence on their part would be ruin to both the Free Church and themselves.

But we have not yet said how this ruinous revolution was effected in Sutherland,—how the aggravation of the *mode*, if we may so speak, still fester in the recollections of the people,—or how thoroughly that policy of the lord of the soil, through which he now seems determined to complete the work of ruin which his predecessors began, harmonizes with its worst details. We must first relate, however, a disastrous change which took place, in the providence of God, in the noble family of Sutherland, and which, though it dates fully eighty years back, may be regarded as pregnant with the disasters which afterwards befell the country.

Such of our readers as are acquainted with the memoir of Lady Glenorchy, must remember a deeply melancholy incident which occurred in the history of this excellent woman, in connection with the noble family of Sutherland. Her only sister had been married to William, seventeenth Earl of Sutherland,—" the first of the good Earls ;" " a nobleman," says the Rev. Dr. Jones in his Memoir, " who to the finest person united all the dignity and amenity of manners and character which give lustre to greatness." But his sun was destined soon to go down. Five years after his marriage, which proved one of the happiest, and was blessed with two children, the elder of the two, the young Lady Catherine, a singularly engaging child, was taken from him by death, in his old hereditary castle of Dunrobin. The event deeply affected both parents, and preyed on their health and spirits. It had taken place amid the gloom of a severe northern winter, and in the solitude of the Highlands ; and acquiesing in the advice of friends, the Earl and his lady quitted the family seat, where there was so much to remind them of their bereavement, and sought relief in the more cheerful atmosphere of Bath. But they were not to find it there. Shortly after their arrival, the Earl was seized by a malignant fever, with which, upheld by a powerful constitution, he struggled for fifty-four days, and then expired. For the first twenty-one days and nights of these," says Dr. Jones, " Lady Sutherland never left his bedside; and then at last, overcome with fatigue, anxiety, and grief, she sank an unavailing victim to an amiable, but excessive attachment, seventeen days before the death of her lord." The period, though not very remote, was one in which the intelligence of events travelled slowly ; and in this instance the distraction of the family must have served to retard it beyond the ordinary time. Her Ladyship's mother, when hastening from Edinburgh to her assistance, alighted one day from her carriage at an inn, and on seeing two hearses standing by the way side, inquired of an attendant whose remains they contained ? The reply was, the remains of Lord and

Lady Sutherland, on their way for interment to the Royal Chapel of Holy-rood House. And such was the first intimation of which the lady received of the death of her daughter and son-in-law.

The event was pregnant with disaster to Sutherland, though many years elapsed ere the ruin which it involved fell on that hapless country. The sole survivor and heir of the family was a female infant of but a year old. Her maternal grandmother, an ambitious, intriguing woman of the world, had the chief share in her general training and education ; and she was brought up in the south of Scotland, of which her grandmother was a native, far removed from the influence of those genial sympathies with the people of her clan, for which the old lords of Sutherland had been so remarkable, and, what was a sorer evil still, from the influence of the vitalities of that religion which, for five generations together, her fathers had illustrated and adorned. The special mode in which the disaster told first, was through the patronage of the county, the larger part of which was vested in the family of Sutherland. Some of the old Earls had been content, as we have seen, to place themselves on the level of the Christian men of their parishes, and thus to unite with them in calling to their churches the Christian minister of their choice. They know,—what regenerated nature can alone know, with the proper emphasis, that in Christ Jesus the vassal ranks with his Lord, and they conscientiously acted on the conviction. But matters were now regulated differently. The presentation supplanted the call, and the ministers came to be placed in the parishes of Sutherland without the consent, and contrary to the will, of the people. Churches, well filled hitherto, were deserted by their congregations, just because a respectable woman of the world, making free use of what she deemed her own, had planted them with men of the world, who were only tolerably respectable ; and in houses and barns, the devout men of the district learned to hold numerously attended Sabbath meetings for reading the Scriptures, and mutual exhortation, and prayer, as a sort of substitute for the public services, in which they found they could no longer join with profit. The spirit awakened by the old Earls had survived themselves, and ran directly counter to the policy of their descendant. Strongly attached to the Establishment the people, though they thus forsook their old places of worship, still remained members of the national Church, and travelled far in the summer season to attend the better ministers of their own and the neighbouring counties. We have been assured, too, from men whose judgment we respect, that, under all their disadvantages, religion continued peculiarly to flourish among them ;—a deep-toned evangelism prevailed; so that perhaps the visible church throughout the world at the time could furnish no more striking contrast than that which obtained between the cold, bald, common-place service of the pulpit in some of these parishes, and the fervid prayers and exhortations which give life and interest to these humble meeting of the people. What a pity it is that differences such as these the Duke of Sutherland cannot see. !

The marriage of the young countess into a noble English family was fraught with further disaster to the country. There are many Englishmen quite intelligent enough to perceive the difference between a smoky cottage of turf and a white-washed cottage of stone, whose judgment on their respective inhabitants would be of but little value. "Sutherland, as a country of *men*, stood higher at this period than perhaps any other district in the British empire; but, as our description in the preceding chapter must have shown,—and we indulged in them mainly with a view to this part of our subject,—it by no means stood high as a country of farms and cottages. The marriage of the Countess brought a new set of eyes upon it—eyes accustomed to quite a different face of things. It seemed a wild, rude country, where all was wrong, and all had to be set right,—a sort of Russia on a small scale, that had just got another Peter the Great to civilize it,—or a sort of barbarous Egypt, with an energetic Ali Pasha at its head. Even the vast wealth and great liberality of the Stafford family militated against this hapless country : it enabled them to treat it as the mere subject of an interesting experiment, in which gain to themselves was really no object,—nearly as little so as if they had resolved on dissecting a dog alive for the benefit of science."

Mr. Miller might have gone farther to shew the cause of the desolation which overtook the Sutherlanders, for he was aware of it, but for want of positive proof he was deterred. There was mighty cause to believe in Sutherlandshire that there was not a drop of the Sutherland families blood in the veins of the first Duchess of Sutherland. As tradition in the country went, when she an infant came under the guardianship of her Grandmother, a cousin or a second cousin of hers of the name of Betsy Wyms of the same age, and complexion with Betsy Sutherland, was brought home to the Grandmother to be her companion, the children lived happy, and grew together, but Betsy Sutherland grew taller than her companion. The gentlemen of Sutherland were very mindful of their heiress, and were sending her presents of the produce of the county, such as fowls, venison, butter, cheese, &c., yearly, and the family officer of the name of John Harall, was always entrusted with the mission ; in this way John became well acquainted with the young heiress and her companion, on his arrival she always (after she was four or five years of age) met him at the gate entrance, and made great work with him, she could scarcely be prevailed upon to go to bed that night he arrived, but getting little news from him. When she was about eight years of age, the news came home to Sutherland that a sudden death deprived her of her companion, Betsy Wyms : and a great lamentation was made as Betsy Sutherland was so very melancholy, and refused to accept of any other companion. Next Martimas John Harral was despatched with presents more than ordinary, and letters of condolence to the young heiress, and wishing the day might soon arrive when they would see her in Sutherland, and sitting on her mother's chair in Dunrobin Castle. John Harral arrived in Edinburgh, and at the gate of Leven Mansion, rang the bell, observed the young lady coming as usual, skipping down among the shrubbery, and her maid following, the gate was opened and the young lady grasped him by the hand ; John was dumbfounded and in his confusion of mind asked where was Betsy Sutherland, (as he used to call her) ; I am Betsy Sutherland was the reply ; no my dear says he, you are Betsy Wyms ; the maid whirled the young lady about, and John did not see her face again for years ; John delivered his commission as usual, and was discharged that same night, instead of remaining a week or a fortnight as usual. John came home disappointed and disheartened, and told his plain story but full of mystery. The heiress was removed to a boarding school in England, and could not be seen by another Sutherlander to recognise her until she came to raise a regiment in Sutherland : what confirmed the fraud upon the minds of the people was a singular anecdote. The first night she landed in Sutherlandshire a mildew or hoar-frost fell that night, in June, which destroyed the crops of that year, and almost every green growth in the county, and did yet not reach upon either the neighbouring counties of Caithness or Ross, and it is said that that mildew never rose yet. One thing is clear that at the time Betsy Wyms was reported to be dead, that a commission was bought in the East India Company for the proper heir of the estate, who was then only a young boy ; though ever so young he was despatched to that cemetery of enterprise, where he soon died, none being then to claim the estate but his two orphan sisters, the investigation to the fraud ceased, but the Duchess had the generosity of settling a portion of £15 upon each of these presumptive female heirs, but when they became old and infirm, occupying a small garret room in the Candlemaker Row, Edinburgh, the portion was reduced by Loch to £2 each, yearly. I knew them, I often visited them in this forlorn condition, I petitioned her Grace twice in their behalf, but to no purpose ; at last I got them on the west Kirk parish poor roll. They were taken into the poor house and died there.

The former part of this short but singular narrative, be it correct or incorrect, I give it as I heard it from my father, and many more of the old men who lived in that age, and who had too much cause to believe it to be correct, for they were almost ever since governed and treated with an alien's iron and fiery rod.

, I am sorry that for the present I must lay aside many important communications bearing upon the clearing system of the Highlanders which corroborates and substantiates my description of it, such as letters published by Mr. Summer and Mr. Donald Ross, Glasgow, Mr. Donald Sutherland, which appeared in the Woodstock *Sentinel* a few weeks ago, but above all I regret how little I can take from the pen of Mr. Mackie, Editor of the Northern *Ensign*, Wick, Caithness, N.B., a gentleman who since the appearance of his valuable paper proved himself the faithful friend of the oppressed, the indefatigable exposer of their wrongs, terror of oppressors, and a chastiser of their tools, apologizers and abettors, though his pecuniary benefits would be to sail in the same boat with his unprincipled contemporaries in the north of Scotland, but he chose the better part. and there is a higher promise of reward for him than worm Dukes, Lords, Esquires, and their vile underlings could bestow. The following is among the last of his productions on the subject.

'WILLING HANDS FOR INDIA.'

Over this title *Punch* of last week gives a very exciting illustration. A towering cart load of ingathered grain, with a crowing cock on its summit, forms the background ; while in front a recruiting officer and a party are cheered by the excited harvesters coming forward with reaping hooks in their hands, to volunteer for India, the banner borne by the officer representing the British lion in the act of springing on the Bengal tiger. The recruits, not yet returned from the harvest field, are all enthusiasm, and are eagerly rushing to enrol themselves among the avengers of the butcheries that have been perpetrated in our Indian empire.

The newspapers of the south report that the recruiting in certain districts has been most successful, and that already many thousand young men of promise have entered the line. It is remarkable, however, particularly so, that all reference to the district from which the main strength of our regular army was formerly obtained is most studiously avoided. May we ask the authorities what success the recruiting officer has now met with in the Highlands of Scotland? Time was, in former exigencies, when all eyes were turned in that direction and not in vain. Time was, when, in only five days, the county of Sutherland alone contributed *one thousand* young men ; and when, in fourteen days, no fewer than eleven times that number were enrolled as recruits from the various Highland districts. Time was when the immortal Chatham boasted that ' he had found upon the mountains of Caledonia a gallant though oppressed race of heroes, who had triumphantly carried the British banner into every quarter of the globe.' Time was when *Punch* would, in such an illustration as that of last week, have included in its representation some half-dozen kilted Celts, shoulder to shoulder, issuing from the mountain homes, and panting to be let loose on the Indian bloodhounds.

Why not now? Answer the question, my Lord Duke of Sutherland. Tell her Majesty, my Lord, why the bagpipes of the recruiting party are silent in Sutherland, and why ' no willing hands for India ' are found in your Grace's vast Highland domain. Tell her how it happens that the patriotic enthusiasm which at the close of the last century was shown in the almost magical enrolment of thousands of brawny Sutherlanders, who gained world-wide renown at Corunna, at Fuentes d'Onor, at Vittoria, at Waterloo, and elsewhere, is now unknown in Sutherland, and how the enrolment of one man in that large county is a seven year's wonder. If your Grace is silent the answer is not wanting, nor is her Majesty ignorant of it.

And yet the cursed system which has disheartened and well nigh destroyed that ' race of heroes,' is pertinaciously persevered in by the very men who, of all others, should be the first to come forward and denounce it. ' Willing hands for India,' say *Punch*. ' No,' says high bred lords and coroneted peers ; gives us game preserves, deer forests, and sheep walks. Perish your bold peasantry! and life to the pleasures of the forest and the mountain heath.' And thus it is that landlord after landlord is yearly weeding out the aborginies, and converting Scotland into one ponderons deer forest. Not a year passes without seeing hundreds of unoffending men, women, and children, from Cape Wrath to Mull of Galloway, remorselessly unhoused, and their little crofts added to the vast waste. And now that Britain for the second time in four years has again to invoke the patriotism of her sons, and to call for aid in the eventful crisis in India, the blast of the recruiter's bugle evokes only the bleat of sheep, or the pitiful bray of the timid deer, in the greater part of those wide regions which formerly contributed their tens of thousands of men to fight their country's battles. Oh, had Chatham been alive now, what a feeling would have been awakened in his manly breast as he surveyed the wreck which the Loch policy has occasioned ; and with what crushing eloquence would he have invoked the curse of heaven on that system. Meanwhile, Britain misses her Highland heroes, and the imperilled troops in India, with the unoffending women and children, must wait the tardy arrival of ' willing hands' to assist them, while, had the Highlanders of Scotland been as they once were, in one week more men would have been raised for India than would have sufficed to have effectually crushed the Indian revolt, had spread itself from the foot of the Himalaya mountains to the most distant district of our Indian empire.

Let Highland evictors, from Dukes to the meanest squires, beware. Popular patience has a limit ; and it seems to me that the time is rapidly nearing when, if Parliament remains longer silent, the people of the country will arouse themselves, and, by one united expression of their will, drive back to its native den the foul and disastrous policy which has depeopled the Scottish Highlands."

Brave John Mackie keep on your armour, you have now another English Duke, no doubt a sporting one, to watch, who will finish the desolation of the Langwell Estate, which the scourge, Donald Horn, commenced some years ago. You never had a higher dignitary before in Caithness than a Lord. Now that you are to be honoured and blessed by a Duke, a sporting Grace, I predict that in a few years Caithness which has been hitherto an exception among all other Highland Counties; may be ranked in the same category with Sutherlandshire—(*Ichabod, glory departed, desolation*)—for his Grace of Portland's retinue will consist of other Graces, and Lords who must be supplied with sporting ground for themselves, while there is an estate in Caithness which money can purchase or to lease, Caithness lairds cannot resist the temptation of their long purses. We have proof positive of this in the parishes of Reay, Thurso, and Halkirk what devastation was made there, to gratify that insatiable monster in human shape, John Paterson of rotten, and infamous memory, to the everlasting disgrace of the Gordons and Sinclairs who indulged that *man*, what will they not do when they have to gratify English graces and lords? But it is not what they have done, or what they will do, should be the question with us, but what have we done and what are we to do? We have a very important duty to perform, and the sins of omission and the sins of commission are equally as henious, and as culpable in the sight of Heaven. Much has the British nation to account for, for these sins of omission. With folded arms, and callous indifference they have seen county after county in the Highlands of Scotland depopulated, the people ruined, oppressed and dispersed; they have tolerated, indeed countenanced, a systematic policy, which anyone might see with half an eye, would end in the alienation of the people, the enfeeblement and ultimately in the disgrace of the nation. In the year 1747, the very next year after the *Cumberland* massacre of the Highlanders upon Culloden field, and his nine months ravages and murder in that country. According to Gartmor's manuscript, the Highlands could raise 52,800 able-bodied young men from the age of 18 to 36 years. It is evident that many years prior to this date agricultural improvements were not much studied in either Scotland or England, more especially in the Highlands, on account of continued internal war and broils, about throning and dethroning legitimate and illegitimate sovereigns; but if the Highlands of Scotland could then raise 52,000 men, I ask, under proper and wise management, how many soldiers should the Highlands raise in the year 1857? At the lowest estimate we cannot say less than 67,000, only allowing the population to increase one-third during a period of one hundred and ten years. What would such an invincible celtic army be worth to the British nation to-day? who laughed and sneered at their calamities and dispersion some years ago, and who would practically say, they may go to h—l if they choose, but we and our sons must have deer stalking ground. I ask, what would such an irresistible body of men be worth to Britain to-day? Would they not be worth more than all the deer, grouse, game, bulls, bullocks, rams, sheep, and lambs, all the sporting gents, foresters, shepherds, dogs, and aristocratic scions in Britain, and all the German legions that Germany can produce to boot. Tell them John Mackie, and proclaim it in their ears through your widely circulated and well read *Ensign*, that on former emergencies of less importance than the present, there was no difficulty in raising regiments in the highlands—take them to their own records, and they will find that 6,000 were raised or embodied in one year, 8,000 in another four years, and twenty times that number willing and ready if required; 2,000 of these were from Sutherlandshire, where there is not one willing man to be found now, and I question if a score, or even two, willing to be soldiers are to be found throughout the whole highlands. The patriotism so characteristic of highlanders is completely destroyed, and that for years past. But Britain will find out that if she is to maintain her former envied position among the nations of the earth that it will be by her own sons, and not by aliens or confederating with foreigners, upon whose constancy very little reliance can be placed. Woe to kings, and rulers who forsake, oppress, and disperse their own people, and have to look up to strangers and aliens for succour in time of need. Britain has dealt treacherously with her own people. *The mountains of Caledonia, from which at all times her principle succour did come to her in time of need are desolated.* Britain is now in need, and in vain looks to these mountains for the invincible host, for they are not there, and it is to be feared that she may look in vain to (the mountain) God, to whom her sires looked for succour, and who often accompanied her armies, and host, while they were councelled by Him, fighting the battles of civil and religious liberty at home and abroad, and dealing justly with his people. But who can say but it is upon the scorching plains of India and through the instrumentality of Mahomedans, Pagans and other idolators, where her eyes are to be opened, and convinced of her past shortsighted folly and sinful policy, although hitherto blind to see her folly, and deaf to the dictates of humanity, and sound reasoning, to the instruction and commands of God, his prophets and apostles, to the remonstrance of philosophers, and all who had her real interest at heart ; and although it is generally believed that it is similar British tyranny, shortsighted, cruel policy, and mal-administration, which depopulated the Highlands of Scotland, ruined Ireland, and beggared two-fifths of the nation is the cause of the outbreak in India, and the horrifying massacres, and inhuman deeds perpetrated by these uncivilised deluded savages ; yet it behoves every son of Britain wherever he is to be found, to join in the demonstration, demanding the abolition of her game laws, and every other law known and proven to afford these accursed vermin of the aristocratic tribe an opportunity of oppressing the industrious people, and detrimental to the progress and prosperity of the nation, and endangering her dignity, her safety, yea her very existence. Utopianism, utopianism, many will cry out ; but it is not more utopian to demand the abolition of the game laws, which costs the nation more than half a million sterling yearly for banishing and imprisoning poachers, and which have been the cause of many a bloody, murderous affray, preserving animals, and birds which consumes more than three millions sterling worth of human food every year, besides the many thousand acres of land lying waste to afford them room for amusement and solitude, than it was to demand the abolition of the Corn Laws and Slave Laws. Many excellent men of high standing in Society are devoting their time demonstrating the necessity and legality of abolishing, not only the Game Laws, but the Laws of Entail and Primogeniture, the Hypothec, &c. Will you not follow their example ?

THE FREEHOLD MOVEMENT AND HIGHLAND CLEARANCES.

A stirring meeting, fully reported in the *Daily Express* of Monday, was held in Queen Street Hall, Edinburgh, on Saturday, when powerful speeches were made by Messrs Beal (from London), Taylor (from Birmingham), Dr. Begg, Mr Duncan M'Laren, Mr Dove, and others, The meeting was most enthusiastic, and gave every indication of energy and decision.

Mr Beal, in the course of his speech, said,—In England, they had looked with stern indignation at some acts which had taken place in the northern parts of Scotland, in regard to those great clearings of which they had heard so much. (Applause.) Such things might be prevented if the influence of the tenantry and of the mass of the people, who were now deprived of the suffrage, were brought to bear on the system of Parliamentary representation by means of a freehold movement. The counties would not then send as their representatives some twenty or thirty men who lacked the intelligence and the progressive spirit of the age. (Hear, hear.) The landlord influence would then be destroyed, and the people's poet would then be no longer able to say as at present—

> I have driven out peasants, I have banished them forth,
> There is hardly a Celt on the hills of the north.

If their own members opposed them, instead of assisting them in the movement, they could yet look confidently to the support of a large body of the English statesmen.

Mr. Dove, with his usual manly independence, spoke out nobly, as follows:—He looked upon this movement as the first thing which he had seen in his day that was calculated to break up that aristocratic influence that had long preyed upon this country of Scotland. (Applause.) When they saw men hounded out of the Highlands as they had been—(cheers and hisses)—let them ask themselves what possible measure could save that Highland population except a freehold movement, which should root them into the soil of Scotland. (Cheers.) That population had been driven out of their country, and now they had only the sea and the sea-shore left to them; but he (Mr. Dove) told them, as he told Scotland, that this movement was the best movement which they had seen in their day, and the most calculated to benefit the whole population of the Highlands of Scotland. (Loud applause.) This very day he was a Scottish Rights' man, and would remain so. He did not care one single farthing what any might say on that subject; he would say that he was a Scottish Rights' man, and would always be so. (Laughter and cheers.) And that very day, finding that they could do very little for that Highland population in any other way, he had been engaged with his friend Mr. George Wink, the Secretary of the Scottish Rights' Association, in endeavouring to found a fishery, and to furnish to these people their boats, lines, nets, and everything which could keep them at home. (Cheers.) Now, he did not know that he should have used the word himself; but they had been told of their subserviency to the landlords; and Mr. Duncan M'Laren had used the words bad lawyers. He did not mean to say that he would have used the word, but in his opinion they were all bad lawyers. (Mr. M'Laren—I meant that they were giving bad law, and not that they were bad men.) Mr Dove said he knew perfectly well Mr M'Laren's meaning—that they were giving a wrong explanation of what the law of England was, and that they were either ignorant or maliciously misleading the people of Scotland. But his (Mr. Dove's meaning was very different; for he told them that they were bad lawyers, because they had cleared out that Highland population in many cases illegally—(hisses and cheers)—and he told them that two or three years ago down at Knoidart, they took the sick people out of their houses, pulled those houses down, and left the inmates exposed to the winds of heaven. (A voice—'They had no right to the land,' and cries of 'Order')—and he told them that they pulled down the barns there in which the people could have been sheltered. Now, it was quite true that the law unfortunately gave them the power to pull down the houses, but not the barns, which would have in some measure sheltered the poor people. But, nevertheless, they had done so, and the people had remained unsheltered ; and he, (Mr. Dove) said that, if as Scotchmen they permitted such things to go on, they were not worthy of the name. (applause.) He hoped he had expressed his meaning pretty plainly, which was, that he was a Scottish Rights' man, and as such he could look any Englisman in the face.

We hope to give this great movement due attention at an early date. *Good* speed to it.

ODE ON SCOTLAND'S LOVE OF INDEPENDENCE.

SCOTLAND's hills and dales can tell,
How bravely foemen she could quell,
What hosts before her vanquish'd fell
    On many a well fought day.

For liberty her red cross flew ;
For liberty her sword she drew ;
For liberty her foes o'erthrew ;
    She could not be a slave.

When Rome's proud eagle was unfurl'd,
And floated o'er a prostrate world,
Defiance, Caledonia hurl'd,
    And scorn'd the haughty foe.

When Scandinavia pour'd her swarms ;
Fill'd all her coasts with dire alarms,
Then Scotland dauntless rose in arms,
    Her heart was proud and brave.

Like ocean wave rush'd on her foes,
Like ocean's barrier Scotland rose,
And dashed them back and 'round them strews
    Their boasted chivalry.

In freedom's cause she drew her brand,
And freedom still has bless'd her land,
And laurel crown'd she aye could stand,
    'Mid bravest of the brave.

Even when her nobles did conspire,
Chose England as their high umpire,
Her gallant son she did inspire—
    Wallace of Ellerslie.

Who, follow'd by a noble band,
Defended well their native land ;
And Cambuskenneth saw the stand
    They made for Scotland there.

But envy ever doth pursue
The brave, the faithful, and the true,
And traitors base this hero slew,
    Whose arm they dare not brave.

Tho' Scotland mourn'd her hero slain,
And prostrate seem'd, she rose amain,
And under Bruce did freedom gain,
    As Bannockburn can tell.

But though our wars with England cease,
And union brings the joys of peace ;
Joys which may more and more increase,
    While time its course shall run ;

Forget we not that patriot band,
Midst blood and death who raised the brand,
And fought for freedom and the land
    Of Scotia brave and free.

J. M. Aim.

Sandwick, 6th January, 1857.

LORDS OF THE GLEN.

(From ' Braemer Ballads,' by Professor Blackie.)

I.

O fair is the land, my own mountain land,
    Fit nurse for the brave and the free,
Where the fresh breezes blow o'er the heath's purple glow,
    And the clear torrent gushes with glee !
        But woe's me, woe ! what dole and sorrow
        From this lovely land I borrow,
        When I roam, where the stump of stricken ash-tree
        Shows the spot where the home of the cotter should be,
        And the cold rain drips, and the cold wind moans
        O'er the tumbled heaps of old grey stones,
        Where once a fire blazed free.
For a blight has come down on the land of the mountain,
The storm-nurtured pine, and the clear-gushing fountain,
And the chieftains are gone, the kind lords of the glen,
In the land that once swarmed with the brave Highlandmen !

II.

O fair is the land, my own mountain land,
    Fit nurse for the brave and the free,
Where the strong waterfall scoops the gray granite wall,
    'Neath the roots of the old pine tree !
        But woe's for me, woe ! what dole and sorrow
        From this lovely land I borrow,
        When the long and houseless glen I see,
        Where only the deer to range is free,
        And I think on the pride of the dwindled clan,
        And the home-sick heart of the brave Highlandmen !
        Far tost on the billowy sea.
For a blight has come down on the land of the mountain,
The storm-nurtured pine, and the clear-gushing fountain,
And the stalkers of deer keep their scouts in the glen
That once swarmed with the high-hearted brave Highlandmen !

III.

O fair is the land, my own mountain land,
  Fit nurse for the brave and the free,
Where the young river leaps down the sheer ledge, and sweeps
  With a full-flooded force to the sea !
      But woe is me ! What dole and sorrow
      From this lovely land I borrow,
      When I think on the men that should father the clan,
      But who bartered the rights of the brave Highlandman
      To the lordlings that live for the pleasure to kill
      The stag that roams free o'er the tenantless hill ;
      What care they for the brave Highlandman ?
For a blight has come down on the land of the mountain,
The storm-nurtured pine, and the clear gushing fountain,
And vendors of game are the lords of the glen
Who rule o'er the fair mountain land without men !

THE HIGHLAND EMIGRANTS.

I

COME away ! far away ! from the hills of bonnie Scotland
  Here no more may we linger on the mountain—in the glen—
Come away ! Why delay ? far away from bonnie Scotland.
  Land of grouse, and not of heroes ! Land of sheep, and not of men !
      Mighty hunters, for their pastime,
      Needing deserts in our shires,
      Turn to waste our pleasent places,
      Quench the smoke of cottage fires.
Come away ! why delay ? Let us seek a home denied us,
  O'er the ocean's that divide us from the country of our sires.

II.

Come away ! far away ! from the river ; from the wild wood ;
  From the soil where our fathers lifted Freedom's broad claymore
From the paths in the straths, that were dear to us in childhood ;
  From the kirk where love was plighted in the happy days of yore.
      Men and women have no value
      Where the Bruce and Wallace grew,
      And where stood the clansman's shieling
      There the red deer laps the dew.
Come away ! far away ! But to thee, oh bonnie Scotland,
  Wheresoever we may wander shall our hearts be ever true.

III.

Far away ! far away ! in the light of other regions
  We shall prove how we love thee to our children yet unborn.
Far away ! far away ! we shall teach them our allegiance
  To thy name and to thy glory, thou beloved, though forlorn.
      At recital of thy greatness
      Shall our warmest fervour swell ;
      On the story of thy sorrow
      Shall our fondest memories dwell.
Far away ! why delay ? We are banished from our Scotland,
  From our own, our bonnie Scotland ! fare thee well ! oh ! fare thee well !

CHARLES MCKAY.

But I have here before me Lord Palmerston's scheme to raise men in the Highlands, and he makes himself sure it will succeed. I am now an old man, and I have read many wicked, stupid, and suicidal proposals, made by Statesmen, and schemes laid down before a discerning public, but as yet I aver that I never read a more stupid, suicidal, and unconstitutional, and surer of failing, than this one now before you, taken from Palmerston's own sweet organ, the London *Morning Post*. I need not comment upon it. The Editor of the *Northern Ensign*, a gentlemen who knows more of the Highlanders that any other Editor living, has done it ample justice. Palmerston, through his organ, the *Morning Post*, after prefacing the article, says: —"The East India Company wants men ; but how are these men to be obtained ? are they to be obtained by volunteering, by increasing the bounty, or by the employment of foreign mercenaries ? He proceeds and says:—

"We would purpose that the peasantry, the artizans, and the working classes of the three kingdoms, should be told that if they enlisted—during the troubles in India for instance—for a limited period, at the expiration of their services they would receive the same kind of treatment which has been extended to the German Legionaries—namely, *a free passage to a British Colony, a respectable outfit, a free grant of land, a house and no rent, and half pay for three years*, the consideration being a few days' drill in the year, and permanent service in the case of some great emergeney. . . . . We believe that the Legislature of Canada would now cheerfully grant millions of acres of wild land of the provinces, to be distributed as rewards amongt the soldiers of the British army. New Brunswick and Nova Scotia would do the same. If Officers and Sergeants at the present time engaged in the recruiting service, were enabled to tell those classes of men out of which the British army is raised, that at the termination of their service they would have a free passage to Canada, a free grant of land, and money enough to build a log-house and to clear a small patch of land, we believe that there would be no dearth of recruits. This plan, we are persuaded, would be more effectual than increased bounty of double pay. If a system of military colonization can be adopted for the special benefit of a few lucky German soldiers, let the same experiment, we say, be tried for the general benefit of the British army."

This scheme, attractive enough at first-sight, is the most positively suicidal which it is possible to propose. Let any sensible, patriotic man ponder it well, in its bearings and results, and we feel assured his very blood will rise within him when he thinks of it. Why, its issue must ultimately be to draw the main strength of the country out of it. Just think of 20,000 militia men, drawn from 'the peasantry, the artizans, and the working men of the three kingdoms,' serving 'for a limited period,' and then sent off to enjoy the fruits of their servitude in a distant colony —just think of this sage proposal being regularly and periodically carried out, and where would the bone and sinew of our national strength be in a quarter of a century ? Toiling away in the 'free land' of Australia, or hewing down the forests of Canada.

We humbly submit to Lord Palmerston and the *Morning Post,* a far more likely and satisfactory method of obtaining militia. There are hundreds of thousands of acres, capable of improvement, but lying in waste and inutility over the Highlands of Scotland. There are in the immediate neighborhood tens of thousands of inhabitants, living in poverty and social discomfort, because deprived of the exercises of their industrial energies, and otherwise prevented from rising in the scale of social beings. Well. There are among these many thousands of young men capable of bearing arms, as the shores of Caithness recently testified, and whose fathers and grandfathers fought and died in their country's service ; but who now moodily refuse to lift a weapon in the same service. To these the offer of a hundred, fifty, or even ten acres of land in the Highlands to each man, with Government security of Tenure, should they pay reasonable rent for it, would be a stimulant which Palmerston, or his aristocratic colleagues never took into consideration. Any other decoyment will most assuredly fail ; for we can tell Lord Palmerston the brightest jewels in Britain's crown would not awake the scintillation of an enthusiastic glance ; but we most surely believe that could Lord Palmerston prevail on certain Whig Dukes and Lords to alter their treatment of their tenantry, and abrogate the policy that is rapidly making the north and north-west of Scotland a prodigious deer forest, there would soon be no fear of raising militia by the thousand.

If, for example, the Duke of Sutherland, the husband of 'the most influential woman in Europe,' were to preclaim from the Meikle Ferry to Cape Wrath, that the Loch policy is to cease for ever ; that the long desolate Straths of Sutherland are to be peopled ; that the humblest tenant in the county is to be treated to a lease on favorable terms ; and that men are to be henceforth preferred to sheep and deer, we verily believe there would be kindled in that county an amount of enthusiasm which it never before witnessed, and which would issue in the raising of such a number of recruits as would astonish even the versatile and sanguine premier himself.

And were a like change to be heralded over the whole Highlands of Scotland, a corresponding result would most surely follow. We assure the *Morning Post* that it would be a far more effectual and nationally beneficial method of defending Britain than casting out the bait of grants of land on foreign shores, and tempting men to fight for a country they are destined to leave. A thousand times rather let the government buy up the myriads of profitless acres at home, give presents of a corresponding quantity of colonial land to the absentee lands, along with a free passage, and give the land at home as a present to recruits, than allow them first to enrol, and then pack them off as felons to Botany Bay. The fact is, the home country stands in need of such men, instead of requiring them to emigrate ; and we see no scheme half so likely to rear a race of invincibles, than restoring to the people the land from which they have been cruelly driven, and evicting those droves of deer that will very soon have their head-quarters within a stone-throw of the largest towns, if the present mania continue to influence many purblind and selfish landlords of the Highlands and Islands. The country *can* want most of its Highland lairds, but it *can not* safely want its Highland inhabitants.—*Northern Ensign.*

What do you think of my Lord Palmerston ? He in the spirit of aristocratic liberality will allow the British soldiers equal benefits allowed German mercenaries ; yes. my Lord, and if they do not enrol themselves upon these conditions, send the press gang, and the ballot box among them, handcuff the stubborn fellows, and force them to swear by God to fight for the East India Company, that they may retain the monopoly of the trade of that boundless territory, and charge what prices they please for the produce; a fac simile of how the unmeasurable territories of valuable land in the north-west of Canada were handed over to the Hudson Bay Company, to enrich a few villians who can keep up the price of skins and fur, that the working, or producing classes, to whom those territories belong, cannot purchase them, hence deprived of the comfort and pleasures of wearing them. But where is there a British soldier to be found who will not frown and spit with disgust upon such propositions, and audacious comparisons ; yes, British soldiers, and German beggars and cowards, to be equally rewarded, and where is a British young man to be found, who is as yet a freeman, who will volunteer to risk his life to fight savages, among the pestilence, and venomous emanations of India, with no better prospect before him than, that should he escape the sword of the Mahomedan, and Juggernaut savage, and plagues of India, on his return home to be packed off to the wilds of Canada to cut wood during the remainder of his life, or perish unprovided and uncared for. Monstrous sophistry, my Lord Palmerston; you may get German mercenaries, as you call them, and town keelies and desperadoes to fill up your ranks, and manure the plains of India upon such conditions, but not Highland, high-minded Scotchmen, and God knows that the British nation has too many German paupers already saddled upon them to feed and clothe, without bringing LEGIONS of the beggarly lowest order upon them to feed and clothe. The fact is, if I am not misinformed, England will soon have the whole of that nursery or kennel of Princes to keep up altogether. Britain had to pay the king of Hanover £21,000 salary a year, it is said that was 3s. 9½d. more than his own nation could afford to allow him. Then our own beloved sovereign, whose hand any emperor or prince in Europe would be proud to obtain unconditionally ; yet Britain had to negotiate with the house of Saxe Coburg and Gotha, and settle £30,000 per year upon one of that family to become her husband; not content with this, he was raised to the rank and full pay of field marshall, and colonel of two or three regiments so that his income can figure no less than sixty or seventy thousand pounds sterling per year, besides, as I am told £37,000 to build stables for his horses, £15,000 to build a kennel for his dogs, a square to break and train them, and dwelling houses for their keepers, without any responsibilities on his part, whether he was competent to discharge the duties of his various offices or not. We have now a young Princess, I believe the loveliest and most enticing creature living; another hungry German Prince

N

smelled the delicious pie, and by some means or another managed to pay his passage to Dover, and it is said that a Government agent paid £2 16s. sterling for his railway fare from Dover to London to meet his spark. It is now said that he has agreed to marry our lovely Princess on condition that she gets £50,000 to fit her out, and that he gets £41,000 annually during her life, to take care of her, and if she should *die*, and leave a family, that suitable provisions should be made to maintain them.

Then we have other four lovely Princesses, should they arrive at the age of matrimony, as I hope they will, they must be divided economically among German Princes upon similar terms no doubt. The short and the long of it is, that should the producing classes of Britain have no more taxes to pay than what is required to keep up Germans and their brood of the high order, that other nations would consider it enormous, leaving the expenses of the *Legions* out of view. Some may say, that I lost sight of my text, "*Highland Depopulation*," yet by looking narrowly into the affair, you will find them closely connected; robbery is robbery by what ever way it is perpetrated, or committed; those who rob the nation of their money, and squanders it away upon other nations, are to a certain extent as guilty as those who depopulated the nation, and disperses her *bones and sinews* to the four winds of heaven, but not so bad. The former party are draining the nation of the blood and sinews of commerce, hence short-sighted and mischievous, yet a nation may redeem themselves from the disasters which their wicked, foolish, profligate, and prodigal Government bring upon them in this way. But the latter party drains away blood and sinews of infinitely more value, and are satanic in the extreme, they do all they can to destroy the very paladium of the nation, which, if once destroyed can never be redeemed—

"Bold peasantry their country's pride,
Once destroyed can never be supplied."

There are many damnatory features in their schemes and conduct that are not to be found in the schemes and conduct of any other class of men under heaven; it is not the millions of brave, patriotic, and industrious people they have banished or expelled from Britain, the only injury they have done and are doing to the nation, they have beggared the rest by forcing the peasantry to manufacturing towns, where vice and crime are in the ascendency; they have glutted the labour market, so that the working classes are entirely at the mercy of employers who can take advantage of every casualty of the season, of every stagnation in trade, and in the money market, so that they can keep the poor workers continually on starvation wages. They do still worse, if that could be, they destroy the confidence which should exist between the government and the governed, they are alienating the minds of the loyal lieges so far, that in a few years, if matters continue to go on as they do, it is to be feared that the peasantry and working classes need not care much who will govern them, Napoleon, the Czar, the fool tyrant of Austria or our lovely and exemplary Victoria. They have done still worse and worse, they have undermined the Gospel of Salvation, they have filled the age we are in with sceptics, infidels, and athe-

ists who can stand now before even the sceptic himself, and defend christianity and maintain that God is just, holy, and impartial; he will tell you
at once, how can you prove that when he is always on the side of the
strong and the rich, and never interferes in behalf of the poor masses nor
aideth them, however much they are trodden down and robbed by the rich;
and when the masses will withstand their robbing rich, and demand even
a portion of their just rights, he is always against them, and will allow
the rich and their tools to hew them down with sabres, and blow them
to atoms with cannons and bombshells. These, and such are the arguments
the sceptic, infidel, and atheist, will advance; but to say the least, this class
in view, abetted by the clergy, who reversed every provision God made
for his people, and abused the power placed in their hands, I say has done
more injury to the cause of Christ, and christianity in the world, than all
his avowed enemies could have done. What think you, a friend
of mine, on whose veracity I can place confidence, was travelling
in the West Highlands, and spent some days in the Isle of Skye, one
day came upon a party of women who were cutting down and collecting heather; he stood a short time speaking to them, when on a
sudden a party of gentlemen appeared upon the top of a ridge of hills
a very short distance from the heather gatherers, and were soon among
them with their dogs and guns; the poor women had by this time had their
creels, or baskets filled, he who seemed to be the chief the gang, asked
haughtily, "what are you cutting and taking away the heather for?" the
reply was, "please your Honour, Lord Macdonald, to bed our cows, to prepare manure for our potatoes." In an instant the monster was engaged
in tramping the creels to atoms, scattering the heather, breaking the hooks
or scythes, and with a face more like an enraged demon than a lord, told
the poor women to go to hell for beds to their cows, and manure for their
potatoes, if they chose, but if they would dare to take away any of his
grouse's food that he would shoot every one of them; one of them said,
trembling, "Oh, my Lord, we are paying rent for this hill," he took up
his gun to a level and swore that he would shoot her if she said another
word; the poor creature let herself down among the heather; his *Lordship*
and party left, went about a hundred yards, halted, consulted a minute,
turned round, levelled their pieces at the women, and bawled out, "you
will be all shot in a minute;" the poor creatures then ran for their lives,
which seemed to afford his *Lordship* and his party of English gents much
amusement. The fiendish lord's grandsires at one period of our Scottish
history disputed the crown of Scotland with no other aid but his own clan,
now he would not get twenty followers, should that number gain the crown
of England for him; you speak, McLeod, not without a cause, of the poverty,
deterioration, and subjugation of the Sutherlanders, and the tyranny of
their Lords, but here is the ultra beyond description, and the poor animal
himself is drowned in debt, every inch of his estates are encumbered,
and it would be but justice should he die a wretched mendicant.

I have made many quotations from many excellent men for various
reasons—I take to myself the credit, and I believe none will dispute it
with me, I say the credit of breaking the ice before them all, that in bring

ing the short-sighted policy of the clearing system, with its direful concomitant results before the world ; but I knew, and do know myself to be a poor man, and however sincere and indefatigable I was and am in the cause, that there is not much credence given to what a poor man may write, say, or do—" a poor man saved a city but no notice was taken of him because he was a poor man,"—Ecles, chap. 9, v. xv ; yet it is a lasting consolation for me to know that men of piety, talent, affluence and influence made a searching inquiry, and investigated my statement, and found them beyond contradiction—indeed more modified and short of what should be told.   Many consultations were held by Sutherland factors and sheep farmers to consider whether I should be prosecuted or not ; but knowing that they had truth to contend with in taking legal steps against me—the resolution that I was so insignificant and poor that few if any would believe what I was writing always carried the majority, and poor Donald was permitted to proceed with impunity.   Silence was considered by my enemies the best policy ; but they had to be silent since before the world when attacked and exposed by men of high standing in Society, whose affluence and influence put them beyond suspicion of telling ridiculous false stories, as laid to my charge by Mrs. Stowe.   Annexed is an extract taken from a sermon preached by an English divine, I wish to God many more of his order would follow his example.   What prompted this man of God, whom I know personally, to come out on such a theme as this ?   That his Divine Master demanded it of his hand, to denounce the oppressors of the poor.   He preached the sermon first ; afterwards he was told that the statements were controverted—he then corresponded with Professor Black, and finding that it was not the case, he preached the same sermon over again with emphasis not to be disregarded.

'A Sermon for the Times,' lately preached by the Rev. Richard Hibbs, Church of England clergyman, Edinburgh, contains the following exposure of Highland depopulation :—

" Take then, at first, the awful proof how far *in oppression* men can go— men highly educated and largely gifted in every way—property, talents, all ; for the most part, indeed, they are so-called noblemen.   What, then, are they doing in the Highland districts, according to the testimony of a learned professor in this city ?   Why, depopulating those districts in order to make room for red deer.   And how ? by buying off the cottars, and giving them money to emigrate ?   Not at all, but by starving them out ; by rendering them absolutely incapable of procuring subsistence for themselves and families ; for they first take away from them their small apportionments of poor lands, although they may have paid their rents ; and if that do not suffice to eradicate from their hearts that love of the soil on which they have been born and bred—a love which the great Proprietor of all has manifestly implanted in our nature—why, then, these inhuman landlords, who are far more merciful to their very beasts, take away from these poor cottars the very roofs above their defenceless heads, and expose them, worn down with age and destitute of everything, to the inclemencies of a northern sky ; and this, forsooth, because they must have plenty of room for their dogs and deer. For plentiful instances of the most wanton barbarities under this head we need only point to the Knoidart evictions. Here were perpetrated such enormities as might well have caused the very sun to hide his face at noonday."

It has been intimated to me by an individual who heard this discourse on the first occasion that the statements referring to the Highland landlords have been controverted. I was well aware long before the receipt of this intimation, that some defence had appeared ; and here I can truly say, that none would have rejoiced more than myself to find that a complete vindication had been made. But, unhappily; the case is far otherwise. In order to be fully acquainted with all that had passed on the subject, I have put myself during the week in communication with the learned professor to whose letter which appeared some months ago in the *Times*, I referred. From him I learn that none of his statements were invalidated—nay, not even impugned ; and he adds, that to do this was simply impossible, as he had been at great pains to verify the facts. All that could be called in question was the theory that he had based upon these facts—namely, that evictions were made for the purpose of making room for more deer. This, of course, was open to contradiction on the part of those landlords who had not openly avowed their object in evicting the poor Highland families. As to the evictions themselves—and this was the main point—no attempt at contradiction was made.

But in addition to all that the benevolent professor has made known to the civilized world under this head, who has not heard of ' The massacre of the Rosses, and the clearing of the glens? I hold in my hand a little work thus entitled, which has passed into the second edition. The author is Mr Donald Ross— a gentleman whom all who feel sympathy for the down-trodden and oppressed must highly esteem. What a humiliating picture of the barbarity and cruelty of fallen humanity does this little book present ! The reader, utterly appalled by its horrifying statements, finds it difficult to retain the recollection that he is perusing the history of his own times and country too. He would fain yield himself to the tempting illusion, that the ruthless atrocities which are depicted were enacted in a fabulous period, in ages long past ; or, at all events, if it be contemporaneous history, that the scene of such heart-rending cruelties, the perpetrators of which were regardless alike of the innocency of infancy and the helplessness of old age, in some far distant, and as yet not merely unchristianized, but wholly savage and uncivilized region of our globe. But, alas ! it is Scotland in the latter half of the nineteenth century, of which he treats. One feature of the heart-harrowing case is the shocking and barbarous cruelty that was practised on this occasion upon the *female* portion of the evicted clan. Mr. D. Ross, in a letter addressed to the Right Hon. the Lord Advocate, Edinburgh, dated April 19, 1854, thus writes in reference to one of those clearances and evictions which had just then taken place under the authority of a certain Sheriff of the district, and by means of a body of policemen as executioners :—'The feeling on this subject, not only in the district, but in Sutherlandshire and Ross-shire is, among the great majority of the people, one of universal condemnation of the Sheriff's reckless conduct, and of indignation and disgust at the brutality of the policemen. Such, indeed, was the sad havoc made on these females on the banks of the Carron, on the memorable 31st March last, that pools of blood were on the ground—that the grass and earth were dyed red with it—that the dogs of the district came and licked up the blood ; and at last, such was the state of feeling of parties who went from a distance to see the field, that a party (it is understood by order or instructions from head-quarters) actually harrowed the ground during the night to hide the blood !'

These things were brought to light during the recent war with Russia ; who can marvel at the sympathising author thus expressing himself, when concluding the astonishing account—

'The affair at Greenyard, on the morning of the 31st March last, is not calculated to inspire much love of country, or rouse the martial spirit of the already ill-used Highlanders. The savage treatment of innocent females on that morning, by an enraged body of police, throws the Sinope butchery into the shade ; for the Ross-shire Haynaus have shown themselves more cruel and more blood-thirsty than the Austrian women-floggers. What could these poor men and women, with their wounds, and scars, and broken bones, and disjointed arms, stretched on beds of sickness, or moving on crutches, the result of the brutal treatment of them by the police at Greenyard, have to dread from the invasion of Scotland by Russia ?'

' What, indeed,'? echo back these depopulated glens.

But enough of the subject of clearances and evictions, of which we had not originally intended to say so much. A regard, however, to the interests of truth and humanity, which we are sure is the cause of God, of God even the Father and Redeemer of all, as revealing Himself in our Lord Jesus Christ, has constrained us to notice these things thus far.

The publications of Mr Ross are recommended to all who may desire further information on this subject. But as concerning the signs of the times upon which we are discoursing, do not these atrocities, viewed too as complimentary of the Knoidart evictions, demonstrate that we are now in the last time, at the end of the age, when, from the beginning of it, it was prophetically declared that ' men shall be lovers of their own selves,' utterly regardless of what others may suffer thereby.

This murderous affair at *Greenyard*, of which the reverend gentleman spoke, was so horrifying and so brutal that I think no wonder at his delicacy in speaking of it, and directing his hearers to peruse Mr. Ross's pamphlet for full information. Mr. Ross went from Glasgow to Green-yard, Ross-shire, to investigate the case on the spot, and found that Mr. Taylor, a native of Sutherland, (well educated in eviction schemes and murderous cruelty of that county) and Sheriff substitute of Ross-shire, marched from Tain upon the morning of the 31st March at the head of a strong party of armed constables, with heavy bludgeons and fire arms, conveyed in carts and other vehicles, allowing them as much ardent drink as they chose to take before leaving and upon their march, so as to qualify them for the bloody work they had to perform. Fit for any outrage, fully equipped, and told by the Sheriff to shew no mercy to any one who would oppose them, aud not allow themselves to be called cowards, by allowing these mountaineers victory over them. In this excited half drunk state they came in contact with the unfortunate women of Green-yard, who were determined to prevent the officers from serving the sum-mons of removal upon them, and keep their holding of small farms where they and their forefathers lived and died for generations. But no time was allowed to parley ; the Sheriff gave the order to clear the way, and be it said to his everlasting disgrace *(but to the credit of the county of Sutherland)* that he struck the first blow at a woman, the mother of a large family, and large in the family way at the time, who tried to keep him back, then a general slaughter commenced, the women made noble resistance, until the bravest of them got their arms broken, then they gave way. This did not allay the rage of the murderous brutes, they contined clubbing at the protectless creatures until every one of them was stretched on the field wallowing in their blood, or with broken arms, ribs, and bruised limbs ; in this woeful condition many of them were handcuffed together, others tied with coarse ropes, huddled into carts and carried prisoners to Tain jail. I have seen myself in the pos-session of Mr. Ross, Glasgow, patches or scalps of the skin with the long hair adhering to them, which was found upon the field a few days after this inhuman affray. I did not see the women, but I was told that gashes were found on the heads of two young females prisoners in Tain jail, which exactly corresponded with these slices or scalps I have seen, so that Sutherland and Ross-shire may boast of having the Nena Sahibs and bis Chiefs some few years before India, and that in the per-sons of some whose education, training, and parental example should prepare their minds to perform and act differently. Mr. Donald Ross placed the whole affair before the Lord Advocate for Scotlsnd, but no notice was taken of it by that functionary, any further than that the majesty of the law would need to be observed and attended to.

In this unfortunate country, you see the law of God and humanity may be violated and trampled under foot, but the law of wicked men which sanctions murder, rapine and robbery must be observed. From the same estate, (the estate of Robinson of Kindeas, if I am not mistaken in the date) in the year 1843 the whole inhabitants of Glencalve were evicted in a similar manner, and so unprovided and unprepared were they for removal at such an inclement season of the year, that they had to shelter themselves in a Church yard, or burying ground. I have seen myself nineteen families within this gloomy and solitary resting abode of the dead; they were there for months. The London *Times* sent a com-missioner direct from London to investigate into [this case, and he did his duty ; but like the Sutherland cases, it was hushed up in order to maintain the majesty of the law, and in order to keep the right, the majesty of the people and the laws of God in the dark.

In the year 1819 or 20, about the time when the depopulation of Sutherlandshire was completed, and the annual conflagration of burning the houses ceased, and when there was not a glen or strath in the country to let to a sheep farmer, one of these insatiable monsters of Sutherlandshire sheep farmers fixed his eyes upon a glen in Ross-shire, inhabited by a brave, hardy race from time immemorial. Summons of removal were served upon them at once. The people resisted—a military force was brought against them—the military and the women of the glen met at the entrance to the glen—a bloody conflict took place, without reading the riot act or taking any other precaution, the military fired (by the order of Sheriff McLeod) ball cartridge upon the women ; one young girl of the name of Matheson was shot dead on the spot, many were woundad. When this murder was observed by the survivors, and some young men concealed in the back ground, they made a heroic sudden rush upon the military, when a hand to hand melee or fight took place. In a few minutes the military were put to disorderly flight ; in their retreat they were unmercifully dealt with, only two of them escaped with heal heads. The Sheriff's coach was smashed to atoms, and he made a narrow escape himself with a heal head. But no legal cognizance was taken of this affair, as the Sheriff and the military were the violators. However, for fear of prosecution, the Sheriff settled a pension of £6 sterling yearly upon the murdered girl's father, and the case was hushed up likewise. The result was that the people kept possession of the glen, and that the proprietor, and the oldest and most insatiable of Sutherlandshire *scourges* went to law, which ended in the ruination of the latter, who died a pauper.

To detail individual murders, sufferings and oppression in the Highlands of Scotland would be an endless work. A few months ago a letter from Donald Sutherland, farmer, West Zorra, Canada West, appeared in the *Woodstock Sentinel*, detailing what his father and family suffered at the hands of the Sutherlandshire landlords ; all the offence his father was guilty of was, that be along with others went and remonstrated with the house burners, and made them desist until the people could remove their families and chattels out of their houses ; for this offence he would not be allowed to remain upon the estate. He took shelter with his family under the roof of his father-in-law, from this abode he was expelled, and his father-in-law made a narrow escape from sharing the same fate for affording him shelter. He was thus persecuted from one parish to another, until ultimately another proprietor, Skibo, took pity upon him, and permitted him in the beginning of an extraordinary stormy winter, to build a house in the middle of a bog or swamp, during the building of which, he having no assistance, his family being all young. and far from his friends, and having all materials to carry on his back the stance of his new house being inaccessible by horses or carts, he, poor fellow, fell a victim to cold and fever, and a combination of other troubles, and died before the house was finished, leaving a widow and six fatherless children in this half-finished hut, in the middle of a swamp, to the mercy of the world. Well might Donald Sutherland, who was the oldest of the family, and who recollects what his father suffered, and of his death, (I say), charge the Sutherland family and their tools with the murder of his father.

But many were the hundreds who suffered alike and died similar deaths in Sutherlandshire during the wholesale evictions and house burnings of Sutherlandshire. But I must now cease to unpack my heart upon these revolting scenes and gloomy memories. I know many will say that I have dealt too hard with the house of Sutherland,—that such disclosures as I have made cannot be of any public service—that the present Duke of Sutherland is a good man, and that in England he is called the *Good Duke*. I have in my own unvarnished way brought to light a great amount of inhumanity, foul unconstitutional and barbarous atrocities, committed and perpetrated in his name, and in the name of his parents, and by their authority. I stand by these as stern facts. Now I call upon his Grace's and predecessors' sympathisers and apologisers to say and point out to me one public or private act performed by any of the family which should entitle his present Grace to be called the Good Duke. I have myself looked earnestly and impartially for such acts ; but could find none, no, not one. I know he never killed or even struck a man or women in his lifetime, nor set fire to a house where a bed-ridden woman was lying disabled by age and infirmities to escape from the flames, he needed not while (as I said before) Loch, Young, Sellar, Suther, Gunn, Leslie, Horsburg, and MacIvor, were appointed by him to advise and superintend the work of brutal destruction and while the Stobbs and Sgrioses, &c. were at their beck to execute their orders at 2s. 6d. sterling per day and their whiskey. The Duke's unassuming, modest, and sheepish like appearance will not entitle him to the appelation of the Good Duke ; neither will his meek, easily approached manners, and readiness to hear poor people's complaints entitle him to the title—for I demand of you to point one complaint of any importance which he redressed, and I will give you and him credit for it. The poor never realized any relief, nor benefit from his interpositions, or from the thousand appeals they made to him ; but the reverse left them more exposed to the wrath and fury of their oppressors, his factors.

What then constitutes his right to the appelation of the Good Duke. I admit that the is not so inhuman, nor so brutal a savage as Lord Macdonald, Duke of Athol, Breadalbane, Colonel Gordon, of Clunny, and many more Highland landlords, but that does not constitute the appelation good Duke : to be more human than these would make him only a little better than *incarnate demons or an host of Nena Sahibs.* My views of rights of property in land are open to criticism; I wish they may be criticised, and that properly, for I find that under that cursed law which affords every opportunity to stupid kings and queens, their selfish ambitious government, and profligate avaricious favourites and capitalists in the days of old, to monopolize the land, created by God for the people without exception, are now in full operation in the Canadas ; I find your government handing large slices of the Canada lands over to one another, and to favourite individuals and companies, as free as Malcolm Ceanmor, King of

Scotland, handed estates to his favourites in the tenth century, in his own word, "as free as God gave it to me and mine, I give it to you and yours." But my Canadian readers the days are coming and approaching when there will be a *scramble* for land in the Canadas, as sure as it was and is in all European nations, and I tell you that this is the age and years, when you should enquire and study the rights of property in land; particularly what right has your own servants, *the Government*, to gift or traffic with monopolisers in your land, and what right have you to abide by the trafficing covenants of stupid kings and queens, and insane Governments who deprive you and your offspring of such immense territories as the Hudson Bay Company now possess. Let it not be recorded that the Canadians of the 19th century will allow the egregious spoliation to continue or remain uncorrected, *yea*, undemolished, for while it remains undemolished minor spoilations will increase ; indeed to all appearance there are very few who are entrusted with the law making and government of the Canadas, who enter either of the Houses with that patriotic spirit which should constitute members of parliament. It is to be feared, indeed it is too evident, that selfishness, and how to better themselves and relations at the people's expense are their motives and principle study while acting for the people. I say, O ! Canadians watch and look, as well as pray, generations yet unborn demand it of you.

Mrs. Harriet Beecher Stowe may be very ill-pleased at my animadversions, and may consider that I went too far with my strictures upon her Sunny Memories. "Those to whom much are given much will be required of them ;" I have no private spleen or animosity against that amiable, talented lady, but I could nor cannot be but sorry for her merchandising the gift of God ; will that lady, however great her talents are, come out now in the face of such a cloud of witnesses, and corroborating evidence as she will find within this little volume and say and maintain that I have been circulating unfounded false accusations against the Duchess and house of Sutherland; well let her peruse the following from the pen of Mr. Mackie, Editor of the *Northern Ensign*, a paper published next county to Sutherland, and say what praise she can lavish upon that family.

WELL DONE, BRAVE HIGHLANDS.

(From the Northern Ensign.)

There is not a man in the civilized world who does not admire the energy daring, perseverance and bravery of the glorious 78th, in their victorious march against the Indian mutineers. Every official dispatch and every private letter concur in proclaiming that those 'brave Highlanders' have not only done their duty, and done it well, but have given another proof to the world of the value of such troops in circumstances of crisis and peril. Even General Havelock, tied down by military and official restraint, seems to have thrown aside reserve, and to have exclaimed, in the hearing of his gallant companions in arms, 'Well done, brave Highlanders!' The country re-echoes the cry. It is heard from the Himalaya Mountains to the Gulf of Manaar, and strikes terror in the breasts of the fiendish revolters. It is heard in every hamlet in the British Isles. The press and the platform catch the echo, and with giant tone swell the strain, 'well done, brave Highlanders' have called forth such eulogistic exclamation. Even Napoleon himself, as he saw the phalanx of Scotch Greys at the battle of Waterloo, could not resist a similar tribute; and the despatches of the Peninsular and other wars, down to the recent Crimean campaign, where Alma, Balaclava, and Inkerman were fought testify to the same. All modern warlike history, from the rebellion in 1715 to the Cawnpore massacre in 1857, teems with the record of Highland bravery and prowess. What say our highland evicting lairds to these facts, and to their treatment of the Highlanders? What reward have these men received for saving their country, fighting its battles, conquering its enemies, turning the tide of revolt, resening women and children from the hands of Indian fiends, and establishing order when disorder and bloody cruelty have held their murderous carnival? And, we ask, in the name of men who have, ere now, we fondly hope, saved our gallant countrymen and heroic countrywoman at Lucknow; in the name of those who fought in the trenches of Sebastopool, and proudly planted the British standard on the heights of the Alma, how are they, their fathers, brothers, and little ones treated? Is the mere shuttlecocking of an irrepressible cry of admiration from mouth to mouth, and the setting to music of a song in their praise, all the return the race is to get for such noble acts? We can fancy the expression of admiration of Highland bravery at the Dunrobin dinner table, recently, when the dukes, earls, lords, and other aristocratic notables enjoyed princely hospitality of the Duke. We can imagine the mutual congratulation of the Highland lairds as they prided themselves on being proprietors of the soil which gave birth to the race of 'Highland heroes.' Alas, for the blush that would cover their faces if they would allow themselves to reflect that in their names, and by their authority, and at their expense, the fathers, mothers, brothers, wives, of the invincible ' 78th ' have been remorselessly driven from their native soil, and at the very hour when Cawnpore was gallantly retaken, and the ruffian Nena Sahib was obliged to leave the bloody scene of his fiendish massacre, there were Highlanders within a few miles of the princely Dunrobin, driven from their homes and left to starve and to die in the open field. Alas, for the blush that would reprint its scarlet dye on their proud faces as they thought in one country alone, since Waterloo was fought, more than 14,000 of this 'race of heroes,' of whom Canning so proudly boasted, have been hunted out of their native homes; and that where the pibroch and bugle once evoked the martial spirit of thousands of brave hearts, razed and burning cottages have formed the tragic close of scenes of eviction and desolation; and the abodes of a loyal and liberty-loving people are made sacred to the rearing of sheep, and sanctified to the preservation of game! Yes; we echo back the cry, 'Well done brave Highlanders!' But to what purpose would it be carried on the wings of the wind to the once happy straths and glens of Sutherland? Who, what, would echo back our acclaims of praise? Perhaps a shepherd's or a gillie's child, playing amid the unbroken wilds, and innocent of seeing a human face but that of its own parents, would hear it; or the cry might startle a herd

204

of timid deer, or frighten a covey of patridges, or call forth a bleat from a herd of sheep; but men would not, could not, hear it. We must go to the back-woods of Canada, to Detroit, to Hamilton, to Woodstock, to Toronto, to Montreal; we must stand by the waters of Lake Huron, or Lake Ontario, where the cry—' Well done, bravè Highlanders!' would call up a thousand brawny fellows, and draw down a tear on a thousand manly cheeks. Or we must go to the bare rocks that skirt the sea coast of Sutherland, where the residuary population were *generously* treated to barren steeps and in-hospital shores on which to keep up the breed of heroes, and fight for the men who dared—*dared*—to drive them from houses for which they fought, and from land which was purchased with the blood of their fathers. But the cry, ' Well done, brave Highlanders,' would evoke no effective response from the race: Need the reader wonder? Wherefore should they fight? To what purpose did their fathers climb the Peninsular heights, and glori-ously write in blood the superiority of Britain, when their sons were re-warded by extirpation, or toleration to starve, in sight of fertile straths and glens devoted to beasts? These are words of truth and soberness. They are but repetitions in other forms of arguments, employed by us for years; and we shall continue to ring changes on them so long as our brave Highland people are subjected to treatment to which no other race would have submitted. We are no alarmists. But we tell Highland proprietors that were Britain some twenty years hence to have the misfortune to be plunged into such a crisis as the present, there will be few such men as the Highlanders of the 78th to fight her battles, and that the country will find when too late, if another policy towards the Highlanders is not adopted, that sheep and deer, ptarmigan and grouse, can do little to save it from such a calamity.

EVICTION BY FIRE IN SUTHERLAND.

Once more has the fire been kindled in Sutherland, to carry out the exterminating theories of the Loch policy. Confessing most heartily that notwithstanding all the antecedents of that system in Sutherland, we are not prepared for this recent case, we proceed to lay before our readers its leading facts :—

"It will be remembered that on the 7th of June last an industrious cottar named Don Murray, with his aged sister, and two little motherless girls were ejected from the hut which they had occupied for many years. After lying for sometimes in the open air, the Rev. Mr. MacKellar, parish minister of Clyne, gave them the use of a cart shed, which they continued to occupy from the date of eviction till Saturday the 17th of this month, their little bits of furniture meanwhile lying in the open air. In the meantime it was found that the Duke of Sutherland had no right to the cot from which Murray and his family were ejected; and that it stood on glebe land, and a case was entered in the Court of Session. Acting under advice, Murray and his family again took possession of the hut, along with part of their furniture, on the date referred to, and immediately on this being done the machinery was set in order for a second eviction. Accordingly, on the forenoon of Tuesday last, public attention was attracted to a dense volume

of smoke rising from the neighbourhood of the manse of Clyne, and it was
soon found that Murray's cabin was on fire, and that workmen were
actively employed in the demolition of its rude walls, the *Magnus Appolo*
of the patriotic and humane labour of love being Mr. Patrick M'Gibbon,
Golspie, who, with crowbar in hand, and with a heart of will, wrought in
the good cause with astonishing energy, assisted (?) by a John Thomson,
cartwright in Golspie, and a youth of some fifteen summers, glorying in
the name of Mackay. The worthy three persevered in the ducal mission till
the miserable hut was razed to the ground. Part of the poor creature's
furniture was soon scattered here and there. A correspondent who witnessed the most part of the proceedings says :—" I stood for a brief period,
surveying the progress of the flames and the torch-bearers, and then turned
away in disgust from the scene, with the reverberation of H.M.S. *Pem-
broke's* guns ringing in my ears, and thoughts occupying my mind that
my pen fails to describe ; but thanking my Maker that I was not born a
Duke and left to tarnish a ducal coronet by such a deed of inhumanity. I
again passed the spot when the work was finished. The walls were completely levelled, and the timbers were still burning ; while the master of
the ceremonies was retiring to a streamlet hard by, to wash his dirty hands.
The outcasts had again to betake themselves to the cart shed, kindly given
to them by the minister of Clyne, every other person in the district being
afraid to do anything for them, or show them any kindness, dreading that
for the simplest act of humanity towards one of the family they would be
similarly treated. I may add that the blankets that Murray's sister had
lying on her straw pallet were burned."

To His Grace the Duke of Sutheland :

May it please your Grace,—

Such is the last act of eviction perpetrated in the name and by the
authority of your Grace. We do not now enter upon the question of right
of property involved in this case, and pending before the legal tribunals
of the country; but admitting that your Grace were found to be the owner
of the few square feet of valueless soil on which that hut stood, we ask
your Grace, firmly, plainly, and boldly, if it is like a "good Duke" to
commit such an act of high-handed cruelty and indefencible spoliation ?
Would it have weakened the case before the court had your Grace allowed
that poor man with his sister and little girls, quietly to occupy *their*
HOME—a home of peace, contentment, and affection, as deep, as sincere,
as lasting, as devoted as Dunrobin's palatial halls can boast of—until at
least it is decided that your Grace had a legal right to *burn* them out ?
Would it have diminished your Grace's happiness ; would it have dimmed
the lustre of your Grace's coronet ; would it have infinitessimally neu-
tralised your Grace's influence ; would it have redounded to your Grace's
discredit, that you had allowed these poor creatures to return and occupy
the little cot which you have now burned and raised ? A thousand times,
No ! ! My Lord Duke, your Grace seems to be forgetful, totally oblivious,
sadly neglectful, of the times and their signs. We are not now living in

the seventeenth century. This is eighteen hundred and fifty-seven, whether your Grace pleases or no, with its enlightenment, its independence, its free press (thank God !) and its noble tendencies to respect the *principles* before persons. Remember, my Lord Duke, what you have done, and where. You have burned out a native of Sutherland, with his little girls; cast them into the open field till a good Samaritan allowed them the use of a cart shed, at a time when public sentiment is being thoroughly aroused to the indescribable and momentous importance of doing everything to encourage the peasantry of this country, and to secure their services in the nation's cause at this deeply perilous crisis. At the very time when the national ear is kept in a state of painful tension, almost hearing the voice of our brothers' and sisters' blood, spilled in oceans on the plains of Hindostan and calling on Britain to send relief; and when we almost see the smoke of desolation rising from revolted Indian provinces, all of a sudden, the smoke of a burning cottage is seen in Sutherland, and a wail of houseless, homeless, burned out *females* is heard from a Scotch county which boasts its possessor to be the husband of the mistress of Queen Victoria's robes. What a state of matters ! Look at it, my Lord Duke of Sutherland. It *cannot*, it must not last. We refrain from implicating in its vileness and guilt even the humblest serf that dared to soil his fingers with the dark deed. The blame, the responsibility is YOURS. THERE IT RESTS, in all its effects and in all its forbidden features. Your Grace may calmly sit in your gilded saloon, surrounded by a loving family, with your fair children prattling on your knee; your Grace's sycophantic followers and servile hangers-on may adroitly conceal from your Grace these and similar proceedings under your name, at your instance, and at your expense ; but the smoke of Donald Murray's cabin *shall* not soon die away; the cries of Donald Murray's children *shall* find an echo; and on the wings of the wind shall be carried the report of this last high-handed act of oppression and spoliation.

Now my dear countrymen my labour is near an end, for if my health continues to decline as rapid as it has been doing for some time back, my pen is laid down never again to be taken up. So far as the Almighty favoured me with abilities, I did not swerve from performing my duty to society even in the face of persecution, oppression, privation, and the forsaking of dear friends and patrons; the most part of my labours are now before you under its deserved title, Gloomy Memories. Gloomy as they are, and thoroughly open to criticism, I challenge contradiction to any one charge I have made against the House of Sutherland or any other depopulating house in the Highlands of Scotland. Come then Mrs. B. Stowe, come you literary scourges and apologisers of highland evictors, vindicate their ungodly and unconstitutional schemes and actions before the world now if you dare. Who have you attempted to crush ? The sincere advocates of the Caledonian Celtic race and the exposers of their enemies. Who have you been calumniating in their moral and religious character, in their brave and chivalrous spirit, so charactersitic of the race, who would, if you could, make the world believe that they were not half so valuable to the nation as sheep and red deer, and unworthy of a home in Caledonia, the nursery of bravery and gallant unconquerable warriors. You vile sycophants, did you ever consult General Abercrombe in Egypt, General Moore at Corunna, Wellington in the Peninsula, and at Waterloo, did you consult Lord Raglan in the Crimea, when proclaiming the taking of the Alma, by the Highland Brigade, and their intrepid bold stand before the Russian cavalry at Balaclava, when the fate of the British army depended that day upon their bravery. What would all the legions of German poltroons, all the deerstalking snobs of England and Scotland, shepherds and dogs to boot, avail Lord Raglan and the British army that day.' What deprived the British army and Generals of the praise of taking Sebastopol ? That the Highland Brigade under Colin Campbell were not brought forward to the first day's assault, they were brought up next day, but the Russians came to learn who they would have to deal with the second day and fled. You hired calumniators, oppressors, and dispersers of the Celtic race, did you consult General Havelock, who it seems never witnessed the undaunted bravery and prowess of Scottish Highlanders before, and ask him what made him exclaim " Well done, *brave Highlanders !*" How many German cowards and town keelies or loafers would he take in exchange for this handful of brave Celts under his command. He would not accept of twenty to one. Did you consult the Generals, and Commanders-in-chief of the British Army at the present time, and they would tell you, however numerous and strong an army sent out upon an emergeney minus of a Highland Brigade, that that army is deficient, and uncertain of success. To enumerate the many victories and laurels the Celtic race gained for ungrateful Britain would be an easy task, had history done them justice ; but when put to the test their enemies will find it a difficult task to point out where they have failed to gain victory where bravery could obtain it. If the few of these men now embodied in two or three regiments are gaining and deserving the admiration of the world, what if Britain could boast of from 50,000 to 70,000 of such men, who would make her afraid ? But alas, the Caledonian nursery, by proper treatment, I aver, from which she could raise that number in time of need, is now a desolation, consigned to feed and rear brute animals. Our beloved Queen taking up her residence in the Highlands during the deer-stalking months of the year, has turned up a curse for the remainder of the people, since then the country is fast becoming one vast Deer Forest. Oh ! my lady Queen, you should show the cruel monsters a better example, than to chase away the few Highlanders you have found upon the Balmoral Estate.

Come, then, you calumniators of my people, apologisers of their destroyers, and extirpators from their own rightful soil—I conclude by calling upon every British subject, every lover of justice, every sympathiser with suffering humanity, to disapprove of such unconstitutional and ungodly doings, and to remonstrate with the Queen and Government, so as to put an end to such systems. Call you upon the world to vindicate and exonerate them.

1 am now an old man bordering on seventy years of age ; symptoms
of decay in the tabernacle convinces me that my race through time towards
eternity is near at an end, when I will have to give an account for what I
write and leave on record. I have devoted the most of this time and the
limited talents God has bestowed upon me, advocating the cause of the wrong·
and oppressed, as I said before, persuaded in my own mind that I could
not serve God in a more acceptable way, nor yet discharge my duty to my
country, my fellow creatures, and co-sufferers, more consistent with the
dictates of humanity, justice, and christian religion, in which I have
been nurtured and educated. (Yes and would spend *ten more lives* in
the same cause if bestowed upon me and needed). .I cannot charge myself
with recording one single false accusation against any one of these High·
land depopulators, yet some of them, or their hired apologists; who dared
not confront me while alive, may attack my character and dispute the
veracity of my statements, and charges against them after I am dead and
gone. Some has the audacity already to question my ability to write such
a narrative as you have now before you, and bestowing the credit of it·
upon some one they know not. I have not much cause to boast of my
abilities displayed in my Gloomy Narrative, only that I have performed
what I considered my incumbent duty in society, and made the best use I
could of all the abilities bestowed upon me, but I challenge them to find
out any one who have put one word or one idea into my head. I wish it to·
be known among my countrymen how willingly Mr. McWhinnie, editor·
and proprietor of the *Woodstock Sentinel*, volunteered to assist me in
revising and reading the proof sheets, I hope he will not loose his reward.
I know my enemies will accuse me of plagiarism ; I deny it, I gave credit to every gentleman from whose writings I have made quotations.

During the time I have been exposing the clearing system in the Highlands through the public press, I have received many private and public
letters from almost every quarter of the empire and her colonies, en-
couraging me in my labour and approving of my actions in very flattering
terms, and passing eulogies upon me, many of which should have a place
in this work only for this, that my enemies and hired critics might
construe them to *self-praise*, hence I have to suppress them ; but to let·
my friendly readers know that my name is still alive in Scotland, and
honourably mentioned there by the real friends and advocates of the
Highlanders, and the unflinching exposers of their wrongs. I here subjoin a speech delivered in November last, by one of the most patriotic
gentlemen with whom the clan Campbell or the Highlanders can claim
connection, viz. Captain Campbell of Borlum :—

A HIGHLANDER ON THE HIGHLANDS.

Last week on the presentation of a handsome testimonial to Captain·
Campbell, Glasgow, by a number of friends and admirers, that gentleman, whose enthusiasm in behalf of the cause of the Highlanders is so·
well known, made the following truly spirited and patriotic reply.

GENTLEMEN,—I feel that my friend the chairman has, in his earnest.
and eloquent address, described my conduct and character in terms far·

above my merits; but I trust the time is yet distant when it will be considered in accordance either with good taste or proper feelings to apply the rules of strict criticism to the innocent exaggerations so natural to gentlemen of kind hearts and generous sympathies, on occasions like the present. My military services have been too brief to deserve the notice taken of them by the chairman. I joined the army at the beginning of the campaign of 1813, in the seat of war—I might almost say the field of bat ?, and was put on half-pay so soon as our arms achieved the peace. I ?ve the satisfaction of knowing, however, that my conduct in presence of ?e enemy was considered by my brother officers as not unworthy of my ountry or my clan; but the fact is, that every Highlander is inspired by nis birth and traditions with the feelings best calculated to enable him to bear himself manfully on the field of battle. The Highlander who does not do so is untrue, not only to the name of his race, but also to the bosom on which he was nursed. That few such have ever appeared among Highland soldiers, is proved by their conduct in battle, from the day of the wild and romantic battle of the Grampians, until that on which the illustrious Havelock gained his ninth victory against such fearful odds, on the arid plains of India. Hence it is that the Lowlander or Celt, whom the novelists and penny-a-liners of modern times seem determined to metamorphose into an Anglo-Saxon, is entitled to credit for having, by his energetic enterprise and skilful industry, covered our plains with palaces and warehouses, and our seas with navies and argosies; the Highlander or Gael is entitled to credit for the patriotism and bravery, the abilities, vigour, and trenchants which still secure to our mountains the proud distinction of having proved in every national extremity the unconquered citadel of our country's independence. Alas, that we have seen the day when the citadel may be ascribed as dismantled and dispoiled of its warlike defenders, not by a brave and noble enemy but by an insidious and unpatriotic friend, aided and abetted by the public apathy. Had the public feeling remained alive to the importance of preserving the clans to their country, the Highlands would have been at this day the best military nursery in Europe—a nursery capable of rearing legions upon legions of strong, brave, willing, and hardy soldiers, eager to enter into the service of their beloved country. Their never was a greater fallacy than the studiously inculcated and generally prevailing impression that the Highlands are incapable of maintaining a large population in comfort and prosperity. The straths, the vales, the glens, and even the far extending wilds of the Highlands, up to an altitude of a thousand feet above the level of the sea, are fertile and salubrious, and under a system of husbandry fitted to grow all the ordinary crops of this country; while the value of the abundance of all kinds of fish contained in the inland and surrounding seas can scarcely be overstrained by the most expansive imagination. Had the old clan system of managing estates been adhered to by the modern proprietors, or in other words, had the country, as of old, been covered with hamlets or clachans, occupied by a rural population, each family possessing a sufficient allotment of the arable land for its own sustenance, and every clachan possessing the whole neighbouring grazings

o

for the payment of its rents, the rentals would have been larger than they now are in the Highlands, and the country teeming with the most virtuous and warlike population in the world. That the population are being expatriated, while such latent resources remained undeveloped, and while the Government are requiring a greatly increased army, is a national disgrace, and may prove a national calamity; but are that disgrace and calamity not to be ascribed more to the infatuated adulation of wealth and rank by the public than to the blindness or apathy of the Government? That such is the case has been painfully confirmed by a paragraph which appeared in the newspapers the other day, showing that the great Celtic Society of Glasgow, from whose patriotism and independence of spirit, as well as its professed object of conserving the poetry, the garb, and the athletic games of the Highlanders, something very different was to be expected, applied for and obtained the patronage of the Duke of Sutherland for the ensuing year. Now, gentlemen, no Highlander possessing a heart worthy of the name, who has perused the history of the Sutherland clearances, written by that brave and noble-hearted man, Donald M'Leod, and which remains until this day uncontradicted, can assign to the Duke of Sutherland a brighter page in the history of the Highlands than has been occupied by another Duke since the battle of Culloden. I have been told that neither the Directors nor the Society have been consulted, nor are consenting parties to the application, and I trust that it is so; but it is humiliating to think that a single Highlander could be found in Glasgow capable of applying for or accepting the patronage of a clearance-maker. Mr Chairman and gentlemen, allow me to assure you that I am at a loss for words in which adequately to express my high sense and heart-felt appreciation of the tokens of approval by which I have this day been honoured by so large a number of gentlemen, for every one of whom I have every reason to feel the warmest respect and esteem; and I beg leave to offer, not only to you who have attended this meeting, the greater number of you from so great a distance, but also, through the committee, to all the other generous donors of this splendid testimonial, my proud and grateful thanks."

Captain Campbell is a gentleman of high birth, moving among the most noble and educated order of society, not among those whose birth and position in the world blinds and deafens to the dictates and demand of Christian humanity, and to disown his country and countrymen even in distress, trampled down and forsaken. Well might he be surprised that a single Highlander could be found in Glasgow, who would be capable of committing such an outrage upon the feelings of his true-hearted countrymen, as to apply and solicit the Duke of Sutherland to become the patron of a Celtic Society of any form; but the one which would please him best, a society to extirpate the Celts, and their name and remembrance from under heaven. I hope for the sake of the Society, and those connected with it, that the anti-highland villain, or villains who gave the call will be discovered and exposed, and he or they will be expelled from the society along with their patron, for a more undeserving or inconsistent *nobleman* elected to be patron of a Highland society could not be found in all Europe

5

LIBRARY
FEB
8
1988
UNIVERSITY OF TORONTO

**PLEASE DO NOT REMOVE
CARDS OR SLIPS FROM THIS POCKET**

UNIVERSITY OF TORONTO LIBRARY

HC
257
S4M34
1892
c.1
ROBA

Lightning Source UK Ltd.
Milton Keynes UK
UKHW02f1858110418
320903UK00016B/798/P